Qualitative
Journeys

Qualitative

Student and Mentor
Experiences With Research

Journeys

Victor Minichiello ▪ Jeffrey A. Kottler

University of New England, Australia   *California State University, Fullerton*

EDITORS

Los Angeles • London • New Delhi • Singapore • Washington DC

For information:

SAGE Publications, Inc.
2455 Teller Road
Thousand Oaks, California 91320
E-mail: order@sagepub.com

SAGE Publications Ltd.
1 Oliver's Yard
55 City Road
London EC1Y 1SP
United Kingdom

SAGE Publications India Pvt. Ltd.
B 1/I 1 Mohan Cooperative Industrial Area
Mathura Road, New Delhi 110 044
India

SAGE Publications Asia-Pacific Pte. Ltd.
33 Pekin Street #02-01
Far East Square
Singapore 048763

Printed in the United States of America.

Library of Congress Cataloging-in-Publication Data

Qualitative journeys : student and mentor experiences with research /
editors, Victor Minichiello, Jeffrey A. Kottler.
    p. cm.
Includes bibliographical references and index.
ISBN 978-1-4129-5676-5 (cloth : acid free paper)
ISBN 978-1-4129-5677-2 (pbk. : acid free paper)
    1. Social sciences—Research. 2. Qualitative research. 3. Mentoring in education.
I. Minichiello, Victor. II. Kottler, Jeffrey A.

H62.Q348 2009
001.4′2—dc22   2008049623

This book is printed on acid-free paper.

09 10 11 12 13   10 9 8 7 6 5 4 3 2 1

Acquisitions Editor:	Kassie Graves
Editorial Assistant:	Veronica Novak
Production Editor:	Karen Wiley
Copy Editor:	Alison Hope
Typesetter:	C&M Digitals (P) Ltd.
Proofreader:	Andrea Martin
Indexer:	Julie Grayson
Cover Designer:	Candice Harman
Marketing Manager:	Stephanie Adams

Contents

Preface

This text and resource book is designed for students and professionals in the fields of social sciences, education, human services, health, and related fields. It is intended for those students who already have some rudimentary knowledge of qualitative research, and can be used in conjunction with a more traditionally structured text. This book, after all, is about the journey that researchers experience.

The first two chapters describe the general nature of a qualitative research journey. Each subsequent chapter tells the story of a research study (both master's and doctoral level) with vivid, compelling descriptions of the struggles, joys, discoveries, surprises, and interpersonal negotiations that take place. Most critically, the parallel stories of both student and mentor reveal the innermost workings of how the qualitative research process unfolds and evolves over time, as well as how all the participants are changed personally and professionally by the experience. A section at the end of each chapter discusses the themes, challenges, and practical issues that have arisen in this particular research experience, helping the student to better appreciate and understand the major concepts highlighted and how to apply these in further qualitative research.

The purpose of the book is to prepare readers, both novice student researchers and their experienced mentor researchers, about the complex journey and partnership they are about to undertake. The chapters portray this research journey not as a sanitized process, as is so often presented in published research articles and conference presentations, but as part of normal human activity and reflective learning processes with all of the accompanying joys, pains, and contradictions.

Unique Features of the Book

Rather than covering the same well-worn territory that is introduced by the dozens of other texts in the field, *Qualitative Journeys* tells the stories of what constitutes qualitative research, what is involved in collecting qualitative data, and how studies were conceived and conducted, as well as the studies' ongoing personal and professional impact. In addition, the following features are somewhat unique:

- There is a focus on research from the perspective of students' experiences—that is, their innermost feelings, reflections, and intellectual growth.

- The stories demonstrate the partnership between students and their mentors, including interactive and relational factors that take place.

- Chapters represent diverse and rich research projects to highlight the methodological challenges associated with undertaking quality qualitative research.

- The narratives engage the reader in a reflective learning process about qualitative research that motivates students to do their own research, not as an arduous task, but rather as an exciting journey.

- Each story discusses research as it is lived, which is the essence of qualitative research.

- Narratives reveal the private and often-hidden aspects of doing research, presenting the realities and struggles as well as the joys and satisfactions.

- Chapters include editors' comments and pragmatic guidance for what works and what doesn't, with accompanying solutions.

- The case studies demonstrate the ways that research is a social production and a collaboration, not only between the researcher and participants, but also between the researcher and student peers, mentors, and auditors.

- This book presents a diverse range of research journeys, not only representing different qualitative methodologies and strategies (ethnography, grounded theory, narrative analysis, phenomenology, discourse analysis, feminist, mixed method, action research), but also within various professions (education, health, social sciences, gerontology, medicine, business, counseling) and cultures (Australia, Nepal, the United Kingdom, and the United States).

- We take a student-centered approach, honoring and valuing the contributions that students make to the development of their professions. The student is always the senior author. This book is, in fact, a celebration of student achievement. By *student-centered* we are referring also to direct dialogue with the reader using engaging prose, reality-based examples, and practical applications.

By drawing on a wide range of different types of qualitative research designs, data collection, context, and analysis, the book provides reflective commentary about how qualitative research can be conducted in a rigorous and dynamic way. The partnership between the students, their mentors, and the editors also reinforces that research is a shared collective process and involves academic engagement with other scholars as part of the learning process.

Structure of the Book

The first two chapters briefly (re)introduce the qualitative research process, reviewing the nature of this exciting method of exploration and investigation. The main features of this approach are described and highlighted. The reader is taken systematically through the component steps in the process, including (1) accessing passion for discovery, (2) learning and planning the methodology, (3) resolving predictable problems and challenges, (4) collecting data, (5) making meaning from the data, and (6) doing qualitative research by means of the relational process. The emphasis is on the skills required to do qualitative research and the human nature of the fieldwork process.

Chapter 2, in particular, describes the language and logic of qualitative research. This includes explaining in a concise manner the conceptual and philosophical foundation of qualitative research, the key methodological features of qualitative data, and how such data are collected, organized, and analyzed as a data set. We also emphasize the distinctly relational features of the establishment of rapport and trust with informants that are so fundamental to doing good qualitative research. The discussion also will address briefly the pragmatics of different data analysis options. This will provide a context for the selected cases that will be presented in the next part of the book, highlighting key aspects related to learning and doing qualitative research.

The next series of chapters (3–16) tell the stories of diverse and fascinating research journeys. In each case, a research student and the mentor write about the processes and discoveries that took place during their investigations. The mentor's comments appear in italics following the student's narrative. You will note that because the contributors represent so many different disciplines and nationalities their language varies a bit. For instance, when describing the faculty member who acts as the guide during the journey, you will see various labels such as supervisor, mentor, committee chair, staff member, faculty member, lecturer, and professor. Likewise, although the academic systems are somewhat different in the American versus European or British traditions, the principles highlighted are universal.

These chapters hone in on particular aspects of the qualitative research process and the relationship aspects of doing qualitative research as the focus of gaining entry into the worldviews of people.

How is this accomplished? When does it work? When and how does it fail? What are the personal tales of such experiences? What can we learn from such fieldwork stories? The stories have commentaries on how qualitative research and data collection and analysis manifest themselves in real projects, how fieldwork challenges are addressed, as well as highlighting the intrinsically developmental process of qualitative research.

Each chapter presents a case with different features and representing diverse fields in the social sciences, health, and education, highlighting some aspect of qualitative research and qualitative research design. There are particular emphases on getting into the mind of the informant and how this is accomplished; the reason for selecting a particular data collection tool and how this was derived; ethical challenges that arise from the doing of qualitative research, some of which were predicted, others that were not; how themes in the data were identified; how grounded theory or a narrative approach is learned and used; and how to use qualitative computer software and using it effectively in the research process.

The chapters contain interwoven narratives alternating between the student and mentor, talking about the journey itself, the mutual learning process, the pitfalls and successes, and the ongoing effects and influence from the outcome. As noted above, in each chapter, the mentor's voice is in italics. The stories are constructed and written in engaging prose. Throughout the stories, you'll find "Editors' Comments," highlighting major concepts, bringing attention to important lessons, and describing particular methodological features that you may wish to consider in your own efforts.

Chapter 17 looks at the lessons learned and main themes derived from all the qualitative journeys. In a sense, this book itself is a qualitative study in which the data collected are the narratives of each research journey. This last chapter presents a synthesis and analysis of what was gleaned from these narratives, highlighting the lessons learned for conducting research. It draws on the rich material presented in the previous section to highlight how qualitative research can be conducted in a methodologically sound and rigorous manner and guided by the principles of qualitative methodology. The editors draw on the learning experiences of the students and mentors to show how the pragmatics of doing qualitative research can be better conceptualized, understood, and put into practice as they embark on their own qualitative research journey.

Acknowledgments

We are primarily appreciative to our students who inspired this project through their passion and excitement for their research journeys. We wish to thank David Plummer, who worked with us for many years and provided important insights into the qualitative learning process. Leigh Kelly, Sue Whale, and Robyn Rogers provided outstanding administrative support. Finally we are grateful to our Sage editing team, including Kassie Graves, Veronica Novak, Karen Wiley, Alison Hope, and Andrea Martin, who were so supportive throughout this journey.

We are especially appreciative of the courage and honesty of our contributors, who have been willing to talk so openly about their struggles and challenges.

Victor Minichiello, Armidale, Australia

Jeffrey A. Kottler, Fullerton, California

About the Editors

Victor Minichiello is professor of health in the School of Health and dean of the Faculty of the Professions at the University of New England in Armidale, Australia. Victor is a sociologist, gerontologist, and public health researcher. He is the author of ten books in the field of aging, sexual health, and research methods. In addition, he has published more than one hundred research articles in medical, health, and social science journals. He has successfully supervised more than fifty doctoral and master's research students across diverse nations including Australia, Canada, China, Hong Kong, Thailand, and the United States. His most recent textbooks include *Contemporary Issues in Gerontology: Promoting Positive Ageing* (Routledge/Allen & Unwin) and *Handbook of Research Methods for Nursing and Health Science* (Prentice Hall/Addison Wesley).

Jeffrey A. Kottler is professor in the Counseling Department at California State University, Fullerton, and a doctoral program supervisor at the University of New England, Australia. He is the author of more than seventy books in the fields of counseling, education, and social science, many of which employ qualitative research methodologies. Most recently, he has completed a series of five books that involved interviewing prominent theoreticians in counseling and therapy about their most memorable counseling sessions. Some of his best-known books include *On Being a Therapist, On Being a Teacher, Making Changes Last,* and *Bad Therapy.* Jeffrey is also cofounder of the Madhav Ghimire Foundation, which supports the education of at-risk and neglected children in Nepal.

About the Contributors

Comstock, Dana L., PhD, is a professor and chair of the Department of Counseling and Human Services at St. Mary's University, San Antonio, Texas. She also has a part-time private practice specializing in women's issues, including pre- and perinatal loss and trauma. She is the editor of *Diversity in Development: Critical Contexts That Shape Our Lives and Relationships* (Wadsworth/Brooks-Cole, 2005). Among her many publications are chapters in *How Connections Heal* (Guilford Press) and *The Complete Guide to Mental Health for Women* (Beacon Press).

Couch, Danielle, MPH, is a consultant with an Internet health services company, *Health1st,* where she works with clients on the delivery and evaluation of online health services and programs. She is also assisting with two research projects with the School of Public Health at La Trobe University that are investigating dating practices. Her professional and research interests include health promotion, online service delivery, and online research methods.

Davidson, Patricia, PhD, is professor of cardiology and chronic care at the School of Nursing and Midwifery, Curtin University of Technology, and director of the Centre for Cardiovascular and Chronic Care in Sydney, Australia. Her clinical and research interests include management of chronic disease (particularly heart disease), models of care, and palliative care in nonmalignant conditions. She is currently working on a number of national projects, including an investigation of the use of oxygen in end-stage heart failure, palliative care in heart failure, women's health and chronic disease, transitional models of palliative care, strategies to promote self-management, and the development of the nursing role in primary care.

Donovan, Raymond, PhD, is adjunct senior research fellow at the National Centre in HIV Social Research, University of New South Wales in Sydney, Australia. His research interests include the culture of public hygiene, design history and theory, gender studies, government of conduct, sociology of public moralities, representations of contagion, and visual sociology. He is a member of the Australian Socio-Graphic AIDS Project (AGAP); the Southeast Asian Socio-Graphic AIDS Project (SEAGAP); the Design History of HIV/AIDS Public Health Campaigns (DHAP); and the Documentary Chronology of HIV/AIDS Project (DCHAP).

Edwards, Helen, PhD, is a lecturer at the School of Education at the University of New England, Australia. She is an adult and early childhood educator and occupational therapist with research interests in indigenous education and disabilities. She is currently working on a number of projects investigating the sharing of knowledge between indigenous nations and the impact of aging on people with disabilities and their families.

Gilchrist, Heidi, PhD, is a lecturer at the School of Public Health at the University of Sydney. She is a physical therapist and public health professional with particular research interests in women's health and physical activity and leisure. She currently teaches public health in the medical program at the University of Sydney.

Grbich Carol, PhD, is a professor at the School of Medicine at Flinders University. Her research interests lie in qualitative health research and she is currently evaluating the delivery of palliative care services and the legal aspects of dementia. She has written several books: *Qualitative Research in Health: An Introduction* (Allen and Unwin/Sage), *Health in Australia: Sociological Concepts and Issues* (Prentice Hall/Pearson), *New Approaches in Social Research* (Sage), and *Qualitative Data Analysis* (Sage). She is the Editor in Chief of the *International Journal of Multiple Research Approaches.* She has supervised doctoral students since 1992, most of whom have become senior academics or senior executives in the health field.

Hays, Terrence, PhD, is a senior lecturer at the School of Education at the University of New England, Australia. He is a music educator and performer. His research interests include psychosocial aspects of music in people's lives and music performance. He is the Artistic Director of the Australian National Seniors' Choral Festival and Australasian Piano Summer School. He has recently cowritten *In-depth Interviewing* (Longman/Prentice Hall).

Hu, Wendy, PhD, is senior lecturer in Medical Education at the Western Clinical School, University of Sydney. Wendy is a family physician and medical educator with research interests in health-care communication and the interplay of values and uncertainty in clinical decision making. She has published in peer-reviewed medical journals, including *British Medical Journal* and *Health Expectations.* Currently she is researching mentoring, workplace-based learning, and other modes of informal learning for medical students.

Leary, David, PhD, is an adjunct senior lecturer at the School of Health at the University of New England, Australia. He is also the director and senior counselor of the Come In Youth Resource Center, a counseling service located in Sydney. He lectures in a number of counseling programs and provides clinical consultation and supervision in government and nongovernmental agencies. He has also published works on youth suicide, HIV, confidentiality and ethics, male sex work, and adolescent counseling.

Liamputtong, Pranee, PhD, is a professor at the School of Public Health, La Trobe University, Australia. Pranee has a particular interest in issues related to cultural and social influences on childbearing, childrearing, and women's reproductive and sexual health. She has published many papers and books in these areas. Pranee has also published several books on research methods, including *Health Research in Cyberspace: Methodological, Practical and Personal Issues* (Nova Science Publishers, New York) and *Researching the Vulnerable: A Guide to Sensitive Research Methods* (Sage).

Lunn, Suzanne, ProfD, is policy and research officer for Independent Schools Queensland (ISQ), Australia. Her work involves reviewing a range of national and state education initiatives in the light of their implications for ISQ and its member schools. A primary focus of her research is the growing quality imperative of integrating information and communication technology within the educational process, and identifying ways in which ISQ can best support its schools to meet the challenges required of twenty-first-century schooling.

Malin, Connie L., PhD, began her educational career as a special education teacher in a general education elementary classroom. She also worked as a preschool director in New York where she ran family literacy programs to assist parents in learning to develop and maintain active literacy skills with their young children. She went to the University of Nevada, Las Vegas, for her PhD in special education. All of that brought her to cofound Innovations International Charter School of Nevada and to serve as its chief educational officer, where she uses her qualitative skills on a daily basis.

Maple, Myfanwy, PhD, is a lecturer at the School of Health at the University of New England, Australia. She is a social worker and lectures in mental health and counselor ethics. Her research interests are in the areas of suicide, traumatic grief, bereavement experiences in families, and mental health and well-being. She is currently working on a number of narrative inquiry projects in these research areas.

McCann, Pol Dominic, PhD, works as a research associate at The National Centre in HIV Social Research at the University of New South Wales, Australia. His fields of interest are gender, sexuality, and blood-borne viruses. He has published his research in refereed journals on the role of homophobia on shaping the gender presentation of men in the West, and is currently researching the injecting drug-using community in Sydney.

Phillips, Jane, PhD, is program manager of quality and professional development at Cancer Australia in Canberra, Australia. She is a registered nurse with research interests in palliative care, chronic disease, health services reform, and health promotion. She has published a number of articles and book chapters related to her doctoral work, and is working on a national project investigating the role of oxygen for people with end-stage heart failure.

Putney, LeAnn G., PhD, is an associate professor at the University of Nevada, Las Vegas, with an early career background in secondary education. Her research focuses on long-term, in-depth ethnographic investigations into individual and collective learning and development in elementary and secondary classrooms. LeAnn's publication record includes refereed research journal articles, book chapters, and a coauthored book, *A Vision of Vygotsky.* LeAnn cofounded Innovations International Charter School of Nevada and brings to the school her expertise on ethnographic research and her work with classroom teachers on constructing academically successful and socially responsible classroom and school communities.

Regmi, Kiran, PhD, MD, MPH, is chair of the obstetrics/gynecology department of Bharatpur Hospital and one of the few physicians working in the remote villages of Nepal. She is on the faculty of the College of Medical Science and reproductive health advisor for Family Planning of Nepal. Kiran is cofounder of the Madhav Ghimire Foundation, which provides educational scholarships for at-risk and neglected children in Nepal.

Reicherzer, Stacee, PhD, is faculty staff with the Master of Science in Mental Health program at Walden University. A passionate social change agent, Stacee has written extensively about the complexities of transgender lives, including gay, lesbian, bisexual, and transgender identity development; transgender experiences; and the cultural bias in the diagnosis of gender identity.

Scott, John, PhD, is a senior lecturer at the School of Cognitive, Behavioural, and Social Science at the University of New England, Australia. He is currently working on two projects associated with sex work and masculinity and violence. His most recent books are *Crime in Rural Australia* (Federation Press), *How Modern Governments Made Prostitution a Social Problem: Creating a Responsible Prostitute Population* (Mellen Press), and *Perspectives in Human Sexuality* (Oxford University Press).

Sheridan, Alison, PhD, is a professor in the School of Business, Economics, and Public Policy at the University of New England, Australia. She has published widely on women's experiences in paid work. Her most recent work focuses on gender and governance.

Smith, Larry, PhD, is a professor at the School of Business, Economics, and Public Policy at the University of New England, Australia. His particular areas of interest and research are business management and leadership and work-based learning. Recently, he was a member of an international team that undertook a World Bank–funded review of the higher education system in Vietnam. He is editor of the *International Journal of Business Policy*. His most recent publications have been the Australian Government Research Report to the OECD on informal learning pathways, and *Approaches for Sustaining and Building Management and Leadership* (Adelaide: NCVER).

Smith-Ruig, Theresa, PhD, lectures at the School of Business, Economics, and Public Policy at the University of New England, Australia. She teaches human relations and management at both undergraduate and postgraduate levels. Theresa's research interests are in the areas of career development and diversity management. She has numerous conference papers and journal publications in these fields.

Sullivan, Gerard, PhD, is an associate professor at the Faculty of Health Sciences at the University of Sydney. Gerard has also held positions in the Faculty of Education and Social Work at the University of Sydney, where Heidi Gilchrist completed her PhD research. Gerard is a sociologist with research interests in minorities' access to health, education, and public services. He has published extensively in the field of gay and lesbian studies.

The Personal Nature of Qualitative Research 1

Victor Minichiello and Jeffrey A. Kottler

You already have some familiarity with qualitative research methods, whether you realize it or not. Regardless of how many courses you've taken, much of your life has been spent investigating issues and subjects that intrigue or confuse you. You set upon a mission to read what you can on the subject, talk to people who might know things that are relevant and useful, observe circumstances and contexts in which this phenomenon is often present, and compare what you have learned to what you think you already know. Then you try to make sense of everything you've collected and arrive at some sort of theory or synthesis to explain what you sought to understand. This process is not much different from what you will learn in this book. We aim to teach you a more systematic, strategic, and effective way to go about researching what you most want to know and understand.

In this first chapter, after introducing ourselves to you through our own personal qualitative journeys, we will review some of the basic concepts and principles that are part of this research strategy. Although this book can stand alone as a text or resource, you will need to consult other sources to learn the more practical dimensions of actually conducting your own studies. Our goal is to increase your understanding of qualitative research by capturing your interest within the stories of two dozen journeys undertaken by students, and the methods they used. Each narrative highlights some of the most important ideas regarding the conceptual and pragmatic challenges that you will face.

Victor Minichiello's Qualitative Journey

My passion for doing qualitative research can be traced to my undergraduate studies. I have always loved both new adventures and talking to people. I enjoy finding patterns within conversations, but struggle when working with numbers or appreciating, let alone understanding, mathematical formulae. I was taking two research method courses in the same semester: one qualitative, the other statistics. I looked forward to the qualitative classes and listening to the fieldwork stories of my professor, reading the books or articles he assigned, and doing the assignments. This course was a joy and hit a chord with me that reverberates to this day. In contrast, I found it difficult to remain awake while listening to my statistics professor talking about means, central tendencies, chi-squares, multivariate analysis, and regression equations, and I hated reading the assigned books and doing the assignments.

It was, however, an assignment in the qualitative course that launched me on my own journey as a researcher. So powerful was this fieldwork experience that I have used it to teach others about the concept of establishing rapport ever since (Minichiello, Aroni, & Minichiello, 2008; Minichiello, Madison, Hays, & Parmenter, 2004). So what was the assignment? Our professor, a prominent second-generation sociologist of The Chicago School, went around the room assigning topics to each student. We were asked to conduct three or four interviews. When he came to me he said, "Your topic is to understand the funeral business through the eyes of the funeral directors." For a nineteen-year-old, this was a very unusual, not to mention disturbing, topic. Or so I thought at the time. I had never even entered a funeral home nor attended a funeral.

After the initial shock wore off, I found this topic both challenging and exciting, perhaps because death holds such a morbid fascination for most people, including me. Who do I interview first? How do I approach these people? What questions do I ask? Do I really want to understand the funeral business from someone else's perspective? After all, what is there to really understand? People die and the funeral industry prepares the body for its public farewell and physical disposition from our world. Big deal. End of story. Literally. Well, to cut a long story short, my first interview is still alive with me today. That is where I learned much of what I now understand about the power of conversation to elicit amazing data. One of the most important aspects of doing qualitative research is establishing rapport. You need special interpersonal qualities to conduct such research, a topic we will discuss later.

Fortunately, for my first research experience I located an enthusiastic interviewee. He had wanted to tell his story for some time and I came along at the right moment in his life. He was keen to tell me that funeral directors are business people, grief counselors, and managers. This immediately challenged my way of thinking about *them* and some of the misconceptions I had in my own mind.

Within a few minutes of our meeting, the funeral director asked me if I wanted to see the showroom. I had no idea what he was talking about since I had never been in such a place before. But the wise words of my professor stayed with me: "Be courteous, open to exploring new adventures and ideas, and prepared to take some risks in order to establish rapport; this is a key feature of people trusting you and letting you into their world as an honored guest." I accepted the invitation not really knowing where I was going to end up.

I soon learned that the showroom was where the coffins are displayed. I nervously entered the room, and he gave me a tour and information about the coffins. My eyes caught the attention of a particular coffin priced at more than $12,000 (a lot of money at the time). I asked, "Why is this one so expensive?"

The response that followed was one that I had not anticipated. "Why don't you try it out?" he replied. And here is where the human interaction skills come into play when you are doing qualitative research. This invitation created a dilemma for me. If I refused the invitation, the informant could interpret this as a sign that I had negative attitudes toward his profession. This might be his test to see if he could trust me. If I accepted the invitation, the cost would be having nightmares (which I have had since) about the experience. I cautiously slipped into the coffin and learned many important things about these structures. More important, though, was what I learned with respect to qualitative research: I learned how dynamic and fluid qualitative fieldwork is and that my action was important in winning the informant's trust and confidence.

Qualitative research suits my personality. I enjoy talking to people, asking them questions, exploring their experiences. I'm curious about what people do and why they think, feel, and act the way they do. Having said this, I am also a practitioner of quantitative methods. I have conducted many large-scale survey studies, and I appreciate how much knowledge can be gained through the analysis of quantitative data.

All of my fieldwork experiences have some elements of complex human interactions and I have grown as a result of these experiences. Here I provide a sample of how qualitative studies have impacted me, both personally and professionally. I have always felt that older people get a raw deal in our society. In one study, I worked with a number of my colleagues to interview older people about their experiences of ageism (Minichiello, Browne, & Kendig, 2000). What I learned was that older people have their own language to talk about their experiences of being discriminated against that center around being seen as old and being treated as old. Our study highlighted how, despite our best intentions, many interactions with older people can make them feel like second-class citizens. As a result of this research I have aspirations to be an activist so that I can minimize the impact of ageism in my own (and other people's) later life. I was inspired by interviewing older people who, rather than wanting to accept situations as they are and ignore the unpleasant consequences of ageist interactions, wanted to negotiate for themselves and others new images of aging and find ways to minimize the impact of ageism on their lives. These people were working out ways to prevent others from seeing them as old and treating them as old. In the same way that feminist research has changed how sexism is played out in society, I hope that studies like this can produce greater awareness and actually change behavior.

Another area that interests me is HIV/AIDS, and how people who have it live with their disease (Minichiello, 1992). The first challenge that I faced was coming to terms with my own risk of contracting HIV/AIDS as a gay man. I found these interviews powerful and haunting. One of the major themes that emerged was the theme of family members ostracizing and abandoning their sons after discovering they were gay. The impact of this disclosure during a time of illness had huge consequences for all concerned, including the health-care system. It forced me to discuss these issues with my partner and family in ways that I probably would have not done otherwise. For example, I always found it difficult to discuss my sexuality with my father, but this research taught me that my hesitation rested with me rather than with my father.

I also directed a study that examined how male sex workers negotiate the context of selling sex to another man (Browne & Minichiello, 1995). I was interested in this topic because the issue of HIV/AIDS had emerged on the scene and because all the studies focused on the female sex industry. I thought that this was strange, because the male body is now being portrayed as a commodity as well, not to mention that HIV/AIDS in most Western countries is transmitted via male-to-male sex. The interviews allowed me to see how important sex is for males; both gay and nongay identifying men were seeking sexual experiences with other males. This was eye opening for me because it challenged my understanding of how sexuality is defined in society versus what really appears to be going on. My most fulfilling research experiences have been similar to this experience in the sense that my view of the world has been altered as a result.

Through the interviews, I discovered that commercial sex is not really seen as *sex* by some workers, and discovered the significance of the concept of work sex for public health. I was able to work with this concept to educate sex workers about the importance of engaging in safe practices and teaching their clients to do the same. As a result of this work, we developed public health campaigns about safety in the sex industry. One of the most rewarding aspects of this work is that Australia enjoys one of the lowest rates of HIV transmissions via the sex industry in the world. I'm proud to say that our health promotion campaigns have played an important role here.

Jeffrey Kottler's Qualitative Journey

I was born a qualitative researcher, as most of us were. What I mean by that is that I have always been naturally curious and trying to make sense of the world, and especially to make sense of where I fit in the grand scheme of things. I remember doing an investigation in high school for an assigned paper in which I was searching to explain my impatience, why I was always in a hurry to get things done and move on to the next thing. I concluded that it had had something to do with being born premature, six weeks before my anticipated due date. This became an operating assumption in the way I lived my life—it was an explanation that justified my behavior, if not explained it: "Sure I'm impatient, but what do you expect? I couldn't wait to jump out of my mother's womb and get started."

It was a lovely theory that helped me to make sense of my behavior, even if it was neither very psychologically sophisticated nor probably very accurate. About the time I began my academic career, my father had a right-hemisphere stroke, destroying the part of his brain that controlled his left side as well as a number of cognitive functions, including some inhibition. It was during one of our conversations soon after the incident that I asked him a question I had always wondered about—why he married my mother. As long as I could remember, I had never seen my parents show much affection. Instead, I only saw them bicker and argue endlessly. By the time they divorced when I was twelve, I was in many ways relieved that maybe the tension in our house would ease. But it never made sense to me for why they had been together, since they seemed to demonstrate so little love.

Stroke addled, my father blurted out a family secret: my parents had been forced into a shotgun wedding because my mother had gotten pregnant with me (this was considered scandalous during these times). They predated their marriage certificate so it would show that I had been born nine months after the wedding, when in fact I had been born six weeks previous to that. In other words, I had been a full-term baby and had never been premature! My whole definition of self collapsed in that moment. I was so stunned I could do nothing but laugh hysterically. (My father thought it was pretty funny as well and had been dying to tell someone after all these years.)

As you can imagine, this got me thinking. I considered all the other assumptions that we might hold about our realities and how they are constructed, often based on data that are imperfect, biased, and certainly subjective. I was by that time already a practicing therapist so I was certainly familiar with the ways human beings inform (and delude) themselves. I also was quite taken with how much I could learn from people if I practiced respectful listening, asked a few probing questions, and reflected back what I heard. It was simply amazing the stuff that would come out of such conversations. At the time, I had clients who were prostitutes, drug addicts, corporate CEOs, circus performers—you name it. And I was getting the education of a lifetime. Naturally, I was impatient to learn more.

My journey as a researcher has consistently followed a path of confronting a question that perplexes me, one that literally keeps me up at night trying to figure out what is going on. While still a graduate student, I harbored my own deep secret that I was crazy, that someday I would totally flip out. I had struggled with depression on and off throughout this time, just as my mother had throughout her abbreviated life. I was convinced that if people only realized how crazy I really was that nobody would ever talk to me again. So I launched a research project to study the history of deviant behavior, especially among those who are extraordinarily creative. This would become a journey that would last the next thirty years, and would culminate finally in a study of such "divine madness" (Kottler, 2006).

It turned out that I was able to attain a state of emotional stability during these early years, mostly as a result of the therapy I received as a client. By then, though, I was hooked on the methodology of finding out what I most wanted to know by talking to people. Since that time, every instance in which I am bewildered by an issue that is of great importance to me and for which I can find no satisfactory answers in the existing literature is the impetus for me to begin another research project.

Being amused and fascinated by the things I do when I'm alone, stuff I've never admitted to anyone before (pretending my house is under attack by aliens, talking to myself in strange voices, and so on) led me to wonder what everyone else does behind closed doors. I interviewed more than five hundred people during a ten-year span about what they do when they're alone and what that means for them (Kottler, 1990).

When my academic department was embroiled in conflict and I could find no useful material to get at the essence of such disrespect I began another journey to discover the ways that people externalize blame for their own misery (Kottler, 1994). When I started to become aware as a therapist how my personal and professional lives intersected, I started to talk to other clinicians about their own experiences (Kottler, 1987). In spite of all I accomplished in life, I still felt like a failure much of the time and wondered why professionals spoke so infrequently about their own struggles with imperfection. This led to two different studies, more than a decade apart, in which I interviewed prominent practitioners about their worst failures (Kottler & Blau, 1989; Kottler & Carlson, 2002). It also led me to investigate how clinicians struggle with their most difficult, challenging clients (Kottler, 1992; Kottler & Carlson, 2003).

I had an experience in which I stopped crying for many years, and then started to become more emotional after a near-death experience. What was *that* all about and why is there so little written and understood about the meaning of tears in people's lives? How do men and women cry differently and how is such behavior influenced by culture and context? Another study was launched (Kottler, 1996).

When I became fascinated with the ways my students and clients had transformed me over the years, I set about interviewing the most famous theoreticians about their own reciprocal influence experiences (Kottler, 2006). The same was true when I came back from a trip abroad a radically different person and wondered how other people's lives are transformed by travel experiences that shook up their worlds. I interviewed scores of people about the ways that trips had changed their lives as a result of being strangers in a strange land (Kottler, 1997).

Most recently, I am embarked on several other journeys (remember: I'm still impatient even if not born prematurely), studying the ways that students and professionals are impacted by their involvement in social justice projects (Kottler & Marriner, 2009), as well as another project interviewing distinguished theoreticians about their most creative breakthroughs (Kottler & Carlson, 2009). In each of these cases and so many others I could name, my journeys begin with intense curiosity to make sense of something that eludes me. After consulting existing research and literature, I still feel like there is something significant that is missing. And the way I prefer to explore these areas with so little understood is to identify those individuals who are in the best position to inform me about their own experiences. It is from such investigations that new theories are developed, new phenomena are understood, and professionals in a variety of disciplines can be better informed about concepts that can guide their practice.

Whereas I have been fortunate enough to be able to publish my work, it is the journey that is as important as the outcome in qualitative research. Whether anyone else ever read what I had discovered, I still experienced the joy, satisfaction, and greater wisdom of exploring those issues that interest me the most. That is what makes doing qualitative research so incredibly exciting for me and why I am so delighted to share more of this process with you.

Your Own Personal Dimensions

You can't understand qualitative research without understanding your personality—that is, your own motives, interests, values, and goals. What are you searching for and what is that journey really about? It is not just about advancing knowledge and science, but also about pursuing a personal agenda. This is not only legitimate to acknowledge but important to the process. It is a distinguishing feature of the approach that differentiates it from quantitative methods in which objectivity and detachment are the hallmarks.

As should be immediately evident in our research journeys, qualitative methods embrace and honor subjective experience—not only of the informants and participants, but also of the investigator. Many of the phenomena we explored were intimately connected to our own most cherished interests. That is not to say that we jettisoned academic rigor and scientific process; on the contrary, some of the greatest contributions to the advancement of knowledge occurred from qualitative studies. Think of Sigmund Freud's theories, based on a few case studies, or Jean Piaget's developmental stages, based on in-depth observations of a limited sample of children. Darwin's theory of evolution was based largely on the constant comparison method that is such an integral part of data analysis in qualitative research. Before Galileo or Einstein attempted to measure the properties of the universe, they first built theories grounded in observational data.

All knowledge is *socially constructed*, meaning that all beliefs and assumptions occur within a personal and cultural context. The topics that are chosen, how they locate that study within a body of knowledge, the approach that is selected, the procedures that are employed—are all influenced by the researcher's perceptions. Contrary to what you might think, this is not necessarily a weakness, but rather a strength of the approach, particularly if the researcher engages in rigorous self-reflection and careful analysis.

In the next chapter, we review many of the most important features of any qualitative study, describing some of the theoretical and methodological concepts. We also provide a context for the narrative journeys represented in each chapter, including the methodological decisions that were made and the assumptions that guided those choices. Somewhat unique in our treatment of the subject is an effort to present the material in the most accessible way possible.

References

Browne, J., & Minichiello, V. (1995). Finding meanings within male sex work: Social contexts and safe sex interactions. *British Journal of Sociology, 46*, 598–622.

Kottler, J. (1987). *On being a therapist.* San Francisco: Jossey-Bass.

Kottler, J. (1990). *Private moments, secret selves: Enriching our time alone.* New York: Ballantine.

Kottler, J. (1992). *Compassionate therapy: Working with difficult clients.* San Francisco: Jossey-Bass.

Kottler, J. (1994). *Beyond blame: A new way of resolving conflict in relationships.* San Francisco: Jossey-Bass.

Kottler, J. A. (1996). *The language of tears.* San Francisco: Jossey-Bass.

Kottler, J. A. (1997). *Travel that can change your life.* San Francisco: Jossey-Bass.

Kottler, J. A. (2006). *Divine madness: Ten stories of creative struggle.* San Francisco: Jossey-Bass.

Kottler, J., & Blau, D. (1989). *The imperfect therapist: Learning from failure in therapeutic practice.* San Francisco: Jossey-Bass.

Kottler, J. A., & Carlson, J. (2002). *Bad therapy: Master therapists share their worst failures.* New York: Brunner/Routledge.

Kottler, J. A., & Carlson, J. (2003). *The mummy at the dining room table: Eminent therapists reveal their most unusual cases and what they teach us about human behavior.* San Francisco: Jossey-Bass.

Kottler, J. A., & Carlson, J. (Forthcoming). *Creative breakthroughs in therapy.* New York: Wiley.

Kottler, J. A., & Marriner, M. (2009). *Changing people's lives while transforming your own: Paths to social justice and global human rights.* New York: Wiley.

Minichiello, V. (1992). Gay men discuss social issues and personal concerns. In E. Timewell, V. Minichiello, & D. Plummer (Eds.), *AIDS in Australia* (pp. 142–161). Sydney: Prentice Hall.

Minichiello, V., Aroni, R., & Minichiello, V. (2008). *In-depth interviewing.* Sydney: Pearson/Prentice Hall.

Minichiello, V., Browne, J., & Kendig, H. (2000). Perceptions and consequences of ageism: Views from older persons. *Ageing and Society, 20*, 253–278.

Minichiello, V., Madison, J., Hays, T., & Parmenter, G. (2004). Doing qualitative in-depth interviews. In V. Minichiello, G. Sullivan, K. Greenwood, & R. Axford (Eds.), *Handbook of research methods for nursing and health science* (pp. 411–446). Sydney: Pearson/Prentice Hall.

An Overview of the Qualitative Journey 2

Reviewing Basic Concepts

Victor Minichiello and Jeffrey A. Kottler

Like any journey, doing qualitative research is an adventure, with all the accompanying excitement and stimulation, as well as the challenges to confront. Even with an itinerary and a rough plan for how you expect things will unfold, there are always surprises, twists and turns in the road, and unforeseen obstacles that must be negotiated. In spite of all the preparation you might do in the form of reviewing literature, studying maps of the terrain, talking to others who have traveled the roads before you, the one thing that you can count on for certain is that you will not end up where you thought you might. That is why qualitative research requires a degree of flexibility and fluidity while venturing into new territory, skills that mark you as an explorer in the tradition of Columbus, Vasco de Gama, Magellan, Marco Polo, James Cook, Charles Darwin, Margaret Mead, or Helen Thayer, the first woman to reach the North Pole in a solo expedition.

Rather than enduring hardships at sea or in the wilderness, you will encounter your own forms of adversity in the form of ambiguity and confusion, yet there is no intellectual enterprise that is more fulfilling and satisfying. During an era in which it seems as if everything has already been discovered, you have the opportunity and the privilege to advance knowledge in your discipline by describing unique experiences, explaining complex phenomena, creating new meaning, developing theories—all based on the data that you collect. As a relative neophyte to research, what could be more exciting?

A Certain Reluctance

Many of the texts that introduce you to the methods and strategies of qualitative research may seem unnecessarily obtuse and confusing. You are exposed to a bewildering new vocabulary, dense philosophical concepts, and procedures that appear at first to be both unscientific and ambiguous. When contemplating a qualitative journey, whatever initial reluctance you might feel might be intensified by explanations that fail to make the process explicit. On the contrary, you are bombarded with terms like *social constructions*, *bracketing*, *discourse analysis*, *phenomenology*, *epistemology*, *hermeneutics*, terms that seem incomprehensible, especially after they are supposedly explained.

In this introductory chapter, we will review and simplify what this journey entails, as illustrated in our own stories that preceded this chapter and the dozen more that follow it. While it is beyond the scope of any overview to cover many of the details that are involved in this research enterprise, the purpose and goal of this book is to highlight this experience through the stories of those students who completed these adventures. We first wish to cover some of the major concepts that are involved in most qualitative studies, thereby addressing some of your confusion and uncertainty about what to expect. This also will allow you to follow the journeys of our contributors with at least a rudimentary familiarity with the major ideas.

You already know this much: qualitative researchers use data collection techniques to explore new territory. They interview people or observe them in their natural settings so they can learn from them about what they are thinking, and, more importantly, why they think or act the ways they do. This process is not that unusual from what you already do quite naturally: you try to make sense of what you see, experience, and encounter. For example, in the workplace or at school you frequently see people doing things that appear incomprehensible. Why would someone choose to sit in the back of a classroom by himself, knowing that it will make it so much more difficult for him to engage in the discussion? On the way to the university, you noticed cars slowing significantly going north, even though there had been an accident on the *southbound* side of the road. On campus, you see a group of friends standing around in a circle. Rather than speaking to one another, though, each is engaged in conversation *with someone else* on their respective phones. On campus you notice social groups that all seem to be partitioned according to their gender and race, but spy one group that appears to represent every conceivable segment of diversity. "What is different about them?" you wonder. There are a hundred such questions that you consider every day, almost every hour. Why do people behave the way they do? What is it like for people to think or react in ways that appear to be so different from the ways that you would? What are people experiencing inside themselves as they go about their most meaningful activities? What sense can you make of what is happening around you—or inside you?

You may feel a degree of reluctance to explore questions like this that seem so complex, so ethereal, so difficult to understand, much less measurable in any way. Whatever tools and skills you picked up in quantitative-type courses don't seem to lend themselves to describing or explaining such phenomena, at least to the depth you might like. Yet the *interpretive approach* that underlies qualitative methodologies holds that individual thinking, as well as collective action, has intelligible meaning that can be identified, described, explored, analyzed, and synthesized into coherent themes. This requires that you view the phenomena from the perspective of those you are studying. It means getting outside yourself in ways that are completely different from what is required in quantitative studies that value objectivity and detachment so highly.

Qualitative journeys may not seem particularly difficult or complicated if all it involves is watching or talking to people. Nevertheless, many beginning researchers feel overwhelmed and discouraged because of previous associations they have with research procedures. Students often equate research methods with complicated sets of mathematical equations, a long and sometimes difficult list of instructions underpinning procedures for data collection, incomprehensible computer models for analyzing data, and the use of technical scientific language that is so removed from everyday communication.

Qualitative research certainly has its own set of technical terms, complex concepts, and challenging procedures, but we believe that ultimately training in this discipline helps you not only to find the answers and knowledge that most intrigue you, but also to become a far better listener and problem solver. These qualitative journeys can enrich your personal experiences, heighten your enjoyment of work, improve the intimacy of all your relationships, and learn a method for discovering what interests and perplexes you the most.

Different Ways of Knowing

Before we review what qualitative research is all about, we first want to make a simple but important point about what is considered valid knowledge. You might immediately wonder what makes any knowledge valid or invalid. Isn't anything that you know or believe you know considered valid, at least in the sense that it is your perceptions or opinions? In one sense, this is assuredly so. A hospitalized schizophrenic patient manifesting florid hallucinations, or someone tripping on a psychedelic drug may hold knowledge about the world—that we are actually all dead but living in an alternative universe—but is that a real, valid, or legitimate perception? Before you reject this idea out of hand as crazy, consider the assumptions and beliefs that people have held for generations that have since been found to be flat wrong. Doctors used to think that infections were caused by evil spirits. Virtually everyone once believed the world was flat or that our planet was at the center of the universe. All of these assumptions were considered truths and unassailable knowledge that couldn't possibly be conceived any differently.

Knowledge is never fixed: it evolves. It is intimately connected to context related to history, culture, language, and the ways that you come to acquire that knowledge. If you want to advance knowledge through the research process, you have to first acknowledge that the approach you take, whether through conversation, observations, surveys, controlled experiments, or analyses of documents, will produce a certain slice of that phenomenon. If you study victims of bullying by interviewing them, or observing behavior in schools, you will most likely learn something different from what you would learn if you read victims' private diaries.

If you are interested in new knowledge, you have to understand there is a multitude of ways that you could study the phenomenon, each of which will tend to highlight certain facets. You could compare schools that have antibullying programs with those that do not, measuring the impact of these interventions. You could interview bullies, victims, and bystanders about their different perceptions and experiences of certain incidents. You could do a historical analysis of bullying behavior in the media, focusing on the ways that incidents have been reported through the ages. You could study the notes of school personnel describing their reactions and perceptions of bullying episodes. You could compare the incidence of bullying in North America versus school systems in central Africa to measure the influence of socioeconomic and cultural factors. You could study one individual case in which bullying resulted in several school shootings. All of these different qualitative and quantitative approaches testify to valid and important ways that issues can be explored, producing results that focus on areas of greatest interest and importance. It is the accumulative knowledge of *all* of those sources that gives us the best understanding of any phenomenon such as bullying.

Different Approaches to Collecting Data

Some time ago, a psychologist named Richard LaPierre wanted to examine the discrepancies between what people *say* versus what they actually *do* (Deutscher, 1973). You notice this all the time: People report that they are neither racist nor homophobic, yet use slurs against particular groups.

People say they will stop bad habits yet persist in the addictions in spite of compelling evidence of how harmful they are. People say they wash their hands after using the toilet but rarely do. The reality is that people say lots of things that are not actually related to their actions. LaPierre was especially interested in how this plays out in perceptions of racism.

LaPierre (Deutscher, 1973) used two different methodologies to capture this aspect of human behavior. He conducted his research in the early part of the twentieth century in California when discrimination on the basis of race was all too common. He collected his data using the qualitative tool of *participant observation,* which means that he visited natural field settings where he could unobtrusively watch the ways that people behave. In this case, he focused on restaurants and hotels that employed Chinese immigrants to observe the ways they were treated by patrons. He followed up these observations by distributing questionnaires to the mostly white patrons about their attitudes toward Chinese service personnel.

LaPierre found that the customers were more likely to say that they would discriminate against Chinese people in a questionnaire than in an actual observed situation, demonstrating two points. One, very different results about discrimination were received, leading to quite different conclusions about the extent to which Americans discriminated against Chinese people. Second, what people say about themselves and others can be at odds with what they do in real-life situations (for a detailed discussion of this study see Bernard, 2006; Deutscher, Pestello, & Pestello, 1993).

One of our students replicated this study (Minichiello, Aroni, Timewell, & Alexander, 1990) by comparing the ways that motel clerks responded to bikers (motorcyclists) who attempted to rent a room for the night. When the receptionists were asked about their level of comfort serving those customers who appear to be in motorcycle gangs, the majority said they would be unwilling to provide such individuals with service and would feel very uncomfortable if confronted with such a situation. Yet when these same clerks were actually faced with this situation—a biker standing at the counter asking for a room—most were perfectly willing to provide friendly service and rent a room.

So, how do you interpret such results? You can reach different conclusions about attitudes toward Chinese immigrants or bikers, depending on which data you examine. If you relied solely on the questionnaires distributed, you would say that discrimination against these minority groups is rampant and universal. Yet if you relied on observations of actual behavior, you might reach a different conclusion—people may hold certain prejudices and biases, but that doesn't necessarily mean they will act on them in a given situation. Interestingly, both sets of data are valid and reflect the contradictory nature of human beings.

These different ways of studying behavior reflect their underlying philosophical approaches that guide the research process. Each of these approaches brings certain assumptions to the journey, certain operating principles, parameters, goals, and procedures that are consistent with the preferred way of knowing about the phenomenon you are studying.

So What Is Qualitative Research Anyway?

Qualitative research originally emerged as a strong reaction against the prevailing view during the early part of the twentieth century in both Europe and North America that people could—and should—be studied in the same way as physical objects. Human beings were considered not much different from rocks, flowers, or planets. There was a belief by scientists that the same patterns that were being observed with physical matter like gravity or glacial movement also could be applied behavior. Within social sciences, particularly anthropology and sociology, some researchers believed that people's behavior was not so easily predicted and measured, especially if the goal was to uncover deeper patterns that might explain the nature of human experience. Surveys and carefully controlled experiments were incredibly useful, but had limitations in the kinds of data that were revealed. Such researchers developed alternative methods that involved observing people in their natural environments like villages, schools, and workplaces. They also found it extremely revealing to actually talk to people about their experiences, as well as examine diaries and letters that were written at a very personal level. It is probably no surprise to you to discover that although these studies were extremely rich and revealing, this method was criticized as being too soft and unscientific to have a place within academic disciplines.

Qualitative researchers argued that there was room for multiple ways for acquiring knowledge, each of which could complement one another. For one thing, people can interpret situations and make decisions that deviate from the norm or from what is expected. They use language to describe their thoughts and experiences. They are capable of controlling their reactions in line with the meaning they attach to these situations. Rather than apologizing for the subjective nature of this approach, qualitative methods actually have several advantages that allow a researcher to investigate issues and topics that might otherwise remain barren. Table 2.1 summarizes some of these strengths (Plummer, 2004).

Qualitative researchers believe that there is no fixed way of thinking about the world and that different people can experience the same events but think about them or interpret them very differently. This, then, provides a useful model to help explain why people from different backgrounds behave in such diverse ways in response to apparently similar

Table 2.1   Contributions of Qualitative Research

Strength of the Method	Applied Example
Exploring unchartered or underdeveloped territory in areas where phenomena are poorly understood	Studying the meaning of crying and tears in people's lives as a form of communication
Examining experiences, behavior, phenomena in a social context that takes into account various perceptions and realities	Looking at childbirth experiences from the perspective of new mothers, their husbands, mothers-in-law, and obstetricians
Describing human experience in vivid, deep, and meaningful ways	Presenting narratives of parents whose children committed suicide
Developing new theories to account for phenomena	A model for conceptualizing and treating attention deficit disorders among homeless youth
Discovering new ways of understanding the world and its inhabitants	Exploring people's experiences with stress associated with learning new technology
Changing or shifting the dominant paradigms of an era to consider alternative ways of knowing or experiencing	Feminist approaches to examining styles of leadership within organizations
Studying aspects of human experience that are influenced by oppression, marginalization, prejudice, and stigma	Examining the ways that elementary school age girls and boys both feel limited by their gender roles
Making interdisciplinary links between intellectual fields and scientific domains in order to synthesize what is known about an issue or topic	Bringing together literature from health sciences, education, humanities, social sciences, neurobiology, and the media to understand loss of memory during the aging process
Intensively studying single cases of phenomena that represent unique or meaningful examples of interest	Observing operations within an organization that is noted for its high employee morale and work satisfaction
Combining qualitative inquiry with quantitative studies to deepen, broaden, or better focus and describe results obtained	Gathering examples from interviews and focus groups to highlight data obtained from questionnaires

situations. As one example, sex workers and clients can be engaged in the exact same physical activity (having sex), yet interpret the experience quite differently. The client may receive intense sexual gratification, even a degree of intimacy, yet the sex worker can report feeling aversion, boredom, or just a routine day at work (Browne & Minichiello, 1995). Even within these two groups, there is remarkable variation in the reported experiences, just the kind of data that is difficult to pick up in overly structured studies. You may discover a similar pattern in your own research efforts—remarkable and fascinating differences in how people perceive, live, and report their experiences.

Features of Qualitative Research

In contrast to quantitative research, which relies on measuring outcomes through statistical analysis, qualitative methods are defined by a notation system comprising words, images, and language. Rather than assigning numerical values to data that are collected, qualitative researchers examine transcripts of conversations, listen to and view tapes, study oral and written records, and review other images contained in media and art. This material is often coded—transformed into more accessible and usable forms—but still is preserved in language rather than converted to numbers.

Table 2.2 highlights some key differences between the two research approaches. You will note, in particular, that people who are studied in qualitative research are referred to not as *subjects* but rather as *participants* or *informants*, meaning that they are active collaborators in the process, treated as coequals and experts about their own experiences. There are some important requirements for anyone attempting to undertake a qualitative project. These include the following five characteristics:

1. **Inductive thinking**. In contrast to the Sherlock Holmes school of deduction in which the detective or quantitative researcher predicts outcomes or logically forms conclusions based on empirical facts that have been tested, inductive methods are far more expansive. Your goal is to observe and listen as carefully as possible and then generalize larger principles that may explain the phenomenon.

2. **Flexibility**. Whereas quantitative researchers are encouraged, even required, to be precise, consistent, structured, and totally prepared, qualitative researchers are masters of improvisation and thinking on their feet. You are constantly reading and responding to whatever is

Table 2.2   Key Characteristics of Qualitative and Quantitative Research

	Qualitative	*Quantitative*
Conceptual framework	Concerned with understanding people's experiences from the perspective of the participants	Concerned with discovering facts in terms of cause-effects
Assumptions	Assumes a dynamic and negotiated reality	Assumes a fixed and measurable reality
Reasoning processes	Inductive (from specific to general) and circular, alternating back and forth between data, analysis, and literature	Deductive (from general to specific) and linear, operating in a sequential series of progressive steps
Methodology	Data collected through observations of what is happening in the real world, or talking with people in a conversational style	Data collected by measuring things via instruments or conducting experiments
Participant role	Active informants about their experiences and perceptions	Subjects of experiments or respondents to questions
Primary tools	Interviews, focus groups, observations, review of documents	Structured questionnaires, predetermined measurement devices, or tools to collect and measure data
Sampling	Small, strategic samples not presumed to represent population	Large samples, randomly selected, presumed to represent larger groups
Data analysis	Data reported in words or text, analyzed by themes	Data reported via numerical values and then statistically analyzed
Data classification	Coded and classified into themes and concepts	Classified by variables
Outcomes	Propositions developed that synthesize themes and lead to rich descriptions, models, and theories	Hypotheses tested between independent and dependent variables

happening in the moment, adjusting your protocol to fit the unique requirements of every situation or context. Depending on how participants are responding, you will continually evolve your inquiry and even change the fundamental nature of your research question. The most valuable data often emerge in unexpected and surprising ways, *if* you remain open to what is unfolding before you instead of remaining stuck in your own expectations and predictions about what you think you will find.

3. **Inquisitive nature**. We are not talking here about being prying or nosy, but in being inquisitive in a respectful, sensitive manner designed to encourage people to share what may be private, personal thoughts. The focus of the research is to get inside the other person's mind, heart, and soul, to penetrate the private, protected domain. This is what makes qualitative studies so powerful: they reveal material that previously has been hidden, disguised, sanitized, or beyond awareness. You will need to develop the skills to building trusting relationships with participants such that they will be willing to talk about things that may be challenging, difficult, or even painful.

4. **Reflective listening**. Relationships are *everything* in qualitative research. The quality of your data will depend on how comfortable, safe, and supported your participants feel, sharing what they are thinking, living, feeling, and perceiving. You will need solid interview skills to reassure people, invite them to talk in meaningful ways, probe and prompt when needed, but mostly listening extremely well—and communicating your intense interest in such a way to encourage deeper exploration. Once the participant senses the slightest critical judgment from you, the least disrespect or disinterest, your interview will be compromised.

5. **Insightful analysis**. One of the most challenging aspects of a qualitative project is living with the data to the point that meaningful themes emerge. This means immersing yourself as fully as possible into the material, allowing it to speak to you over time. Qualitative researchers often most enjoy collecting their data, which often means talking to people about a topic of great personal interest. Once you develop some basic interview skills and practice them in some pilot sessions, you also will find yourself enjoying the process immensely, continually saying to yourself, "I can't believe what I'm hearing!" or "This is incredible!" However (and this is a big however), there is a lot of apprehension and frustration associated with making sense of the data you've collected. What does it say? What are the most important themes? How do you synthesize so much material, collected over dozens, perhaps hundreds, of hours, and find

the essential components? The answer to these questions is that you will develop the ability to think analytically about what you encounter. Your mentors will help you with this, as can some more experienced peers, but basically you will learn to ask yourself, "What is this really about?" "What are the patterns that I've heard over and over again?" "How does this material relate to what has been done before?" "What are the connections between what I am reading (or hearing, sensing, or observing) and what has occurred previously?" There's no shortcut for this process but the good news is that you will carry these skills with you for the rest of your life, forever able to think more analytically about the things you observe and experience.

In this brief overview, it is not our intent to deal with the complex philosophical issues associated with qualitative research, nor to describe all the complex and detailed parts of the process, which are covered in standard texts on the subject. Our goal instead is to simplify and highlight some of the most important concepts that will be useful to you when reading the narrative journeys that follow.

Editors' Comment

Sources to Consult

This book is likely one of several sources that have been recommended to assist you in becoming a skilled qualitative researcher. It is beyond the scope of our purposes to introduce you to the seminal works in the field. However, it is imperative as part of your journey that you devote time to reading the classics, especially those directly relevant to your chosen methodology and topic. For example, any self-respecting ethnographer would be familiar with Garfinkel (1967), a grounded theorist with Glaser and Strauss (1967), a phenomenologist with Husserl (1963), and a participant observer with Spradley (1980).

Of more contemporary interest, there are several websites that list all the journals that publish qualitative research studies, as well as publishers that distribute specialty books on the subject. Here are a few of our favorites:

Qualitative journals:

http://www.slu.edu/organizations/qrc/QRjournals.html
http://www.nova.edu/ssss/QR/calls.html

Qualitative books:

http://www.amazon.com/s?ie=UTF8&index=books&field-keywords=Qualitative&page=1
http://www.sagepub.com/home.nav?display=cat&catLevel1=&prodTypes=any&level1=Course1007&level2=Course1008&currTree=Courses&_requestid=238425

Variations on a Qualitative Theme

Thus far we have been talking about qualitative research as if it were a single entity, a homogeneous method that everyone understands and agrees with, practices universally, and talks about in the same terms. Nothing could be further from the so-called truth. In fact, there is tremendous variation (as there is in all human enterprises) in the ways that qualitative researchers talk about their craft, the language and preferred terms they employ, and the philosophical assumptions that guide their process.

Before we discuss some of the major qualitative methodologies (yes, there are many), we first want to mention some of the theoretical and data analysis paradigms that led to the construction of the approaches. It is way beyond the space limitations of this chapter to discuss these theories in any depth or detail. You might wish to consult other sources (see Denzin & Lincoln, 2005, for a review) to develop further your appreciation for the conceptual basis for qualitative research.

Some scholars (Habermas, 1987) have attempted to make clear distinctions between philosophies, methodologies, and research methods within qualitative research. To confuse matters further, *phenomenology*, for instance, is considered both a philosophy (Husserl, 1963) and a methodology that relies on certain techniques (Embree, 1997; Moran, 2000). In addition, followers of a particular theory like *symbolic interactionism* often use research methods such as *grounded theory* or *thematic analysis.* The boundaries are sometimes blurred. For the sake of simplicity, we include an overview of some important theoretical traditions that you are likely to encounter in your work.

The theories to which you align yourself depend on several factors, including your views of the world, your preferred line of inquiry, and the preferences of your mentors. The variability is not unlike what you could do if you wanted to take a photograph. You could choose one among many lenses—wide angle (grounded theory), telephoto (discourse analysis), fixed (action research), or zoom (ethnography). You could use a variety of filters (feminist theory) to highlight certain colors or contrast. You could use a narrow or wide depth of field, blurring the background or keeping everything in focus. You could take a portrait (case study) or landscape (purposeful sampling), a horizontal or vertical alignment. You could use film, slides, or digital capture. You could adjust the settings for color or black and white, muted or saturated color, high or low resolution. Even in choosing the camera, you could use a point-and-shoot, digital or film, 35 millimeter, rangefinder, medium or large format. With all these choices, each producing a different outcome, you would then have to consider the person holding the camera. Taking photographs, like doing qualitative research, is not just about the tools and methods employed, but also about the photographer's unique viewpoint.

CONSTRUCTIVIST THEORY

Each of the theories we summarize represent attempts to understand how people perceive and make sense of the world, as well as what motivates them to act the ways they do (Andrews, Sullivan, & Minichiello, 2004). Almost by definition, most qualitative researchers generally take a *constructivist* view of society, looking at the ways that people give meaning to their experiences and their interactions with others (Sarbin & Kitsuse, 1994). While often misunderstood and far more complex than we can describe briefly (we won't even begin to differentiate it from *social constructionism* at this point), this theory originated as a way to locate human behavior and experiences in the context of their particular social environment and cultural identities. Central to this theory is that social phenomena do not exist as natural events or objects in the world, but are brought into existence by human social activities that have important implications for how they should be studied (Searle, 1995). Rather than taking the existence and character of social phenomena as given, seeking to identify causal relationships among them, one should study and document the processes by which they have been given meaning and come to be accepted as *shared* reality (Berger & Luckmann, 1967).

What it is that we know, or think we know, about what it means to be a man or woman, gay or straight, rich or poor, black or white, or anything else, is determined in large part by the cultural scripts with which our parents, teachers, media, and a thousand other sources have indoctrinated us since childhood. In order to make sense of any human experience we would thus have to examine it within these social constructions. This may seem rather obvious now, but it was a radical position when first introduced, one that transformed most academic disciplines and gave birth to qualitative research.

SYMBOLIC INTERACTIONISM

One of the long-standing theories associated with qualitative research uses the process of human interaction to understand meaning in people's lives. There are three core principles to this theory, as identified by one of its founders (Blumer, 1969): meaning, language, and thought. The first idea refers to just what you'd think it is—the *meaning* that people ascribe to their interactions with others or even with objects, as well as the ways they experience and behave toward them.

Second, the *language* that we use helps us to negotiate this meaning through symbols. Third, *thinking processes* negotiate the interpretation of these symbols.

Let's say that you are interested in the rather unique and varied ways that people relate to their cell (mobile) phones. These are ubiquitous objects, now found within the possession of practically every person in the industrial world. There are some individuals who even have two or three phones with them at any moment in time and can often be found talking, texting, or emailing a portion of every hour of the day. The interesting question, however, is, "What is the particular *meaning* of this device in people's lives?" For some, it is a conduit of intimacy for friends and family. Others might relate to this object as a business tool that allows them to make sales and accumulate wealth. It can be experienced and related to as a terrible intrusion and annoyance, or an unholy temptation of the devil, or a source of security in the case of an emergency. It is an object that represents far more than merely an electronic device—it is a friend, an enemy, a distraction, a source of entertainment and amusement, or a plague of modern life. Symbolic interactionist theory allows you to investigate this phenomenon from the perspective of the meaning that people attach to their cell phone experiences.

POSTMODERN AND FEMINIST THEORIES

These theories were developed primarily in reaction to the prevailing positivistic (supposedly objective and empirical) ideas of the time. In the case of *postmodernism*, there was a realization that new technologies led to new forms of knowledge, not to mention changes in the social systems that structure the world. Postmodern theory rejects assumptions that there are clear cause-effects; reality is instead often fragmented, indeterminate, and chaotic. It takes into much greater account the ways that culture, language, gender, and especially issues of power influence the beliefs we hold.

People share their views with others in the forms of stories, narratives, discourses, and texts, material that can be analyzed or deconstructed in order to discover underlying assumptions and hidden meanings. (For a detailed discussion of narrative analysis, see Bruner, 1990, and Polkinghorne, 1988.) It is a theory and also set of research practices that reject the *grand narrative*—one single way of seeing and explaining the world in which we live (Holzman, 2006).

Often considered similar to postmodernism, but more focused on several core issues of gender, oppression, and power, feminist theory looks at the ways that dominant patriarchal hierarchies have maintained inequities within culture (Nicholson, 1990). Research, in particular, is an enterprise that has been dominated by male values (objectivity, detachment, logic, cognition, control, measurement) for generations. Feminist theory and research practice challenges the assumptions that reflect the dominant values of male culture.

ETHNOMETHODOLOGY

Unlike symbolic interactionism, this theory is less concerned with the content of understanding than with the methods or ways that meaning is established and shared within a cultural group. Ethnomethodologists start out with the assumption that social order is an illusion, a fabrication; reality is far more fluid and chaotic. Because of the human need for at least the perception of coherent order in the universe (and community), there is often a consensus among people about universal assumptions that guide and rule daily life. These are related to family, social, political, and economic structures. They form the basis of values and laws within a society.

Ethnomethodology, meaning *folk methods*, was a theory developed by Garfinkel (1967) at about the same time that symbolic interactionism was created. Its intent was to look at the ways that people produce and share their social rules that guide behavior. You would immediately recognize that this would be an especially useful approach for anthropologists who seek to understand the underlying structures and patterns of cultures. It also has formed the basis for *participant observation* studies that can occur within any group or organization. If, for instance, you wanted to look at the deeper patterns by which adolescents live and operate within the world of video games, you could do so by actually entering that cultural domain to understand it from the inside.

PHENOMENOLOGY

We warn you without apology: this theory is a tough one to grasp—and no wonder since its aim is to uncover the *essence* of human experience (Embree, 1997). Essences of anything are ethereal and difficult to pin down. Phenomenology (fi-nŏm' -nŏl'-jē —practice pronouncing it), quite simply, has as its goal to understand someone else's world as if you were standing in her shoes. Like the other theories mentioned, the aim is to understand the meaning that people attach to their experiences, but the focus is to investigate more deeply the internal world as it is seen, felt, intuited, and thought by the individual (Moran, 2000). It is the most subjective of all the theories and sees that as its major contribution since it can access material that might otherwise remain private and mysterious. For example, in Terrence Hays's research journey described in this book, he describes the ways that older people relate to music in their lives.

DISCOURSE ANALYSIS

This theory focuses on examining texts and talk (discourse) within their cognitive, social, and cultural contexts. It seeks to analyze and decode the hidden motives and meanings of ideas that dominate society with particular focus on issues of power, manipulation, and control. It goes beyond the superficial and literal to uncover less obvious meanings that people associate with ideas (Gee, 2005). In McCann's chapter within this book (Chapter 14), he uses this theory to understand the ways that men give meaning to homophobia. By examining the role of language and the power dynamics that underpin what McCann calls "boyhood communication" that occurs in a variety of settings (schools, sports, bars, fraternities) jokes emerged as a powerful communicator of ideas about gender. The discourses of social power were highlighted by analyzing the underlying currents of derogatory humor that enforce certain values associated with masculinity. Certain men, who display any effeminate or nontraditional masculine traits, often become targets of ridicule to ostracize them or force compliance.

GROUNDED THEORY ANALYSIS

We saved grounded theory analysis for last because it is among the most popular methods in qualitative research. This theory originated from the work of Glaser and Strauss (1967), who developed one of the first systematic methods of qualitative analysis. Essentially, they provided a means by which to think about data collected that lends itself to identifying codes and themes. The goal is to develop a theory that explains or at least better understands the phenomenon, a theory that is carefully grounded in the material that was collected.

Basically, the analysis of the data includes a detailed examination, interpretation, and breaking down of the textual data (usually transcripts) into its descriptive and conceptual elements, and then reconstructing those components into a meaningful whole. The relative success of this enterprise depends on your ability to:

1. ask deep-level questions about the data, ferreting out meaning on multiple levels;

2. make comparisons between people, situations, and contexts: "If this seems to be true for one person, why is this not the case with another?";

3. identify concepts and linkages between concepts found in the data, within and between individuals;

4. classify concepts into meaningful categories; and

5. refine these categories to develop a meaning explanation of the phenomena under study. These refinements often result in the development of a theory.

The chapter in this book by David Leary, Victor Minichiello, and Jeffrey Kottler (Chapter 4) describes the journey of using grounded theory analysis to develop an understanding of the life experiences of young male sex workers who work on the streets. A proposition that emerged from the analysis is that involvement with sex work is fundamentally about involvement with people. Another chapter, by Kiran Regmi and Jeffrey Kottler (Chapter 5), develops a deeper understanding of the ways that childbirth is conceptualized by new mothers, their families, and health professionals in the rural areas of Nepal that have among the highest maternal mortality in the world.

You may notice from this last section that we are slowly transitioning from the theoretical to the more practical dimensions of doing qualitative research. We began with some of the more complex, abstract theories that form the basis for qualitative journeys and are now moving slowly (probably more slowly than you wish) to the ways that these ideas lead to particular ways of operating within the journeys themselves.

Grounded theory analysis, just described, is one of several approaches designed to make sense of whatever you uncover—or discover—in your own investigations. Regardless of the approach you take, using thematic analysis, narrative analysis, or discourse analysis, your goal is to collect something from the field and then find meaning in your data. This information can be analyzed in a multitude of ways, depending on your ultimate goals and the suitability for your particular interests and research questions.

A Time Out to Catch Your Breath

Student: I am totally confused.

Mentor: About what?

Student: Well, all this theory stuff is great and all . . .

Mentor: Meaning you can't see what all this stuff is about and why it is even introduced to you when all you want to do is finish this study and get on with your life.

Student: You read my mind.

Mentor: Putting that point aside for a moment, what are you feeling confused about?

Student: Back to my project. You helped me formulate my research question. I know what I want to study now.

Mentor: That's encouraging.

Student: Yeah, sure, but how the heck do I figure out which methodology to choose? There are all these theories and stuff but I'm not clear how they translate into getting into my research question. Besides, they all sound pretty much the same. They just seem to use different language, most of which I can't really understand anyway.

Mentor: What is it that you want to find out?

Student: What do you mean?

Mentor: What outcome do you want when this journey is over? Do you want to describe the essence of some human experience? Do you want to develop a theory to explain things? Do you . . .

Student: You've lost me.

Mentor: Look, each of the theories and their corresponding qualitative approaches is designed to get at particular aspects of your question. Are you primarily interested in describing people's experiences, understanding the social context under which the experiences emerge, understanding the fine-grained meaning of what they're saying, developing a theory to explain what the phenomenon, or perhaps just studying one case that is especially intriguing to you?

Student: Am I supposed to know the answer to that?

Mentor: Hmm. Perhaps not quite yet. But at this point it is important to understand that you have choices, and whatever decisions you make at this early stage, you're likely to change your mind once you get into the study.

Student: So, then, it's okay to be confused?

Mentor: I'd be seriously worried about you if you were not.

Do you feel any better? Or at least realize that you are not alone? We want to reassure you that at this point in your journey feeling bewildered and a bit overwhelmed is not only normal, but expected as part of the process. After all, what would you think would happen when exploring new territory, using unfamiliar tools, in challenging terrain, venturing pretty much on your own?

In order to address some possible concerns you might have about converting theory into action, we also mention several of the major methodologies that are used in qualitative research. While each of the tools might share similar compatible features (in the same way that all cameras have

Table 2.3   Major Qualitative Methodologies

Method	Uses	Strengths	Limitations	Example
Grounded theory	Develop a proposition or theory to promote understanding of an issue or topic	Provides high conceptual level	Time consuming, high analytic skills, sophisticated data analysis tools	Development of a model to conceptualize and treat sexually reactive teenagers based on interviews with counselors
Phenomenology	Understand the essence of people's experiences	Exposes unique ways of thinking and relating to the world	Philosophical roots complex and difficult to understand; requires skills for interpreting text; challenging	Women's experiences of leadership within organizations
Narrative	To describe the major plots within people's life stories	Preserves the integrity of people's experiences and connects life events	Selective in its focus: allows the participants to control what is revealed	Aboriginal men's stories of grandfathering, told through rituals
Case study	Intense exploration of a single individual, organization, or incident	Provides in-depth description and analysis over time	Totally dependent on a single case that may be unique and not a common experience	A university's recovery from a traumatic act of violence
Ethnography	Participant observation of a culture or subculture	Studies phenomena in their natural environment	Very time consuming; complex to negotiate researcher's role within the culture	Social or dating networks within fitness centers

lenses), each of them offers distinct advantages that allow you to match the method to your interests and goals. Table 2.3 reviews a few of the most common qualitative methods (there are others), including how they might be used.

One Final Point

This book is all about lived learning experiences and applied knowledge converted into practice. It is time for us to be even more honest with you. Despite our best attempt to make qualitative research methods comprehensible and accessible, this concept chapter is still formed in the discourse and structure of a textbook. It does not begin to capture the imagination, creativity, and—most of all—the excitement of the research journey.

Perhaps with a subject as complex and multifaceted as qualitative research it is impossible to present an overview that is absolutely gripping and totally engaging. That, after all, is why this book is structured around narratives of adventure and expedition into unknown realms. What follows is a series of stories that talk about the challenges, joys, disappointments—the *realities* of doing research. They were written by students (and their mentors) who were just a little further along the road than you are right now.

References

Andrews, I., Sullivan, G., & Minichiello, V. (2004). The philosophical and theoretical context of qualitative research. In V. Minichiello, G. Sullivan, K. Greenwood, & R. Axford (Eds.), *Handbook of research methods for nursing and health science* (pp. 59–70). Sydney: Pearson/Prentice Hall.

Berger, P., & Luckmann, T. (1967). *The social construction of reality: A treatise in the sociology of knowledge.* New York: Doubleday.

Bernard, H. (2006). *Research methods in anthropology: Qualitative and quantitative.* Lanham, MD: Rowman AltaMira Press.

Blumer, H. (1969). *Symbolic interactionism.* Englewood Cliffs, NJ: Prentice Hall.

Browne, J., & Minichiello, V. (1995). The social meaning behind male sex work: Implications for sexual interactions. *British Journal of Sociology, 46,* 598–622.

Bruner, J. (1990). *Acts of meaning.* Cambridge, MA: Harvard University Press.

Denzin, N., & Lincoln, Y. (2005). *The SAGE handbook of qualitative research.* Thousand Oaks, CA: Sage Publications.

Deutscher, I. (1973). *What we say/what we do.* Glenview, IL: Scott, Foresman and Co.

Deutscher, I., Pestello, F., & Pestello, H. (1993). *Sentiments and acts.* New York: Aldine.

Embree, L. (1997). *Encyclopedia of phenomenology.* New York: Springer.

Garfinkel, H. (1967). *Studies in ethnomethodology.* Englewood Cliffs, NJ: Prentice Hall.

Gee, J. (2005). *An introduction to discourse analysis: Theory and method.* London: Routledge.

Glaser, B., & Strauss, A. (1967). *The discovery of grounded theory: Strategies for qualitative research.* Chicago: Aldine.

Habermas, J. (1987). *Lectures on the philosophical discourse of modernity.* Cambridge, MA: MIT Press.

Holzman, L. (2006). Activating postmodernism. *Theory & Psychology*, *16*, 109–123.

Husserl, E. (1963). *Ideas: A general introduction to pure phenomenology*. New York: Collier Books.

Minichiello, V., Aroni, R., Timewell, E., & Alexander, L. (1990). *In-depth interviewing: Researching people*. Melbourne: Longman Cheshire.

Moran, D. (2000). *Introduction to phenomenology*. London: Routledge.

Nicholson, L. (1990). *Feminism/postmodernism*. New York: Routledge.

Polkinghorne, D. (1988). *Narrative knowing and the human sciences*. Albany: State University of New York Press.

Plummer, D. (2004). Demystifying qualitative research: The heart of the matter. Unpublished manuscript, School of Health, University of New England, Armidale, Australia.

Sarbin, T., & Kitsuse, J. (1994). *Constructing the social*. London: Sage Publications.

Searle, J. (1995). *The construction of social reality*. New York: Free Press.

Spradley, J. (1980). *Participant observation*. New York: Holt, Rinehart & Winston.

Locating and Understanding Voices in Narrative Inquiry

3

A Journey of Discovery

Myfanwy Maple and Helen Edwards

T his chapter describes my (Myfanwy's) experiences as a doctoral student and one of my mentors (Helen) in the application of narrative inquiry methodology to a research study, a study that examined the parental stories of the death by suicide of a young adult child. We have structured the chapter in a manner that allows you as the reader to experience a narrative mode of writing and to think about how to analyze data using this method. As the dialogue is developing, we will take turns in providing you with a view of the research, the analytic process, and the ways in which narrative inquiry can be used with relation to a particular study.

We start with an overview of the choice of methodology and then recount my interview experience with one participant that occurred around the halfway point of the research project. We chose to do this to illustrate the absence of a linear path in narrative inquiry, and highlight an interactive, engaging, one-step-forward, two-steps-back kind of journey. This approach to writing not only represents a way to analyze the data, but also demonstrates how narratives can inform the work in a way that honors the whole. This chapter differs from others in this text as it also follows the developing narrative between the two of us, doctoral student and mentor. Some shared life experiences and disciplinary expertise in the allied health professions helped to develop our relationship. These shared experiences opened us to open communication, a feature vital to a successful student-mentor relationship.

Why Narrative Inquiry?

In some of our initial meetings, we discussed the gaps in the research literature in relation to suicide, in particular the associated poor understanding of family grief (Maple, 2005a). We also talked about the possible range of methodologies that could address these gaps and answer the research question that had emerged: How do parents live through and live with the suicide of their young adult child (Maple, 2005b, p. 3)?

Editors' Comment

Matching of Objectives and Approaches

It is interesting that Myfanwy chose a narrative perspective among several possible choices. It's important to realize that whatever approach is selected, you have to find one that matches your objectives. In this case, she wanted to hear the voices of parents and their stories. This provided the optimal way for her to understand the issues that parents were telling in a way to keep their stories intact. She started out using another approach, grounded theory, but abandoned it because it was generating themes that were generic but not representative of the individual voices that she wanted to highlight and honor. As a side note, it also should be mentioned that she had to advocate strongly for this approach in order to convince her mentors. There is always a wide menu of choices from which to select those items that best suit particular goals and to generate the kind of data desired.

✳ ✳ ✳

Myfanwy and I (Helen) discussed grounded theory in some detail (Glaser & Strauss, 1968) and Polkinghorne's (1995) two types of narrative methodology, paradigmatic and narrative cognitions. Grounded theory and paradigmatic narratives appeared to focus too much on the commonalities and overall frameworks arising from the data. Myfanwy argued the value of taking a narrative cognition or inquiry approach, "noticing the differences and diversity of people's behavior" (Polkinghorne, 1995, p. 11). Narrative inquiry provided mechanisms that "retain the complexity of the situation in which an action was undertaken and the emotional and motivation meaning connected with it" (Polkinghorne, 1995, p. 11) as the focus of analysis.

✳ ✳ ✳

In reflecting to the supervision team on my understandings of suicide grief and from an awareness of the interviews that had been completed, I determined that narrative inquiry was the methodology that would enable my study to reach a deep understanding of the unique elements of the parents' stories. The term *narrative* was taken to "refer to a discourse form in which events and happenings are configured into a temporal unity by means of a plot" (Polkinghorne, 1995, p. 5). Because I am a social worker with previous research interview experience, Helen and I were confident in my ability to gather data. Narrative inquiry provided a framework to analyze and produce explanatory stories from the mass of data gained from the interviews.

A narrative methodology seemed to me like a natural choice for this research. I liked the distinction that narrative inquiry gave by steering clear of mining the data for themes and the danger this has to depersonalize and decontextualize the stories from the participant. The orientation toward understanding the story within the teller's social situation, locating not only what is said and not said, but also the way in which events are placed and the importance given to them (Gilbert, 2002), was critical to a sound study in the area of suicide bereavement. I carefully examined and took note of my own assumptions and understandings about the experience of loss through suicide in a process of bracketing to allow me to immerse myself in hearing the experience as voiced by the participants (Gubrium & Holstein, 2003).

Once I had settled on the broad methodological stance that I would take, I had to work through the various schools of thought within narrative to find the right mode for this research. Ultimately, I settled on narrative inquiry—primarily the work of Donald Polkinghorne (1988, 1995). The analytic focus of this approach is the plot of the narrative—the way narrators configure their stories and the meanings they attribute to the events within. Due to the intimate and sensitive nature of the research topic, it was very important to honor parents' stories. This study required a methodology that would allow me to explore the full breadth of their experiences through the stories they told during long, in-depth interviews. About halfway through my interviewing, my choice of methodology was confirmed when I interviewed Kate.

Listening for Meaning—An Example From Kate

Kate was the thirteenth parent I interviewed about the experience of losing a young adult child to suicide. It was in reflecting on Kate's story that I really had to sit back and think—her interview was so different from the others. At first, I could not put my finger on why it was so different. All the parents before her had told me unique stories regarding their deceased son or daughter. The stories were all so different that I was starting to panic about trying to make sense of the narratives. Thus far, the only analysis I had done was written reflections on the interviews, reflections on the data gathered, and my own thoughts about the process. How was I going to make sense of all these data? I was desperately hoping the answer would emerge—as the qualitative methods textbooks had promised.

When I interviewed Kate, everything suddenly looked different. At first I did not understand exactly what it was that was so different. Like the other parents I had spoken to, Kate shared with me experiences of her daughter over the years, from when she was young until the day she died and since. But in her voice was a quality that I had not yet heard from the other parents. Her dialogue revealed something that had not been present in the stories I had previously heard. The way she spoke made her daughter, Sallie, come alive. Her voice was so full of pride and love for her daughter, and her dialogue was breathtaking. To this day, four years later, I can still hear her voice in my head. I share some of her story here to illustrate the type of data I collected, and how interviewing Kate changed my study, the analysis, and how it ultimately directed the findings of my research.

> I (Kate) had been told in a lot of different ways. Eight times she had tried to take her life and so when someone, at first I am sure they were cries for help, then they became really, she usually slashed her wrists and took sleeping tablets and antidepressants, but the last time she gassed herself. . . . It was as if I could see her go into this pit of blackness and she would feel herself slipping into it and she would do things to avoid slipping into it and find herself at the bottom of the black pit and to get out would take a lot of energy and struggle until the day came when she went into that black pit and she said "I know I haven't got the energy, it's not worth it, I cannot get out, and I cannot bear the thought of living the rest of my life." . . . So I guess that was the end of the story, but it was also the end of a hell of a lot of pain and suffering, sadness, and dysfunction and none of us would wish her back because it is too painful, too hard. . . . How could she, how long did she have to continue with that black depression and her hopes and dreams, you could see them gradually being torn down.
>
> I am just grateful that I have been able to get up again, but get up with an arm missing and I am constantly thinking of her. . . . And it is a pleasure, I love to think about her. . . . It is like where you have a cenotaph and the little light flickering eternally, it's like I have got that burning inside me all the time, a little Sallie Light that's always going to be there and it is precious and don't touch it. It is my hallowed spot and I want to have it there and it is never going to go out, so I carry that little light everywhere, that little Sallie Light.

After a lot of thought, I became aware that there was not an ounce of shame in Kate's voice, nor was she concerned that I, or others, may judge her negatively (something all the parents commented on experiencing in relation to their child's death). She had already experienced that and had consciously chosen to ignore such behavior. While the other parents I had spoken with all expressed their love of their child, Kate was not ashamed of the way in which Sallie had chosen to die. In fact, Kate was proud that her daughter had chosen to end the suffering that she experienced throughout her life and knows now that her daughter has found a peace that was not available to her in life.

Editors' Comment

The Art of Listening

One of the distinguishing features of qualitative journeys is that researchers must listen carefully, attentively, and analytically to the experiences that are described. It takes considerable training and practice to learn to withhold your own biases, preconceptions, and expectations in order to hear clearly what is being said, rather than "hearing" what you anticipate will be expressed. Qualitative interviewing involves opening yourself up to explore, and being surprised with what you learn. It means taking on a position of respectful curiosity, prompting open sharing in such a way that you don't overstructure and guide the conversation, but instead allow participants to tell their own stories in their own unique ways. This is remarkably difficult to do since often you must surrender control and a position of authority.

Another stark difference in my interview with Kate was that she knew prior to Sallie's death that her daughter would take her own life. There had been previous attempts—as there had been for other families—but Kate, unlike others, could understand the need for her daughter to do this and ultimately saw Sallie's actions as justifiable considering the pain that her daughter was suffering in life.

So, in terms of the analysis for my research, this was a breakthrough. Let me go back and give you an overview of my research to place this breakthrough in perspective. Then I will highlight the way in which narrative inquiry helped me to understand these parents' stories and ultimately write up the research in an accessible manner, uncovering some important aspects and new understandings of parental bereavement through suicide.

The Research Project

For this research, I set out to interview parents after the suicide of their young adult child to gain a beginning empirical picture of their experiences. I wanted to gain some insight of what these parents experienced before, during, and after the death by suicide of their son or daughter.

While there had been a lot of research focused on youth suicide prevention, little attention had been paid to those who have been intimately affected by a suicide. My rationale for this study was that in addition to learning more about parental grief and appropriate support for those bereaved through suicide, this intimate knowledge also could help unlock more understandings of why young people in Western cultures are vulnerable to suicide.

To answer the research question, I wanted to delve deeply into participating parents' stories, while allowing them to tell their narrative in any way they were comfortable doing so. To do this, I used a variety of design strategies, including allowing the parents to choose whether they wished to be interviewed alone or with their partner, allowing them the choice of where the interview would take place (their home, my office if they were local, or a public place). Parents also were given the opportunity to choose their own pseudonym, to protect their own and their child's identity. I used a single open-ended question to begin the interview. After that, I only used prompts from their story to explore an issue more deeply or to gain clarification. The question I developed and used was this:

> I would like to hear about your experience of losing a young adult child to suicide. You can tell your story in any way you feel comfortable, perhaps beginning with telling me a bit about before [child's name]'s death, and then your journey since the suicide.

This question was carefully worded to provide the participants with a guide to the research focus—that is, the story of their experience. The interviews typically lasted for between one and three hours. Most interviews were with one parent, four were with both parents. From the outset of the project, in the research design, I instinctively sensed that it would be important to honor these parents' stories in every way I could, and I wanted a method that could offer this.

Editors' Comment

Flexibility in Design

In quantitative research, there is a strong emphasis on standardizing procedures, keeping everything consistent and the same. Such consistency adds to the perception of objectivity and precision. Yet in qualitative studies, the possibility of such consistency is contested. Nevertheless, it is critical to demonstrate flexibility, adapting your approach and sensitivity to the context and each individual as illustrated by Myfawny's methodological choices. Some participants will require a bit more structure than others will. Some will tell their stories with little prompting except an initial inquiry or two; others will stop and start, looking for a bit more direction. Depending on the relationship you develop, the personality of the participant, and their responsiveness at any moment in time, you will need to make continual adjustments in your style and approach.

RECONCEPTUALIZING THE DATA

✳ ✳ ✳

As a part of Myfanwy's supervisory team, I (Helen) was conscious that she was deeply immersed in the stories and listening for the meanings that parents were sharing. It was necessary to remind her that in order to analyze the narratives, she had to step back from the first-hand experiences to make sense of it. In narrative inquiry, Polkinghorne (1995, p. 177) explains, "the goal of analysis is to uncover common themes or plots in the data. Analysis is carried out by hermeneutic techniques for noting underlying patterns across examples of stories." In relation to the data, this type of analysis made sense to enable Myfanwy to explore the meanings that parents attributed to their experiences through the story they told. It also provided her with a way to understand why some events were talked about and others were not, and the influence of the social context.

✳ ✳ ✳

While I was committed to the use of this method for the study, I discovered there were no clear steps that described how to do narrative inquiry analysis. Unlike most quantitative and qualitative methods that clearly provide generalized steps for undertaking the analytic process, narrative inquiry looks to understand meaning within story. As I read further in methods texts and examples of research using this method, I realized that, while there were clear foci of narrative inquiry (primarily the plot, in this instance), there were limitless ways in which the focus could be directed.

Primarily due to this lack of clear direction, I was overwhelmed by how this was done and underwhelmed by my ability to do it. A sense of desperation threatened to overcome the whole process, and there were moments when I thought that I should review my choice of method. While this may seem absurd to those with a more traditional scientific orientation to research, I realized over time that the lack of formal analytic steps allows for a freedom and flexibility of data analysis that may be lost when using other methods.

Editors' Comment

Overwhelmed With Data

It is perfectly normal and to be expected that you will sense that you are drowning in your own data, and that you will be uncertain how to organize or make sense of everything you have heard and witnessed. And how could you not feel this way, considering the innumerable hours you've spent with your participants and the thousands of pages of text that you now must review and analyze? What are you going to focus on and how do you know that is what is most significant? It takes patience and perseverance to give yourself permission to remain bewildered during this transitional period between data review and synthesis. Most researchers eventually discover meaning in their data, as illustrated in this section.

✻　✻　✻

Myfanwy discussed these internal conflicts with me (Helen) regarding the analysis of her data. In response, I shared my experiences of using knowledge visualization approaches (Burkhard, 2005; Edwards, 2003) to examine data. I indicated that visual representations of information, such as metaphors, drawings, and photographs, had been key elements for my own thesis development. Several of the other doctoral students I was supervising also had found rethinking narrative materials helpful, doing so from a range of visual and other perspectives. This gave Myfanwy an idea for a starting point to examine the data in terms of understanding how parents chose what they do and do not say.

✻　✻　✻

USING METAPHORS TO UNLOCK DATA

Metaphors provide a mechanism to relate, compare, and make meaning of new knowledge with lived experiences. In the process of debriefing with one of my peers, I describe below, using the washing line metaphor, how I interpret the stories that have emerged from my interviews. At the same time, I adopt Lincoln and Guba's (1985) verification strategies through peer crosschecking, an important way to enhance the rigor of qualitative research studies.

In trying to explain the data in a simplified version to a peer one day, I described how each parent appeared to peg pieces of their story on a piece of string and that this string could easily break, letting all the pieces fall. The pieces would then have to be readjusted in the next telling. This simple explanation led me to using a metaphor of a washing line as a concrete way to begin to think about my data analysis. I listened again to the tape-recorded interviews and thought about the ways in which each part of the narrative was presented to make up the whole. As my voice was limited in the interviews, the parents' stories were free flowing, influenced only through my presence, body language, and occasional comment.

Viewing each part of the story as a piece of clothing, with each parent having basketfuls of clothing that could be used to make up each story, and viewing the washing line as the plot, the choice between what will and will not be hung out each time the story is told was fluid. This fluidity means that feedback from the audience is interpreted each time a story is told, and that this feedback directs how the items will be hung out next time.

The washing line that holds the pieces of clothing in place for the story to have meaning for the parent and for me, the listener, is the plot. I began to understand how parents changed the composition of the contents of the washing basket and the order the items were placed in it, depending on how I responded to what I was being told. Sometimes they added more pieces to explain something further, or sometimes they left some items in the basket if they did not feel safe to hang it out at that time. These choices ultimately affected the composition of the plotline and thus the story of their experience. The washing line was tentative and vulnerable to breakage, and sometimes it needed to be restrung depending on audience approval or disapproval, or depending on the social setting in which the parents told their story.

Uncovering this washing line, or the plot, of each parent's story was quite difficult. As you can imagine, each story was very emotive, telling of a young life cut short. Trying to understand these stories in terms of how they were held together was challenging, to say the least. Delving into the depths of the story—why each parent told me of particular experiences, gave preference to some situations, less to others—was challenging for me. At the same time, this process was also very exciting. I was honored that these parents had chosen to be so open with me, honest about their experiences and sharing of their child's life and death. I was moved by the experiences of these parents, and still am. This topic opens up a vulnerability for all parents that, no matter what they do for their children, some children will die. I acknowledge this vulnerability in my own parenting, but I was not aware at the time that this also may have had an emotional impact on my supervisors, as Helen explains.

UNDERSTANDING NARRATIVE IMPACT

✣ ✣ ✣

Reading the suicide narratives as I (Helen) responded to Myfanwy's thesis drafts disturbed my sleep and impacted my dreams. My own and extended family members were approaching young adulthood at the time and I was challenged by thoughts of, "What if it were them? How would I deal with such an experience?" Such visualizations brought emotions to the surface that I worked through at another level.

✣ ✣ ✣

It was during this period of using metaphors to explore the plot that I (Myfanwy) came to understand what it was in Kate's story that seized my attention. Understanding that Kate both knew that her daughter would die by suicide and had no shame in discussing Sallie's life and choice for death began my deeper awareness of narrative inquiry as a method. I realized how a plot is used to hold together each story, and how each story is influenced by the individual narrating it. I had had one of those Aha! moments. This event allowed me to take the pressure off myself, enabling me to believe that I could succeed. As a consequence, I freed up my thinking on other aspects of the data, which led to me exploring different ways of examining the similarities and differences between and across the stories of these parents.

With this new insight guiding me, I reexamined the data and found that another mother also had predicted that her son would die. While this mother was not proud of her son's action, nor did she accept them, she certainly was prepared for the fact that he would die young, well before he eventually did. I began to understand that while some parents were prepared for their child's death prior to their suicide, others definitely were not. In fact, they had never imagined such an event occurring in their family. There was also a group of parents positioned in between. While they had not thought their child would die, these parents could realize, after the event, that there had been clear signs that their child was suicidal. By the time each interview was finished, all parents' narratives had a plot that could be described as preparing before, preparing after, or never preparing for their child's death by suicide (Maple, Plummer, Edwards, & Minichiello, 2007).

While this plot of preparedness, as it became known, was a monumental discovery in terms of my research, it was not enough—there was so much more to each interview. There were the obvious things that I expected to find having read the literature—disenfranchised grief, stigma, and grief differences between men and women, to name a few. There also were smaller groupings of interesting data. For example, a number of mothers attributed the suicide of their son to emotional distance displayed by the child's father.

LOOKING BROADLY

When I looked more broadly, I began to see that what shaped these parents' stories was the way in which society—and themselves—silenced their narratives. These parents were unable and often unwilling to talk about their child. This was in direct contrast to their desire to do just that. In addition, these stories were ongoing. They do not finish with the death of the child. The parents remain in an ongoing, evolving, dynamic relationship with their child postdeath. This continuing bond had been explained elsewhere (Klass, 2000; McCabe, 2003); the data from my study added weight to an emerging field of grief and bereavement literature.

As I write this, I am aware that the process sounds clear and clean cut. Let me assure you: it was not. Searching through hours and hours of transcribed interview data, trying to understand what was going on between the lines, trying to establish what was holding these parents' stories together, what difference and similarity meant in and across the interviews was painstaking, extremely time consuming, yet ultimately very satisfying.

During this analytic phase, I needed support from my mentors to act as sounding boards while I was making sense of the data. I talked through my reflections during team supervision sessions, but was able to deepen my understandings more fully in one-on-one explorations. While my two more-experienced mentors were able to help me to think philosophically about these findings in relation to the research literature, it was Helen, only newly graduated with her own doctorate, who listened and reflected with me for hours while I tried to make sense of the data. Helen helped me to understand where my own narrative—the doctoral thesis—fitted into the big picture.

INTERCHANGING ROLES

✳ ✳ ✳

Due to a parity of research experience, we interchanged our roles often, moving from learner to expert and back. Our relationship helped to create a comfort zone where it was safe to admit confusion, to not know a way forward, to ask for help, and to reject information surplus to current needs. There were questions raised, as much in a process of interpersonal exploration as in project management. We each listened and put forward possible options, but ultimately Myfanwy was self-directing and self-affirming. I (Helen) became conscious that a primary focus of mentoring doctoral students was about supporting the appropriation of knowledge. New directions emerged for us both that were not apparent when working in isolation.

✳ ✳ ✳

Early on in the emergence of our professional relationship I indicated in an email that the feedback I was receiving from Helen "was so refreshing to have . . . since I commenced this long and arduous journey . . . during my reflections I was thinking how wonderful it was to have someone to talk to about my project and how it is going and the things I should be getting under control (especially the formatting)."

✳ ✳ ✳

I (Helen) was tentative about the direction I should be taking as a beginning supervisor, and about what sort of feedback I should be giving, as seen in the following email to Myfanwy: "I went in this morning's session not quite knowing what best to do, say etc. . . . . What is important to me is that the time is useful to your purposes, so I am very open to structuring or doing things in a way that will meet that need. Obviously, it is not possible when you have given me such a volume of material to discuss each response in a supervision session. Would it be useful to you to take my written comments away to digest and then a few days later to meet again to give you the chance to challenge or ask for further explanation of what did this mean? Why would you have suggested that? How did you interpret what I wrote, because it does not appear to link to what I intended? Or whatever other questions you might think are worth exploring."

✳ ✳ ✳

FINDING CLOSURE

In the text above, there is an email I (Myfanwy) sent to Helen about halfway through the research journey. As explained earlier, I was totally overwhelmed at the time by the amount of data narrative inquiry produced, how to manage and massage it into a dissertation that would fit university requirements and provide new insights into parental bereavement through suicide. I was also aware of the need to honor the experiences of the participating parents.

Throughout the whole journey, I sensed it was very important that the parents involved in the study were given the opportunity to retain ownership of their stories as much as possible. One way that I did this was with regard to pseudonyms. Rather than randomly assigning pseudonyms to the parents and their deceased child, I asked whether they wished to choose their own aliases. Most parents wanted to do so, and used names that were important to them, often nicknames for their deceased child. All were grateful of the opportunity to do this, and thanked me for my thoughtfulness.

Another matter that I had predicted being a potential issue in researching in this area was ending the research relationship. I was very careful throughout the process to keep parents a part of the process, ensuring they were kept up to date with the status of the research, sending them reports every six months. They all received a final four-page summary of the research. At the time of the interview and again when this report was sent I told the participating parents that the report signified the end of their commitment to the research. Many parents chose to keep in touch over the ensuing years, often through a Christmas card at the end of the year.

As I conducted some of the interviews in my local rural area, I became aware early on that I would meet some of the parents while conducting everyday life—at social outings, at the supermarket, around town. At the conclusion of the interview with local parents, I discussed this possibility and a decision was made on how this would be handled. Some parents wished to be acknowledged in social situations, others did not—the choice was theirs and I have honored their choice to this day.

I had considered both of these issues prior to the research, but as is the nature of the research process, I could not predict all the sticky moments. One that became apparent early on was that in many cases I was of an age at the time of the interview that was close to the age of the child that had died (or the age that he or she would have been now). In addition, as the research was of such a personal nature all the parents wanted to know how I had come to study suicide. I had to give something of myself in developing rapport with the parents. Many research texts warn of not doing this, and my professional inclination was certainly to refrain from doing this. So, while it seemed unnatural at the beginning, I soon realized that I was asking of these parents something much more personal, and that I owed it to them to share a little of me. So, if parents asked about me—my motivation for the study, my family life, or commented on my age in relation to their child—I willingly had a short conversation about this. While at the beginning I was a little uncomfortable with this, I am glad that I shared with the mothers and fathers who so generously shared their experiences with me. Had I not done this, I believe I would not have received the depth of data that they ultimately shared with me (Hiles, 2002).

VICARIOUS TRAUMA

The other side of engaging in sensitive research topics is the potential that these interviews could negatively affect my own health and well-being through vicarious trauma. I carefully arranged debriefing sessions with the university counseling service prior to setting out to interview. I did attend a couple of these sessions, but contrary to what I had been led to believe by colleagues prior to the interviews (that I would be traumatized by opening up old wounds), I found the opposite to be true. The stories the parents told were traumatic, yes. However, I also was incredibly privileged to be told the stories, to provide a new avenue for these parents to express their experiences, and ultimately to share this new learning in broader ways—through publishing, presentations, professional training, and support for bereaved parents.

Editors' Comment

Personal Challenges Elicited by the Process

This qualitative journey describes vividly the ways that this kind of research can be so informative and fulfilling, yet also disturbing and evocative. It takes a lot of emotional energy and resilience on the part of the researcher to remain with the participant—and the data—when it reveals such agonizing stories. Whereas objectivity and rigor are defined as a form of detachment in quantitative research, the qualitative scholar has to find attachment in order to gain understanding, yet do so in a way that she doesn't lose herself in the process. *Bracketing* means recognizing your own assumptions and biases, owning them, but keeping them in perspective so they don't pollute and prejudice what you've heard and observed.

In looking after myself with regard to the content of the interviews, it never crossed my mind that perhaps I should have prepared my supervisors, also. When I read the transcripts of the interviews, I can hear the parent's voice in my head. I am not overwhelmed or upset by this, because I also know the parents' story. This knowledge is not available to those who read my data, however. You may have noticed your own reaction to the excerpt from Kate I included at the start of the chapter. Due to the grounded nature of narrative inquiry and the narrative style in which the data are presented, this emotional response to my writing will always be a hazard. At the same time, though, I believe that it is this emotional response that allows us all to understand a little more clearly what it is that these parents have experienced and shared in this research process.

POSTSCRIPT TO NARRATIVE INQUIRY

From the outset of this research, I believed I had to use a method that honored the participants' contribution to the research. I set up stopgaps to ensure that in as many ways as possible the participants' ownership of their stories remained intact. At the same time, I had an obligation to the university and academic community to make sense of the data that these stories provided. I also had an opportunity to build knowledge in the area of suicide bereavement for the benefit of all families experiencing the suicide of a loved one and those professionals who encounter these individuals and families.

I believe that using narrative inquiry was an appropriate choice for this research, and that the outcomes have been valuable for all stakeholders. Most qualitative methods are extremely time consuming, and narrative inquiry is no exception. It is this level of engagement with and immersion in the data that led me to understand in a unique way the narratives that I collected.

POSTSCRIPT TO SUPERVISING
A NARRATIVE INQUIRY PROJECT

✳ ✳ ✳

The opportunity to be a mentor in Myfanwy's doctoral program was stimulating for me. The way she engaged as an adult learner, scheduling each stage of the research and thesis process with advanced notice to supervisors, allowed us to block out spaces in our diaries. When supervision sessions were organized, she facilitated the process with a list of agenda items. This proactive approach made effective use of the supervision period. As Myfanwy's period of candidature grew, so did her confidence. She moved comfortably across to the role of expert in her discipline.

In this situation as a mentor, I found myself embedded in an environment where I was concurrently supporting a colleague to extend her research skills while broadening my investigative abilities and adapting my approaches to knowledge sharing to collaborate effectively with Myfanwy. This development process was significantly assisted by the feedback and modeling received from two very experienced academics who were cosupervising Myfanwy's doctoral work.

The openness of my relationship with Myfanwy facilitated extensive reflective critique sessions about the doctoral process. In these discussions, we explored ways to modify my practices and hers to more fully meet the career and academic goals we aspired to (Pearson & Brew, 2002). Our shared cultural, personal, and disciplinary backgrounds were factors that played a part in supporting the frankness of these discussions. An environment was created where it felt safe to admit not knowing and to work together to learn. Such critique identified gaps and stimulated our desire to build new knowledge.

✳ ✳ ✳

Conclusion

From our immersion among the voices in narrative inquiry, a number of strategies have surfaced that others could usefully apply:

- The student-mentor relationship is a challenging relationship to develop and nurture; it needs time to emerge. It extends over a long period; many external events can influence it. If you can relate in an open and honest manner, the relationship will be fulfilling for you both and new knowledge will emerge in a more seamless way.

- It is important early on to develop and adhere to a scheduled plan of action. From this base, short-term goals should be set. Such scheduling forewarns the supervisors and allows them more opportunity to meet your needs within their overall obligations.

- Make a firm decision on the particular form of methodology as early as possible. Otherwise, much time can be wasted exploring unhelpful possibilities.

- The process of data collection, analysis, and writing up narrative inquiry is complex and convoluted, but over time you will master it. Metaphors and other visualization techniques can enable you to examine the data from a range of perspectives. It also facilitates a back-and-forth dialogue between doctoral student and mentor.

- Expect the unexpected as normal. Work with this to explore the dimensions that open to you. What seems overwhelming and chaotic at the time often is the source of new knowledge.

References

Burkhard, R. (2005). Towards a framework and a model for knowledge visualization: Synergies between information. In S. Tergan & T. Keller (Eds.), *Knowledge and information visualization* (pp. 226–243). Heidelberg, Germany: Springer-Verlag Berlin.

Edwards, H. E. (2003). Quality assurance in aboriginal early childhood education: A participatory action research study. Unpublished doctoral thesis, University of New England, Armidale, Australia.

Gilbert, K. (2002). Taking a narrative approach to grief research: Finding meaning in stories. *Death Studies, 26,* 223–239.

Glaser, B. G., & Strauss, A. L. (1968). *The discovery of grounded theory: Strategies for qualitative research.* London: Weidenfeld & Nicolson.

Gubrium, J. F., & Holstein, J. A. (2003). Analyzing interpretive practice. In N. Denzin & Y. Lincoln (Eds.), *Strategies of qualitative inquiry* (pp. 214–248). Thousand Oaks, CA: Sage Publications.

Hiles, D. (2002). *Narrative and heuristic approaches to transpersonal research and practice.* Retrieved August 5, 2003, from http://www.psv.dmu.ac.uk/drhiles/N&Hpaper.htm.

Klass, D. (2000). Meaning reconstruction and the experience of loss. In R. Neimeyer (Ed.), *The inner representations of the dead child in the psychic and social narratives of bereaved parents* (pp. 77–94). Washington, DC: American Psychological Association.

Lincoln, Y., & Guba, E. (1985). *Naturalistic inquiry.* Beverly Hills, CA: Sage Publications.

Maple, M. (2005a). Parental bereavement and youth suicide: An assessment of the literature. *Australian Social Work, 58,* 179–187.

Maple, M. (2005b). *Parental portraits of suicide narrating the loss of an adult child.* Unpublished doctoral thesis, University of New England, Armidale, Australia.

Maple, M., Plummer, D., Edwards, H., & Minichiello, V. (2007). The effects of preparedness for suicide following the death of a young adult child. *Suicide and Life Threatening Behavior, 37,* 127–134.

McCabe, M. (2003). *The paradox of loss.* Westport, CT: Praeger.

Pearson, M., & Brew, A. (2002). Research training and supervision development. *Studies in Higher Education, 27,* 135–150.

Polkinghorne, D. (1988). *Narrative knowing and the human sciences.* Albany, NY: State University of New York.

Polkinghorne, D. (1995). Narrative configuration in qualitative analysis. *Qualitative Studies in Education, 8,* 5–23.

Radical Reflexivity in Qualitative Research 4

David Leary, Victor Minichiello,
and Jeffrey A. Kottler

During the first part of the Iraq War, journalists often spoke of being embedded within army brigades. This was the only way they could approach the front line of the war on which they were reporting. Being embedded was a mixed experience: they were close to warfare but they also were, in a sense, censored by the structured and dominating experience of being embedded. If objectivity in journalistic reporting were ever a possibility, it was limited by being embedded.

I (David) began a doctoral program after many years of working as a counselor with homeless and otherwise marginalized young people. Over those years, I had formulated key clinical questions, the primary one of which was, "How is it that some young people survive in spite of all the negative and debilitating experiences they encounter?" My research was about this question: about vulnerability and resilience, and the place of relationships (connectivity) in the movement from vulnerability to resilience.

I chose to explore the experience of young males who engage in street-based prostitution, also known as sex work. After approaching forty-four males of various ages and with diverse backgrounds, I interviewed twenty-seven. Young or old, these males are often stereotypically regarded by clinicians and researchers as a small but highly vulnerable population group, and yet one that survives. Understanding this phenomenon was a core aim of my research. While this sounds a relatively simple research task, one complicating aspect of the project was that I was embedded in the environment. The purpose of this chapter is to understand that experience, the place of reflexivity in grappling with the lack of distance from the participants of the study, and with personal history. It is about exploring the tangible and live connection of me, the researcher, to the sex work scene and to those who engage in street-based sex work.

Nausea and Fear

I can clearly remember my earliest and most powerful experience as a research student. It occurred at the end of a research methods seminar. I wanted to explore the ways that counselors help their adolescent clients to manage their vulnerability and develop resilience. I wanted to understand how resilience emerges and what threatens its existence in young people. It was—I thought—a safe and manageable area of research, focusing on the experience and wisdom of counselors.

The professor knew I was a counselor with street kids and she advised me to focus my research on a specific part of my clinical practice. She recommended an academic supervisor. From her perspective, it was a perfect match. I worked with young males engaged in street-based sex work; Victor Minichiello, soon to be my principal supervisor, had significant research experience in a related area. So the specific area of my study emerged, albeit uncomfortably, out of my interest in vulnerability, connectivity, or connectedness. This was combined with Victor's abiding interest in the health sociology of male sex work.

✳ ✳ ✳

I (Victor) was impressed with David's ability to think conceptually and qualitatively. (He had a strong passion to understand the world of his informants.) He was a perfect fit for a qualitative study on male sex workers who worked on the streets. I was conducting a number of both qualitative and quantitative studies on the male sex industry and immediately saw the gap that David's study would fill in the literature. Male sex workers, particularly those who work on the streets, are a difficult population to study, and it is difficult to gain their cooperation to participate in research. David's professional experience and easy manner in dealing with people were ideal traits to possess for the research journey he was about to undertake.

✳ ✳ ✳

The lecturer who initiated the connection between Victor and me (David) was excited by the prospect of new research in an area about which she was also interested. Her level of excitement was matched by my anxiety and discomfort. All I could feel was nausea—a sustained sickness in my guts every time I thought of doing doctoral research on male sex work. While I had a few ideas about why this discomfort was present, I had little clarity. I only knew that it was connected with feelings of vulnerability and with my past. I had never procured the services of a male sex worker and yet I felt shame and avoidance. It was an experience of vulnerability loaded with history, rich in meaning, and connected with notions of flight. I was happy that they came to my place of work for practical assistance and counseling but I was uncomfortable being on their ground where control was lost. The place, the people, and the experience were taboo for me. I couldn't explain why and I wanted to avoid its exploration; the thought of doing research in the midst of these complex and unfathomable feelings was nauseating for me.

Editors' Comment

Personal Motives Underlying Research

It is often the case that the research questions of greatest interest to qualitative investigators are those that are most personally meaningful. We illustrated this in the preface, where we talked about our own experiences that led us to pursue our seminal studies. Rather than apologizing for this personal connection to the data, we prefer to point out that this is among the noblest motives for conducting research. Some of the greatest theoreticians in history—Sigmund Freud, Jean Piaget, Margaret Mead, Michel Foucault, Karl Marx—all chose subjects that were of particular relevance to their own lives. As David has described in this section, the researcher must locate himself in the study so that the context is clearly appreciated by readers, while at the same time such self-reflections open up the possibility of viewing things differently.

The sensation of vulnerability, sickness, and the desire to run away was palpable. It was preverbal, it lasted for weeks, and it created havoc and doubt in my thinking about my future studies. Part of me desired a hasty retreat from the whole idea of research. Yet some awareness of the nonsense in my feelings made me avoid such a rash action. Despite the force of this early research-derived experience, I could neither trace its logical origin nor articulate or explain the significance of its influence. It was an inchoate phenomenon that rummaged around inside me, a chaotic internal dialogue that produced a sense of discomfort and isolation, a degree of fear, and a mass of hesitation. I had no thoughts about the origin of my fear but the discomfort was clear and unavoidable. It begged for understanding. Although clarity was a long time coming, this experience drove my thinking and became a lynchpin for understanding my experiences throughout my research and the writing of my dissertation.

In the early phase of my thinking about this initial experience, all I really knew was that this strange and unspeakable sensation had a connection to my past. That was it, and that was as far as I could go, or was willing to go. Sickness in my guts, a palpable sense of fear in the face of an unavoidable sensation, an experience I couldn't fathom, and the reality of solitude with these sensations: what a way to begin a long and arduous research and writing program.

The dawn of understanding about this early formative experience occurred well into the research process, when memories and feelings from the past were triggered by a certain qualitative in-depth research interview with a young male who worked the street. At that point, and because of my immersion within the research, it was not possible to avoid thinking about these long-suppressed fears. The relevance of an inexplicable memory—of the past bleeding into the present, thereby producing nausea and fear— lingers in my thinking about my particular study on marginalized young males. It also permeates my thinking about qualitative research in general. This dawn of understanding would not have been possible without the use of various forms of peer-debriefing—that is, self-supervision (reflexivity) as the precursor to other conversations, clinical supervision, and, most significantly, through the specific peer-debriefing provided by academic supervision (Spall, 1998).

✻ ✻ ✻

I (Jeffrey) observed from the beginning of our collaboration that David had a lot of emotional stuff connected not only to his topic, but also to the signifi- cance of completing his degree and how it would impact his choices thereafter. The ambivalence that David describes thus far remained a constant factor throughout our work together. Since Victor was the primary mentor for David, my role evolved as mostly a supportive one. From the outset, I recognized how remarkable a study this could be, and how important and unique it could be. At the same time, I also saw how challenging and even dangerous a journey this was for David. As you'll see, this ambivalence played out at every stage of the research process.

Victor, David, and I had an interesting series of discussions about how David should locate himself within this study. What were his personal motives that led him to investigate street kids and male prostitution? What attraction did he feel toward the dark side of human nature? What resonance did he sense toward these kids who had been so neglected and often abused? What part of himself did he see in them? We had talked about him including an introductory chapter discussing what led him to this research question. After consulting with Victor, David decided it would be best to include it in the methodology chapter. Apart from the outcome of this negotiation, it highlighted the cooperative nature of our relationships with one another. Victor and I worked hard to coordinate our efforts so that David would not be triangulated into any differences of opinion that might emerge. Ultimately, we let David make final decisions since it was his study.

✻ ✻ ✻

About This Chapter

Many academic works on qualitative research trace the development of the rational movements within research. The emphasis in the rational is on the reasoned, evidentiary, and logical intellectual movements. Such works also focus on how these lines of thought are crafted into a dissertation, and the role of supervision in this complex developmental process.

In this chapter, and while not ignoring the rational, I (David) trace the development of the parallel path. These are the affective moments or experiences within my research. Specifically, I examine my emotional responses to the mere suggestion of researching street-based male sex work. I also examine the historical depth of my own nonrational experiences within the research and the way it has influenced my scholarly activity. Finally, and far from disconnected from the foci already mentioned, I also examine some core experiences during participant encounters. I present these affective moments as examples of the power and significance of personal responses within research and of the need for such experiences to be captured, thought about, understood, and then incorporated into the research and the academic mentoring process, and not ignored (Brown, 2006; Foley, 2002; Gadd, 2004; Hollway & Jefferson, 2000).

This capturing and thinking about personal emotional experience within the research was dealt with via a process of reflexivity or, as Taylor (1991) refers to it, "radical reflexivity." Various authors refer to the use of reflexivity (or reflection) as a critical element of qualitative research methods (Alvesson & Sköldberg, 2000; Brown, 2006; Finlay, 2002; Hall & Callery, 2001). Foley (2002, p. 473) notes that "reflexivity is the capacity of language and of thought—of any system of signification—to turn or bend back upon itself, thus becoming an object to itself." Taylor (1991) clarifies this approach by indicating that reflexivity may also be a radical action within human experience. As Taylor (1991, p. 304) indicates, "to be interested in my own health, or wealth, is to be reflexively oriented, but not radically. But when I examine my own experience, or scrutinize my own thinking, reflexivity takes a radical turn." Building on Taylor, Rennie (2007, p. 53) indicates, "reflexivity has been defined as self-awareness, and radical reflexivity as awareness of self-awareness." In the qualitative research process, where strong emotions and relationships develop, it is not sufficient simply to be self-aware. What makes for good and sound qualitative research within an environment as complex as my own research is the capacity to be keenly aware of the relational processes and emotional intricacies that develop between the participant and researcher and of what impact this can have on the research. This is where reflexivity takes a radical turn: at the point when I become thoughtful about my own active contribution to the process of experience that is being generated within the research.

In this chapter, I examine how my emotional experiences are combined with the rational endeavor within the research project via a radical form of reflexivity, intensive and reflective writing (a research journal), and through purposeful conversations with academic mentors, colleagues, and peers. I explore the practices in which I engaged in order to bring about a high level of radical reflexivity. It is these practices and the thoughtfulness that is a necessary aspect of the practices that brings the oft-hidden non-rational elements of research to light. Finally, I explore the insights gained from such processes. It is the practice of radical reflexivity that is a central part of creating rigor within the qualitative research process (Brown, 2006; Whittemore, Chase, & Mandle, 2001).

The Path of Emotional Experiences

It may seem strange to begin a chapter on research by focusing on experiences that stimulate nausea, fear, chaotic internal dialogues, and solitude. Such experiences, regardless of their character, are crucial and formative experiences in the life of any qualitative researcher. What is critical is what emerges from such raw and confronting research moments.

✳ ✳ ✳

I (Jeffrey) think it is interesting that David is focusing exclusively on his negative emotional reactions. I sensed, as well, that there was some excitement, arousal, curiosity, intrigue, titillation, joy, and tremendous commitment to this topic. It was clear from the beginning this was not going to be a boring, run-of-the-mill study but rather one that would break new ground. It is wonderful when a student can feel such passion and excitement toward a research topic. When it happens, it almost never feels like work for either of us.

✳ ✳ ✳

While my starting point was one of confusion, during the subsequent months and years I (David) began to make sense of the various emotional experiences connected to the research, to put words to the nausea, fear, excitement, and arousal, and to realize that a doctorate is more than just a rational exercise. It is also a complex experience created by and within my own life. This represents a parallel path in the research process: the path of affective moments or experiences. While many researchers may not view this path as the main game of the research project, it is far from incidental to what is often regarded as the substantive intellectual elements of the research program (Brown, 2006). These internal experiences hold significant authority and sway; this reality is often visible in the outcomes of research.

In my research project, I became aware of the emotional responses I was having to participants in the study. Sometimes mild and at other times volatile, these reactions or responses were a key element of each participant encounter. Allen (not real names) arrived for our interview intoxicated on heroin and repeatedly fell asleep. This was a trigger for frustration, anger, and sadness on my part. Dominic and Jack spoke intensely of sexual abuse, such that the interview was dramatically cathartic for them. I was simply overwhelmed and exhausted by the intensity of the encounter. Damon never made it to the interview. We talked, made several arrangements, but he died of an overdose before we were able to meet. Anton began an interview but left suddenly and promised to return. His body was found at the base of a building with the police suspecting foul play.

It may not be the case with all qualitative research, but this project brought with it a large and fertile groundswell of emotion. There is little doubt that what I experienced was of and within me, but the trigger was the encounter with the research participants and their often-dramatic life stories.

✻ ✻ ✻

At times I (Victor) was concerned that David and Jeffrey were taking too much of a counseling perspective, where the emotional aspect of how David was experiencing this fieldwork process was of paramount importance. I often interjected comments and reminders to focus on the data collection and analysis. With time, however, I realized that it was critical for David to locate his own position within the research. It offered important insights into the data collection and the analysis of the data.

Where such experiences are left unattended within the research field, a lack of insight and attention to the fabric of the research is evident. Where this essential element of the research is ignored, it can result in a lack of attunement to and with the participants. This lack of attunement can result in poor research and be the cause of criticism (Guillemin & Gilliam, 2004; Morrow, 2005). Within this methodological framework, emotional experiences can be stumbling blocks to progress or—if attended to via radical reflexivity, writing, and purposeful conversations—the glue that binds the research within the field of innovative discovery.

✻ ✻ ✻

I (Jeffrey) like the way David is legitimizing a tremendous resource and strength in qualitative research that distinguishes it from quantitative traditions where objectivity and detachment are paramount. It is important, of course, to identify, acknowledge, control, and harness emotional reactions, especially as they may unduly prejudice and distort the results. Nevertheless, one's own strong feelings are critical guides that lead the researcher to explore aspects of a project that may otherwise be ignored or denied.

There is an indispensable link between the rational moments of the research—the first path—and the affective experiences within the research—the parallel path. The way to create a synthesis between the two is via a process defined by radical reflexivity. It is often brought about in solitude, by transparency, through reflective writing, and with a high level of openness to scrutiny that arises from within the researcher but that also occurs within encounters with academic mentors, colleagues, and professional peers. While rigorous conversation and writing are the final stages of radical reflexivity, solitude is a critical element of the reflexive process. It is solitude that allows for the first emergence of the contradictions, discomfort, and connections that require transparency; these then become the basis of conversations aimed at clarifying emergent insights. Conversation can never be a replacement for the solitude in which the scrutiny is carried out and insights emerge.

✳ ✳ ✳

The Past Bleeds Into the Present

My (David's) encounter with participants triggered emotions about the here and now, but it was not only about the here and now. I was there, in the encounter, as they were also, with a past and a history. During many of the research encounters, I was dealing with multiple layers of affective experience because the past bled into my present activity, sometimes in an uncontrolled manner, sometimes creating the nausea and fear of which I have already spoken. It was the lack of control over what was bleeding through from the past that caused a sickness, panic, and fear. Nevertheless, it was in these raw uncontrolled moments that the link between the emotional path and the rational path in qualitative research was clearest and the value of this understanding most evident.

I now understand the emotional experiences that gave rise to my sickness and fear. I can now speak of the power these moments exuded in the earliest stages of my research. It is to these past events and their impact on my research that I now turn.

✷ ✷ ✷

I (Jeffrey) think it is interesting that as the two mentors for David's research, Victor and I are so different in our personalities, backgrounds, professional orientations, and research interests. Because we respect one another and enjoy one another's strengths, our differences became a great resource for David (although I presume they became a frustration at times, as well). Victor and I would frequently bring out different aspects of an issue, based on our personal and professional lenses, just as we are doing in this chapter and in the larger book.

✷ ✷ ✷

From the Beginning

In December 1977, I (David) began work as a nurse at the Sacred Heart Hospice in Darlinghurst, an inner-city suburb of Sydney. It was a twelve-month position taken up the day after I had left a Catholic seminary. This palliative care unit is located adjacent to where young males engage in street-based sex work in Sydney. The Wall, as it is known, is a notorious place with a lengthy and complex history and geography. It has been and in some cases still is a hospital precinct; the location of endless death and dying; a prison; a technical and art college; a church; a park inhabited by grieving visitors, nurses, destitute people, and drug dealers; and a court house. It is noisy and cacophonous, and it is central to my history and the locus of my research.

My first memory of male prostitution was early in my year at the hospice. It was in the winter of 1978. It was 11 PM. After a torrid and draining day of caring for the terminally ill, I had finished work and walked out of the hospice and into Darlinghurst Road, along which The Wall runs. Dressed in a white nurse's uniform, I was mocked and jeered by a scantily clad adolescent, not much younger than me, who had parked his buttocks on the hood of a car. It was a cold night with the wind howling down Darlinghurst Road. He wore cut-off jeans that barely contained what he was selling. He wore a sleeveless lumber jacket, no shirt, and a pair of long sheepskin-lined boots strapped with leather thongs. It was a strange and yet alluring sight after a long day's work. He was cocky and sensual. I was tired and vulnerable. He appeared to be completely at home in the darkness of the night and the exposure of the street. I was uncomfortable, confused, hesitant, and shy. Perplexed by his apparent confidence, I could not help wondering why he was so at ease exposing his body to all and sundry. I was embarrassed, confused about who I was and what I wanted to be, and uneasy with my own sexual identity. He appeared at home; I was the stranger and foreigner. I have a journal note from that first encounter with street-based sex work. It notes the emotional details of that night: trepidation, fear, attraction, and the keen desire I had to know and understand him (Leary, 1978). I was twenty-two; he was probably about the same age or a tad younger.

Infusing, Bleeding Through

What I rediscovered at the beginning of this research—triggered initially by nausea and fear—was that the young man in the sheepskin-lined boots had remained an iconic part of my thinking about male sex work. It was an acute dimension of my understanding of male sex work that arose from my background sense of things (Taylor, 1991, 1993, 1995). It was the past infusing into or bleeding through to the present in an unspoken, inchoate, and yet influential manner. The arousal, discomfort, and even excitement of twenty-eight years ago was awakened. Though occasionally thought about, I had never been able to articulate an understanding of my thoughts and feelings. I was imbued with a sense of strangeness and was aware of a discomforting foreigner within me. My initial and strong reactions at the beginning of this research—nausea, fear, and even repugnance—had more to do with my own unresolved thoughts and emotions about intimacy and sex than about that particular young man on the car hood.

Being seduced by a male sex worker was, at twenty-two, an unfamiliar and confronting experience. It excited and challenged my own need for intimacy. I experienced relief, pleasure, and the promise of a new relationship. At the beginning of this research, all of these emotions were alive and active, hovering out of view in the background but too close to home for my liking. These feelings were first activated by a lecturer's suggestion regarding research and then later, with more vivid connections, in a qualitative interview. It required significant and thoughtful attention if it was not to become problematic within the research process.

At the end of this research and through a rational and affective process to which radical reflexivity was applied, I discovered what it means to welcome and entertain the stranger and the foreigner, within me and within others (Kristeva, 1991). What I engaged in was not simply a *hermeneutic* (interpretative) process (Alvesson & Sköldberg, 2000; McLeod, 2001; Messer, Sass, & Woolfolk, 1988; Ricoeur, 1981; Woolfolk, Sass, & Messer, 1988). What was at play was a type of *double hermeneutic*, or the interpretation of the experience of both the participant and the researcher. Within this complex intersubjective process, which was, in my case, of laying out and exploring the emotions that led to nausea and the fear of the foreignness, I was able to develop a fresh vision of the experience of young males who do sex work at a place called The Wall. I do not pretend to have it all together or, even more, that this is the only part of my background that has been alive and active. At the beginning of and throughout this research, I attempted to explore that which prevented me from creating a place for otherness, for those who, in my fear, I may regard as the foreigner.

Editors' Comment

The Power of Reflexivity

What David has illustrated is the value of reflecting systematically and critically about your own experiences, assumptions, and knowledge. How is it that you know what you know? What do you take for granted? What do you accept as truth? How do you allow yourself to see things differently, even when these alternative viewpoints may contradict or conflict with what you already think you know and understand? The inductive reasoning process within qualitative research is about changing perspectives as a result of what you learned. For instance, David was quite surprised to have his initial beliefs, informed by literature and professional practice, challenged by the results of his study that showed a connection between a sex worker's level of education and resilience in the face of tremendous adversity. If David had not undertaken a critical review of his own personal motives and experience, he would not have generated the type of analysis that emerged from his study.

This approach to my research was not just about adaptation—of me as the researcher adjusting the method to a new and particular research environment. It was about a type of enculturation—of me with my background engaging with the research participants and their environment and of them engaging with me, such that all parties to the research were changed. It can never be said that a full enculturation occurred or that such an experience was ever possible. Nonetheless, and with that caveat in mind, engagement and enculturation did occur and it transformed the research methodology and the research outcomes. Transparency and reflexivity made the methodology and the research more alive, interactive, and dynamic. It is to the exploration of this reality that I now turn, exploring both the affective experiences and the techniques I used to capture, think about, analyze, and incorporate these complex personal experiences.

Mapping Affective and Intellectual Movements in Qualitative Research

It is one thing to experience confrontation within the research and to be aware of the past infusing into the present, but it is another, and more significant, thing to work out what to do with this raw material and how to relate it to the other primary (rational) task of doing qualitative research. It is the task of melding and mapping affective experiences alongside of, and then within, the intellectual endeavor. This reality posed a unique and practical problem within the context of my research.

There were significant realizations that emerged for me from a growing understanding of the infusion of my background issues—of my history and experience—into the research. The most profound realization was that mapping movements and developments in the doctorate was about mapping the entire research process, both rational thought and raw emotion. The mapping of thought and affect, which could not be an occasional exercise or an irregular task that happened accidentally, included noting and processing the emotional experiences from each participant encounter, as well as the rational insights that eventually developed through radical reflexivity.

* * *

I (Victor) think that David was vigilant in maintaining both a personal and methodological log of his study. While it was time consuming, it paid off in the long run. David was in a strong position when he was writing his methods chapter to insert reflections and information contained in his logs. He produced a strong methods chapter on which the reviewers of his study commented positively.

* * *

A significant number of stories that emerged during the interviews that I (David) conducted were difficult to hear. Peter recalled that after he had been in sex work for a number of years, he avoided ongoing sex work by seeking out younger boys for older men, for which he received a monetary commission. Nick recalled a number of incidents where he engaged in serious violence with others also engaged in sex work at The Wall. The violence was against potential clients in sex work, and the result was that the boys gained money and avoided the sex work.

People were hurt and lives were changed and these narratives had an impact on me in real time, but also as they connected with my own history. In the past, though in different circumstances, I was also the subject of physical violence in the form of a violent attack from a counseling client who was psychotic at the time of the incident. It was difficult hearing the violent stories of the participants in my study. Acknowledging the emotions associated with hearing such stories, which often meant recalling my own experience of violence, was an indispensable part of my research. Their telling demanded an active and engaged response from me. Their telling and my acceptance of the responsibility to deal with what emerged within me began a process whereby insight produced clarity within the research, about the complexity and depth of their own experiences and the separateness of my own history and affective responses. The possibility of not being biased against their story and of being able to hear otherness, sometimes in its ugliness, and of being able to respect the foreigner became real only because of a process whereby my own emotions were not ignored or suppressed. Ultimately, what emerged were the credible, uncensored, and real-life narratives of essentially hidden and fearful young males: the participants in this research.

Using a Research Journal

The first strategy for dealing with the infusion or bleeding of the personal into the research environment was the use of a research journal. Throughout my research, I maintained a day-to-day account of the experiences I encountered: historical and other factual material, my thinking on the project, and the emotional experiences that weaved their way through the research project. The research journal was a separate yet interlinked file within the data analysis program (NVivo) into which I also imported the text of each interview (Bazeley, 2007). Each entry within the research journal was dated and, where appropriate, cross-referenced with participant interviews and the theoretical and reflexive memos (Bazeley; Glaser & Strauss, 1967). Mapping the intellectual and affective movements of the research meant that an audit of the research could be carried out by a person external to the research, should that be required (Davies & Dodd, 2002; Finlay, 2002; Guba & Lincoln, 2005).

In my own research, tracking the rational movements was a primary task but no less important than the mapping of the raw internal experiences associated with the research. Once I became aware of the nausea, fear, anger, disdain, or sadness, I monitored the experience through writing and reflection, seeking over time to plot a point or points of origin for the sensation that was initially wordless, whether it was within the here-and-now encounter, from my own experience, or from both sources. It was a process of freeing up my own emotions and thinking so that the foreigner could really exist as he really was within my research.

After interviewing Peter, it was impossible for me not to feel sad and to empathize strongly for the young boys he had introduced to a dangerous and potentially violent world. At ten or eleven years of age they could not have understood the world to which they were being introduced, but Peter did when he had recalled his own induction to this world of sex work, and this complicated my reaction to him. I felt a number of emotions that made thinking about him almost impossible. I recorded my overwhelming sadness and a personalized form of social guilt for not knowing and not rescuing those in his story who were clearly in harm's way. While the sensations and the guilt were not always rational, they were real for me and they colored how I heard his words, read his transcript, and pondered the significant emergent themes. Left unattended, my own emotional experience would have ensured that Peter would never have emerged. Attention was required, and it was this attention to the nonrational that allowed for Peter's emergence.

Other less-harrowing but nonetheless significant experiences also required attention. The unnamed young man on the car hood caused emotional chaos for me in 1978 when I was twenty-two. That experience, embedded in my internalized history, then caused nausea and fear when I began my doctorate, although I did not fully realize the point of origin for those affective experiences. During my eighteenth doctoral interview, further clarity began to emerge about this and other experiences.

It was a hot summer's day and Jules, at twenty-three, was articulate, engaging, self-assured, confident about himself, and comfortable with his trade. However, there was another side to his immediate presentation. When Jules arrived on his bicycle for his interview, he was wearing a pair of board shorts and little else. He was dripping perspiration, and what I initially saw was a naked torso and a highly sensual and sexual man. A fear of and yet attraction to Jules emerged as a primary reaction both during and after the interview. I found it a confusing and confronting experience. I needed to understand this fear and the attraction because it felt similar to my experience in 1978. Both men were handsome and alluring, almost seductive. Both were confident and unabashed about their place in society and about work. As the experience with Jules recalled with significant power the uncomfortable moments of 1978, the blurring of these two experiences made it difficult for me to hear and understand the experience that Jules brought to the research.

I had to admit that I wanted more from Jules. I had a heightened awareness of my own needs within the encounter; but I needed to regain a research perspective. This was difficult when my own aloneness and solitude were being confronted by the beauty of a participant who would have allowed for more to occur. I knew the ground rules and, while I maintained an ethical boundary, I needed to understand the experience and not simply regard it as a near miss. A complex process of radical reflexivity and recording within the research journal allowed me to reflect on the path of my own reaction and to approach a second interview with Jules with a focus on the dynamism of relating in his life, within and outside sex work.

This process of radical reflexivity, and the ensuing analysis of text, allowed me to write about the complexity and fluidity within the relational world of the male engaged in street-based sex work. Relationships shift and move, and those relationships that are normally regarded as being within one frame of reference (e.g., sex work) sometimes morph into other types of relationships (e.g., close friend, occasional nonpaid sexual partners, nonsexual supporter). The development of my insight on relationships within the research began with my own overwhelming experience. Once captured and thought about, these reflections became the source of further questions and the development of new knowledge about the complex relational world of the person engaged in street-based sex work.

✳ ✳ ✳

It is interesting to me (Jeffrey) the ways that David has always talked about the things he has learned from his participants. The interviews were so incredibly interesting that they were better than anything that ever appeared on television. I know that David was having so much fun with his license to investigate the forbidden and secret world of street kids, but it became a problem to convince him to stop collecting data and move on to writing it up. After several years of becoming quite skilled at doing these interviews, David felt a marked reluctance to let go and move on to the next stage of writing up what he had learned. He took a leave of absence for a year to complete some unfinished business and resolve any lingering ambivalence. Once he jumped back into the fray, the thesis seemed to write itself.

✳ ✳ ✳

Through my (David's) research journal, in which I scrutinized my own emotional and rational experiences throughout the research period, I began to understand that their way of being was emotionally confronting, at least to me. Beyond their beauty and their apparent level of public comfort, I don't fully understand why I was attracted to both men, but I was, and this caused moral upheaval and psychological conflict within me. That was my nausea and the origin of my fear: of being discovered as a researcher who became attracted to and confused by his participants.

✳ ✳ ✳

Once again, I (Jeffrey) respect the risks David is willing to take. The same courage that David is demonstrating in the honesty and transparency of this narrative were also evident when he pushed himself to confront his fears. He relied on a lot of resources during this difficult stage: friends, colleagues, and others he trusted. I recall a half-dozen different conversations we had about his blocks and his fears, some of which went far beyond the surface issues of this study.

✳ ✳ ✳

I (David) thought, or perhaps imagined, that they had something that I did not have: freedom to be, a pride in self, and an ability to experiment and challenge social mores. I was hidden, fearful of my own sexuality, unable to live out the side of me that appeared so evident in their lives. Regardless of the reality of the conclusions I drew, these were powerful thoughts and they were contaminating not just my past, but also my present endeavors. Whatever I was hearing in my time with Jules was being filtered through my prior, unreflected, emotional moments. For me to achieve rigor in my research I needed to scrutinize these emotional moments. I could neither deny nor quarantine such events.

Incorporate the Personal: Avoid Bracketing Out!

This raises a second important methodological strategy that emerged for me throughout the research. Where emotional moments are strong and relational dynamics are evident within the research material, as was evident between Jules and me, there can be no pretense that you can research and remain detached or at a distance. The bracketing out of my "views before proceeding with the experiences of others," such as is spoken of in phenomenological research (Creswell, Hanson, Plano Clark, & Morales, 2007, p. 254), is far from feasible. The research method must be robust enough to incorporate such powerful emotional experiences without any pretense that they can be objectively removed. They are not data within the meaning of research; if not actively thought about and critiqued, this emotional material invariably contaminates the collection and analysis of qualitative data (in this case, the data compose the text). A radical level of reflexivity has been critical to this study. A crucial element of the method in my doctoral research was acknowledging and utilizing my reactions, and not bracketing or denying their reality with the resultant (false) notion that this provided me with an objective stance.

In the examples explored within this chapter—that of Peter and Jules—the bracketing of my emotional reactions and responses before, during, or after the interviews would have been a futile exercise and a pretense to an unreal objectivity. They were evident, powerful, and persuasive emotional experiences. They were in my thinking. Left unattended, they would have biased my approach to both participants and contaminated the further gathering of data and the process of textual analysis. The rigorous use of transparency, acknowledgment (not bracketing), and the faithful use of the research journal for recording the analysis of personal experience are all critical elements of the research method I developed throughout my research project. I would suggest that this is a critical element within any study that considers powerful emotions, psychosocial experiences, and relationships, where intimacy, desire, and need are key elements.

* * *

I (Victor) was not surprised that David's analysis paid particular attention to relationships. This is not an accident. It reflects the way he approached the study and how he located his understanding of how informants were talking about their experiences.

* * *

Conversations

A final core strategy in a radically reflexive approach to qualitative research is that of conversation. While solitude and thoughtfulness are required for a reflexive stance in order that insight and connections are able to emerge in both the emotional realm and the intellectual process of the research, as Taylor (1991) indicates, "human beings are constituted in conversation" (p. 314). This is the aspect of the methodology where reflexivity becomes absolutely radical because scrutiny is transparent.

Conversations occurred in a variety of ways throughout the research project. Academic supervisors, while formally important within the conversational process, were not always available and not necessarily the most significant people when it came to understanding the interaction between me (David), my emotional experiences, and the participants. Professional peers, who understood the relational dynamics that occur within the counseling setting, were core to the conversational process. As it was readily available, my own clinical supervision became a forum where the conversation about research interviews took place. Finally, and most significantly, conversations occurred with other doctoral scholars who likewise had an interest in the psychological content of the research encounter.

* * *

Discussing your ideas with people is an important aspect of making sense of your data. I (Victor) have seen this phenomenon occur repeatedly. Researchers present their findings at conferences or discuss it with friends and colleagues and, through their efforts to get others to understand what they are trying to make sense of or through people asking critical questions, the penny drops. It is likely that without this dialogue the ideas would remain unclear or confused.

* * *

My (David's) experience with Jule s was a critical turning point in the research process. Beyond my own reflections, I took this encounter to clinical supervision and to a meeting of my professional peers. In those forums, I was able to explore the vulnerability I experienced with Jules, and the latent needs that emerged within me. Eventually, I was able to develop a new perspective, not just on that encounter, but also on the prior experience to which it was so clearly connected. This allowed me to hear anew his complex methods for relating to others.

Radical reflexivity, through transparency, thoughtfulness, the use of a research journal, and conversation, is critical to qualitative research. Radical reflexivity on the stuff of me that bleeds from the past to the present should never be ignored for it contains power, influence, and potential insight, all of which are critical elements in the process of qualitative research.

Lessons Learned

There is always an educational impact from research. There is also an experiential impact that lingers long after the research is complete. In my research, impressions of the participants were marked onto me: their faces, sadness, joy, achievements, the courage to tell a painful story, and the ability to survive and relate. The narratives of these received experiences were the research space out of which emerged the Eureka! moments of delight at discovery. They sustained me through a lengthy research project. The intimacy of the experience and the fine-grained nature of the Eureka! moments must be embraced in qualitative research. This was the first lesson from my research.

A second lesson continued on the note of relationship and intimacy. I had little idea at the beginning of the research that I would need to deal with events of my own life in parallel to understanding the lives of the participants with whom I made contact. By the end of the research, not only did I understand the necessity of this process, but I also understood the value to the method of incorporating rather than bracketing self, a task I am not even sure is possible.

In drilling down into the data, I began to understand the importance of applying a fine-grained approach to data analysis, of staying with the data and allowing them to unfold and show their potential. A final core lesson involved expanding the notion and experience of this fine-grained approach to include the whole of the project and not simply data analysis. This meant applying a form of checking and crosschecking within each aspect of the methodological process I was using through the interviews, journaling, transcribing, coding, thematic development, chapter writing, all the way to the level of detail within the dissertation. The aim was to establish and maintain rigor and reliability so that the process could be transparent and understandable to any onlooker. Radical reflexivity was imperative in understanding the encounters and the data. An equally fine-grained and doubly reflexive approach was needed for the whole of the research process.

Concluding Remarks

If the primary function of research is to seek and develop knowledge, then the primary task of the researcher must be to plumb the depths of understanding within the research area under consideration. This can only be achieved in qualitative research if a posture of openness is adopted; radical reflexivity is an essential key to that posture. This involves, first and foremost, a willingness to be open about the intricacies and foibles of our human nature. It is this reality along with any expertise in research that we may possess that we bring to the projects we undertake. It is the affective experience contained within this reality that becomes the foundation upon which are built the intellectual pathways of our research. Radical reflexivity unlocks the treasures that give color and hue to our intellectual endeavors. Our emotional experiences must be welcomed and not shunned, embraced and understood and not feared.

Postscript

After the writing of any work, such as this chapter, conversations continue, with colleagues and editors. The aim is to understand further the ideas that have been generated and the writing that has been produced. Some months after the second draft of this chapter was completed I had another conversation with Victor. He noted with some amusement and frustration that I had overused two particular words throughout the chapter: emotion and reflexivity. During the conversation, I was challenged to think about what was happening within me at a psychological level and to reedit the chapter. What transpired through the conversation, and then through postconversation musing, was itself an act of collaborative radical reflexivity. Through Victor's prodding and challenging, the repetition of words translated into an awareness of an emphasis in my thinking that should be noted here: that the raw emotion I experienced in this research, which I associate with intimacy and isolation, remains alive, active, unresolved, and in need of attention.

There is rawness in my emotions when I think of the original events in 1978 and of their connection to my research some twenty-five years later. Such was and is the strength of this stuff that it bled, unknowingly, into the writing of this chapter through an unnoticed overuse of the perceived problem word (emotion) and the perceived remedy (reflexivity). After the conversation and the subsequent musing, I reread the text, reframed some of the work, and attended reflexively to the more than fifty references to *emotion*. As a matter of principle and emphasis, most of the references to *reflexivity* remain. The scholar's journey to be open and transparent in qualitative research never ends.

References

Alvesson, M., & Sköldberg, K. (2000). *Reflexive methodology: New vistas for qualitative research.* London: Sage Publications.

Bazeley, P. (2007). *Qualitative data analysis with NVivo.* Los Angeles: Sage Publications.

Brown, J. (2006). Reflexivity in the research process: Psychoanalytic observations. *International Journal of Social Research Methodology, 9,* 181–197.

Creswell, J. W., Hanson, W. E., Plano Clark, V. L., & Morales, A. (2007). Qualitative research designs: Selection and implementation. *The Counseling Psychologist, 35,* 236–264.

Davies, D., & Dodd, J. (2002). Qualitative research and the question of rigor. *Qualitative Health Research, 12,* 279–289.

Finlay, L. (2002). "Outing" the researcher: The provenance, process, and practice of reflexivity. *Qualitative Health Research, 12,* 531–545.

Foley, D. E. (2002). Critical ethnography: The reflexive turn. *International Journal of Qualitative Studies in Education, 15,* 469–490.

Gadd, D. (2004). Making sense of interviewee-interviewer dynamics in narratives about violence in intimate relationships. *International Journal of Social Research Methodology, 7,* 383–401.

Glaser, B. G., & Strauss, A. L. (1967). *The discovery of grounded theory: Strategies for qualitative research.* New York: Aldine de Gruyter.

Guba, E. G., & Lincoln, Y. S. (2005). Paradigmatic controversies, contradictions, and emerging confluences. In N. K. Denzin & Y. S. Lincoln (Eds.), *The SAGE handbook of qualitative research* (3rd ed., pp. 191–215). Thousand Oaks, CA: Sage Publications.

Guillemin, M., & Gilliam, L. (2004). Ethics, reflexivity, and "ethically important moments" in research. *Qualitative Inquiry, 10,* 261–280.

Hall, W. A., & Callery, P. (2001). Enhancing the rigor of grounded theory: Incorporating reflexivity and relationality. *Qualitative Health Research, 11,* 257–272.

Hollway, W., & Jefferson, T. (2000). *Doing qualitative research differently: Free association, narrative and the interview method.* London: Sage Publications.

Kristeva, J. (1991). *Strangers to ourselves* (L. S. Roudiez, Trans.). New York: Columbia University Press.

McLeod, J. (2001). *Qualitative research in counseling and psychotherapy.* London: Sage Publications.

Messer, S. B., Sass, L. A., & Woolfolk, R. L. (Eds.). (1988). *Hermeneutics and psychological theory: Interpretive perspectives on personality, psychotherapy, and psychopathology.* London: Rutgers University Press.

Morrow, S. L. (2005). Quality and trustworthiness in qualitative research in counseling psychology. *Journal of Counseling Psychology, 52,* 250–260.

Rennie, D. (2007). Reflexivity and its radical form: Implications for the practice of humanistic psychotherapies. *Journal of Contemporary Psychotherapy, 37,* 53–58.

Ricoeur, P. (1981). *Hermeneutics and the human sciences: Essays on language, action and interpretation* (J. B. Thompson, Trans.). Cambridge: Cambridge University Press.

Spall, S. (1998). Peer debriefing in qualitative research: Emerging operational models. *Qualitative Inquiry, 4,* 280–292.

Taylor, C. (1991). The dialogical self. In D. R. Hiley, J. F. Bohman, & R. Shusterman (Eds.), *The interpretive turn: Philosophy, science, culture* (pp. 304–314). Ithaca, NY: Cornell University Press.

Taylor, C. (1993). Engaged agency and background in Heidegger. In C. B. Guignon (Ed.), *The Cambridge companion to Heidegger* (pp. 317–336). Cambridge: Cambridge University Press.

Taylor, C. (1995). To follow a rule. In C. Taylor (Ed.), *Philosophical arguments* (pp. 165–180). Cambridge, MA: Harvard University Press.

Whittemore, R., Chase, S. K., & Mandle, C. L. (2001). Validity in qualitative research. *Qualitative Health Research, 11,* 522–537.

Woolfolk, R. L., Sass, L. A., & Messer, S. B. (1988). Introduction to hermeneutics. In S. B. Messer, L. A. Sass, & R. L. Woolfolk (Eds.), *Hermeneutics and psychological theory: Interpretive perspectives on personality, psychotherapy, and psychopathology* (pp. 2–26). London: Rutgers University Press.

An Epidemiologist Learns Grounded Theory

5

Kiran Regmi and Jeffrey A. Kottler

A grounded theory study of maternal mortality and child morbidity in Nepal was conducted by an obstetrician who had been trained as a quantitative researcher and health policy expert. The research was mentored by a supervisory team consisting of a psychologist, an infectious disease specialist, and a hospital administrator, all of whom were academic qualitative researchers. The study examined the subjective experiences of those participating in the birthing process, including mothers, mothers-in-law, husbands, and health professionals, in order to understand better their cultural perceptions and to reduce adverse outcomes for women and newborns. As is often the case in such a study, the findings were unexpected. The study had a significant impact on changing the nature of obstetric health care in a developing nation.

This chapter focuses on the personal and professional impact of the research process on both the student and her mentor. It explores some of the challenges that were faced negotiating relationships within the research team, as well as with the participants in the study. It also highlights cultural and diversity issues that were such an integral part of the research questions, and the background of the participants, the various professional disciplines represented among those involved, as well as the use of grounded theory as an approach for addressing medical challenges.

Editors' Comment

What Is Grounded Theory, Anyway?

It is unfortunate, perhaps even a curse, that Glaser and Strauss (1967) decided to name their method of qualitative inquiry including the word *theory* as the desired outcome. Ever since then, generations of students have been absolutely terrified by the prospect of developing a major theoretical breakthrough, one worthy of a Nobel Prize. Actually, this is a relatively simple methodological approach that allows the researcher to collect and analyze data simultaneously while forcing comparisons to uncover new insights about the phenomenon under investigation. One reason why it is such a popular approach is its elegant simplicity and sophistication in identifying significant patterns that help make sense.

Delivering a Goat

"That's impossible," I (Kiran) told the patient in my most authoritarian, doctor-scolding voice. "If you leave the hospital under these circumstances, you will not recover. You won't be able to have other babies. You could even die."

I was speaking to my patient as the obstetrician who just delivered her baby, but I also have been trained as a medical researcher and public health official who specializes in large-scale epidemiological studies that help guide future policy decisions for my country of Nepal. I am one of the few physicians who live and work outside the capital city of Kathmandu. More than 90 percent of the people in my country have no access to health care whatsoever. More mothers die in childbirth in Nepal than almost anywhere else in the world.

The conversation with this stubborn, new mother made me feel helpless. This woman had given birth a few days earlier. Her whole uterus, together with a full-term baby, had prolapsed through the vagina. I had managed to deliver the baby through a cesarean section. The uterus was still outside the vagina and would remain there for another week at least. I told her that she had to be hospitalized during that time, and for at least another week after that if she hoped to survive, much less fully recover. Incredibly, she insisted she had to return home immediately.

When I pressed her to tell me what was so important that she was willing to risk her life, the young mother just stared at me with frustration. She nodded her head, indicating that she heard my concern, but she still must leave as soon as possible.

"What is worth risking your life?" I asked again.

It was her goat, she explained. One of her goats was pregnant and she had to return home right away to attend to this delivery.

✤ ✤ ✤

Kiran first consulted me (Jeffrey) about this case in an email message. We had been working together for a few years. When I first met Kiran, she had already completed master's degrees in anthropology and public health, in addition to her medical training, yet she wanted further education in research to help guide her country's health policies in the future. I had visited her country a few times, supervising her research, following her to villages while she made her medical rounds, learning about the context of her work.

Because I am a counselor educator, Kiran was learning not only about qualitative research methodology, but also about counseling skills that could be used in her medical practice. It was especially challenging for her to let go of some of the assumptions about research that she had been using while conducting large-scale, quantitative studies with carefully worded hypotheses and predictions about assumptions. Instead, now she was learning about approaching interviews with both patients and research participants with a far more open mind.

When Kiran told me about this case and asked me how she could make her patient more compliant, I had little in the way of definitive advice I could offer her except to remind her that sometimes the best she could do was to listen with compassion and hope for the best. But Kiran was a doctor who was used to giving orders and having her patients obey. In the beginning, she approached research interviews in the same way, asking a series of rapid-fire questions that generated brief and limited responses. She had to unlearn, or at least adapt, some of the things she had learned as an epidemiologist and as a physician.

✤ ✤ ✤

A Research Question Dear to One's Heart

If the above interaction with my patient had occurred four years earlier at my hospital, I could never have appreciated the woman's priority to value her goat's life above her own. Conducting my doctoral research taught me to appreciate better that, although the discourse of science rules in the common phenomenal world of all humans, the context is so different in each culture. This realization was especially meaningful to me because when any event occurs people generally seek some explanations; the explanations they seek depend on their understanding of processes in nature and in the world. In natural science, understanding usually means searching for strictly material cause-effect relationships. However, in many rural places where I work people live a subsistence existence. I was learning from some of my research interviews that to some families a goat was more important than a mother—wives could easily be replaced.

✳ ✳ ✳

I (Jeffrey) noticed that Kiran had settled on a research question that was critical to her professional interests and dear to her heart. She wanted to understand better why so many young mothers were dying in childbirth, even when medical services were available. Quantitative studies had not previously been helpful in addressing this problem. The answer did not seem to be providing more clinics, or even sending more doctors to remote areas. Even when doctors were available, the women would not avail themselves of the services. Time after time, Kiran would show up in a village and find a new mother lying in a barn, dead in a pool of blood. Kiran could have saved the lives of this woman and her baby, if only she had sought her help.

Kiran wanted to revolutionize obstetric care in rural Nepal in a way that would be far more responsive to the unique cultural and geographical context. Grounded theory was an ideal methodological choice because it would allow her to explore the experiences of new mothers and their families, as well as to make sense of the significant themes that emerged. Her goal was ambitious but critical: integrating (if not creating) a practical, relevant, and useful model grounded in the data she collected from interviews.

✳ ✳ ✳

Some Remarkable Breakthroughs

I stared at Maya's lifeless body with frustration, with anger, and with grief. I examined her heart and lungs—digging through blood and soft tissue. Maya had bled profusely at home, during her travels, and then at the hospital where she had expired. I wondered what would happen to her two children now, just two and four years old. What would happen to her husband who was away working in India, trying to keep the family together? What would happen to her mother-in-law's dream to be surrounded by a dozen grandsons?

Before Maya had finally succumbed to blood loss, she had given birth to a baby girl. I wondered what would happen to this child as well. Would she grow up to be just like her mother? How would she live with the stigma of being blamed for killing her mother? I knew the village would not blame me as her physician since I had arrived on the scene far too late to save her. The family would not blame themselves for failing to help her as she lay dying. They would say it was the will of God, or that she had done something to anger the gods, or that she was too weak and perhaps it was better for all concerned if she died so that her husband could have a stronger wife.

Editors' Comment

Why Grounded Theory?

The reason why grounded theory is so popular is that it allows the researcher to make new discoveries. It provides a systematic framework for collecting and analyzing data at the same time; these two processes are so often separated in traditional methods. The methodology of grounded theory merges these two processes so that the researcher can continuously guide the direction of the analysis, but also so the researcher can use this new understanding to lead the next stage of the process. This approach, so different from any other option within quantitative or qualitative paradigms, generates new insights because it forces the researcher to question continuously what has been found.

Kiran had been trained as a physician and an epidemiologist who was used to conducting large-scale population surveys on health issues, and to collecting routine clinical data from her gynecological patients. She was familiar with the patterns of reproductive health, but that familiarity did not allow her to see the phenomenon as it was lived in the rural communities. She was looking for new forms of explanation that might better inform her practice and government health policies. It took concerted effort on her part to tell her originally assigned mentors that more quantitative studies of mortality among childbearing women had already been attempted with limited results. She was highly motivated to attempt an alternative research paradigm that would allow her to hear more clearly the concerns of those she was most trying to help.

Frankly, the death of a woman in labor was such a common occurrence in rural Nepal it would barely register to anyone that Maya's death could have been prevented. She could have survived if only she had gotten help in time. I wondered what the circumstances were that stopped such a course of action. Why did the family fail to take her for medical care when they could see she was in such bad condition and worsening every minute? Her death struck me as all the more tragic because it could have so easily been prevented.

✵ ✵ ✵

One of the most remarkable things that Kiran learned in conducting her research interviews—and this came as a huge surprise to me as well as to Kiran—was that women were dying not only because of scarcity of medical care, but also because of their belief systems. Once Kiran learned to ask more open-ended, probing questions, what she discovered was that it wasn't actually the wife's decision about whether or not to seek medical care during a complicated pregnancy. It was her husband's mother, her mother-in-law, who called the shots and made the decision. If the daughter-in-law was having medical problems such as vaginal bleeding or abdominal pains, sometimes the mother-in-law believed that no intervention was the best course, and that the situation should be left to the will of the gods. While Kiran (and most of us) might find this difficult to accept, these beliefs were an integral part of their culture.

Another groundbreaking result from Kiran's study, one that has revolutionized the way she runs her obstetric unit, was to find that when new mothers did visit the hospital, they often had horrific experiences with the medical personnel. Within their own villages, when a lower-caste woman gives birth she is often attended by all of her female relatives and the women elders. It is a social occasion with much support and love. The pregnant woman is constantly touched and rubbed and massaged. She is a celebrity.

Yet when these lower-caste women visited the hospital, they were often treated as objects rather than as people. Doctors and nurses would barely speak to them, and were only interested in conducting their tests and running their procedures. The women found the experience impersonal and humiliating, especially when they were subjected to the indignity of having male doctors touch their private parts. Some would rather die than suffer such a torture.

When the women returned to their village after a successful medically supervised delivery, they reported all the indignities that were thrust upon them. They described how snakes were put in their arms (intravenous tubes), how rude the medical personnel had been, and how they had been treated worse than animals. They warned the other women in the village never to go to this place where they would be treated so disrespectfully.

✽ ✽ ✽

What I Learned About Myself

As a physician, I (Kiran) have always seen myself as a lifesaver. As an obstetrician and one of the few women doctors in my country, there are many reasons I should be proud. Most women of my country do not receive much education beyond primary school, yet I have received many opportunities to study at some of the world's best institutions. Rather than leading an academic life, I choose to live in the Chitwan area of southern Nepal, near the border with India. As a physician and surgeon, I have performed thousands of successful operative deliveries to save mothers' lives. As an anthropologist, however, I have found myself struggling with my own convictions. In the process of performing my work, I have routinely separated women from their families by asking them to deliver alone in a foreign hospital delivery room. In a sense, by focusing only on the uterus and birth canal, I have separated a woman's reproductive organs from the rest of her body. I had forgotten that a birthing woman also has a heart that is beating nervously in reaction to some great uncertainties. All the times I was delivering babies and performing life-saving operations I rarely, if ever, stopped to consider what this pregnancy experience was like for the woman.

Many birthing women suffered from psychological trauma during labor. Anu, for example, was hospitalized for her second childbirth. She was lucky this time because her husband was able to remain with her; in the past, he often had to leave suddenly for extended periods because of his job in the military. There had been much violence, strife, and the undercurrents of civil war in Nepal. Soldiers were required to leave their homes suddenly in order to fight Maoist rebels who were seeking to overthrow the government. It was a time of great instability, both throughout the country and in the homes of all the people who were caught in the middle of war.

As representative of my interviews, Anu describes her hospital experience that was marked by shame, confusion, and humiliation.

> When pain was intolerable I called a doctor on duty, but she didn't respond. She didn't even look at me. I pulled her white coat while she was passing by my bed, but she ignored me. I was struggling just to get a word of reassurance. She could've said, "I am busy. I'll attend to you in a while." But she ordered a nurse to put some kind of tubes in my arm. She also instructed the nurse to call her if I didn't deliver in two hours. In about four hours, the nurse took me to the delivery table. There were several young males and females in white coats surrounding the delivery table. Their job was to shout in a monotonous voice "*bal gar, jor gar*" [push down]. Then they said I needed a cut down into my private part [episiotomy]. I didn't like the idea, but they said that it had to be done otherwise the baby could get stuck. Finally, going through all these terrible things I delivered this baby. Now I am asking myself, what have I done to deliver this baby? I simply watched the health workers delivering this baby. (Anu, age 20)

I have been trained as a physician, an anthropologist, an epidemiologist, and a scientist. Dealing with childbirth constructs and practices is always puzzling. After all, I had been taught to measure things and to keep my distance from patients as much as possible. I had long been admonished to not become personally involved with any of my patients. As a researcher, I had been trained to look at the numbers. In both cases, I did not see people, with all their dreams, joys, challenges, and hardships.

I was trying to find ways to better understand human emotions and experiences. After three months of studying various qualitative methodologies, I believed grounded theory analysis would be the best choice to develop a model that could guide clinical practice in my country and others like it. I learned grounded theory from one of my supervisors, but found it difficult to grasp. The whole idea of coding, emerging categories, and themes eluded me. It seemed so subjective and unscientific, at least as I had learned science as a physician. But my other mentor, David Plummer, was also a medical doctor, so he was able to explain to me the ways that all physicians diagnose illnesses in very qualitative ways, developing theories of what might be going on based on the data of the presenting symptoms and tests conducted.

Since the time that I conducted the research interviews for my grounded theory study of childbirth practices in Nepal, I have crossed into territory that I never imagined existed. It has changed who I am as a doctor and as a health professional, but also as a mother, a wife, a daughter, a sister, a colleague, and a friend. At some moments during my research, I felt psychologically disoriented and emotionally shattered. Most of what I had ever learned was being challenged.

I remember, in particular, when I was trying to reconcile the need for confidentiality in my informants' experience with the ways they seemed to be depersonalized and objectified during the data collection and analysis stages. After sharing hours and hours of their vivid life experiences, it seemed discourteous, if not disrespectful, to keep them anonymous, to lock them up in a file cabinet. Then, as mandated by the Institutional Review Board procedures, five years later after the interviews, when I do not need them any more, I will burn these transcripts in a fireplace. It is as if I am destroying a part of their lives.

✳ ✳ ✳

Kiran's research experience exemplifies the powerful ways that a qualitative research journey not only advances knowledge in a discipline, but also transforms the researcher. I have seen the way that Kiran now functions differently as a physician and health professional. I have noticed the ways she now constructs relationships with patients rather than merely administers procedures to them. I have witnessed her dancing with village women, drinking tea in their homes, forging collaborations with indigenous healers and shamans, all in the hope that this will strengthen their bonds as a team.

I have also seen the ways that doing this study changed Kiran as a person. Kiran's father, Madhav Ghimire, is one of her country's greatest writers and the National Poet of Nepal. Because doing and living qualitative research is not just about collecting data and conducting interviews, but also about describing and writing what was revealed, Kiran found her voice as a writer. It has strengthened her identity as her father's daughter and brought them closer. It has also changed me as well, a subject about which I will speak a little later.

✳ ✳ ✳

Challenges I Faced

Completing this qualitative journey forced me (Kiran) to examine the way I practice as a physician and health policy administrator, and challenged me in so many other ways. It may seem as if doing qualitative interviews would be natural for doctors, because that is what we do every day talking to patients to formulate a diagnosis and appropriate treatment. On the contrary, though, it was very difficult for me to learn to think like a grounded theorist, to look at embedded and underlying themes in the transcripts and conversations with informants. The process of coding transcripts was also difficult for me because it seemed that people's words were being scrutinized and analyzed to the point that the people themselves were lost.

English is my third language so it was difficult for me to learn and practice research. I am a Nepali woman and doctor, yet I was studying in a small university town in Australia that was very strange to me. I am used to being in charge, being a doctor who makes life-and-death decisions every day, yet as a doctoral student I found myself sometimes in a subservient role in which I had to be deferential and hide what I knew and understood. This was not at all the case with my mentors and supervisors, but rather with some other faculty members with whom I had to interact.

The cultural challenges were even more complex and interesting because Jeffrey Kottler, my primary mentor, was an American who lived in California. His training was in counseling so he spoke a very different language from what I was used to as a Nepali and a doctor.

It was difficult for me to express my Nepali thoughts in the (Australian) English language. My frustration and confusion were only heightened when my supervisors returned chapters with comments about how they found my writing "rough" and even "incoherent." I had to accept that there were limits to what I would be willing to do writing in a language that was not my own.

A turning point for me occurred when I loaned a book to Jeffrey on constructivism, which was the theoretical framework of my study. I had spent several sleepless nights worrying because I found the book so incomprehensible. I thought I wasn't smart enough to understand this and wanted to give up and go home. There were several times I wanted to abandon my studies because I was lonely, because I missed my family, because I missed my patients and my work, because I was frustrated with the Australian system, because I didn't understand what people were saying or why they were behaving in such strange ways, but this was the worst time for me. When I saw Jeffrey the next day, he practically threw the book on the desk. When I asked him what was wrong, he said the book was so poorly written, so dense and unnecessarily obtuse, that he couldn't make any sense of it. All of a sudden, I felt so much better! Eventually, I was able to let go of my anxiety and enjoy the process as it unfolded.

One of the most interesting and enjoyable aspects of our collaboration were the cultural aspects of our relationship. This was further complicated by the two other members of our committee: an American health administrator and Australian infectious disease physician. Each of the four of us represented different disciplines, religions, cultures, and theoretical orientations. This diversity only enriched our team because there was tremendous respect among us, even with our disagreements.

⁕ ⁕ ⁕

Kiran liked to write like a poet in her manuscript, including Hindu and Sanskrit expressions, and including vivid descriptions of the context of her interviews. Personally, I loved this material and wanted to preserve it, but another committee member believed that it didn't fit the style of a dissertation, at least one on health policy. Another area of debate that was absolutely fascinating was how the study evolved over time, initially investigating only new mothers' childbirth experiences. Based on input from the other committee members, Kiran was encouraged to expand her research, to include interviews with mothers-in-law, husbands, and health professionals. This made for a far more complex and rich study.

Even with my frequent visits to Nepal (which continue to this day), Kiran and I have had to negotiate our language and cultural differences. This is one of the aspects of directing doctoral dissertations that is so exciting and growth producing, the time that I learn as much as my students. Indeed, this collaboration has changed my life in ways that I am now only beginning to understand and integrate into my life.

⁕ ⁕ ⁕

Learning Interviewing Skills

When I (Kiran) was first learning qualitative interview skills, one of my Australian friends happily volunteered to be an interviewee for a practice session. She also organized a dinner, followed by the interview in her house. Jeffrey also attended so he could observe my skills and provide feedback. I remember so well that during this Australian winter night that it was cold outside but we sat beside a warm fire.

The interview began with some general topics so that both of us could become comfortable. Because this woman was an actress, she added elasticity to the interviewing process. She gave me such confidence by helping me whenever she saw me falter. Jeffrey was sitting on a sofa behind me, but I could see his disappointment reflected in the woman's face every time I made a mistake. I was learning to ask questions that were more open ended, and not to stick with my agenda if the informant wanted to lead somewhere else. I had to be more patient and more respectful of the person's pace. This new interviewing style would help me significantly as a doctor as well.

Editors' Comment

Deep Interviewing

Doing qualitative interviewing is not at all a natural skill. It is not about having a questionnaire sitting in your lap or having all your questions prepared ahead of time. It is not about anticipating the answers you will receive, nor about confirming what you think you already know and understand. It is not about a tidy, sanitized process that follows a logical, sequential process. This was challenging for Kiran, who had been trained as a physician and clinical interviewer. In the role of a physician, she proceeded through a checklist of possible hypotheses and diagnoses. This procedure just doesn't work within the qualitative paradigm, which requires a fundamentally different set of skills.

A qualitative interview is about probing within the individualized context that is in front of you. It involves figuring which questions are most relevant and appropriate at any moment of time that will yield the richest possible lived experiences of the participant. It is a fluid, interactive process of engagement in which the next probe stems from the preceding conversation. The questions asked allow both participants to explore a phenomenon at the deepest possible level wherein the researcher can explore inside the mind and heart of the informant.

✼ ✼ ✼

I also remember this session well. At first, I was concerned about whether Kiran could make the necessary adjustments to focusing on feelings and deeper thoughts instead of only medical symptoms. She asked rapid-fire rather superficial questions and didn't go into much depth. She seemed stilted and overly structured.

It was amazing and so gratifying to see the ways that Kiran grew in her skills over time. Of course, it helped that she could eventually conduct her interviews in her native language, with me not looking over her shoulder.

✼ ✼ ✼

Some Highlights From the Study

Although I learned something from each of the interviews I conducted, two especially moved and impacted me. The first was with a woman named Aitu who lived in a little village at the edge of the jungle in the Chitwan District. In order to travel to her small home I took a bus as far as it would go and walked up a bicycle path until that ended in a narrow, slippery lane that was a part of an irrigation channel. It was interesting to watch other people on the road walking with their shoes in their hands so they wouldn't become muddy. Eventually I took my shoes off as well.

It was already late evening by the time I reached Aitu's house. A young man offered me a bowl full of water to wash off my feet. When I spread my palm over the sole to clean it under the water stream, I was startled to see four leeches attached to the bottom of my foot. The villagers thought my reaction of fear was very funny. Leeches were simply a part of their lives. This is how my interview with Aitu began.

A second experience that is strong in my memory occurred on one of the hottest days of the year, during the monsoon. This was during a time of civil war; the Maoist insurgents abruptly called a strike, closing all public activities and government offices. On that same day, I had scheduled an interview with Chameli, which meant I had to walk a dozen or more miles each way to and from her house. As I neared Chameli's village, my tiredness vanished. Life's beauty was there in the blue sky, opening over the paddy fields and riverside. The villagers lead such a simple life without all the complexities that make up our own daily lives. When I first saw Chameli, she was enjoying a mustard oil massage under the hot sun. With a look of happiness and pride, Chameli welcomed me and invited me to sit beside her. This is where and how our conversation took place.

✳ ✳ ✳

Kiran and I (Jeffrey) discussed the importance of these contextual details. Doing qualitative research sensitized her even more to all the details of daily life. She learned to be far more observant, not only of her patient's symptoms, but also of the patient's daily life.

It is also noteworthy that during the civil war the Maoist guerillas, who originated in this same area where they had their headquarters, required all doctors and successful people in the district to pay them bribes in order to avoid being kidnapped and ransomed. Kiran, however, was never once asked to make payments. The Maoists were well aware of how much of her practice was devoted to helping the poorest people in the community.

✳ ✳ ✳

Promoting Social Justice

It is interesting how one can learn so much from a research project that the results can be applied immediately to professional practice. I (Kiran) have said earlier how the interviews I conducted changed the way I practice medicine, and the way I plan health policies. Even though my study was not constructed as social action research, there were certainly some long-term benefits that resulted.

✳ ✳ ✳

It was when I (Jeffrey) was visiting a village near Chitwan, about an hour's drive from the district city, that I first learned about the girls who were disappearing. Kiran and I had traveled to this village so that she could show me where she worked and the settings in which she was doing the research. I was horrified to learn that some of these people were so poor that they could not feed and school all their children. Since girls are not valued as much as boys, they were the ones who were pulled out of school. In some cases, they were married off to reduce the family burden; in others, they were sold to "employers" who promised to find them jobs in India. These jobs were in fact working in brothels as sex slaves. In India, and in other countries, men who are HIV positive believe that having sex with a virgin will cure their disease. These girls, some as young as eleven years old, are then infected themselves and eventually make their ways back to their village.

I told Kiran that we had to do something about this. We had already learned from her research study that one reason why women would not seek medical care was because they found it humiliating to be examined by male doctors. But what if we could grow a whole generation of women doctors? What if we could identify girls from the lowest caste, those who are academically gifted but who are otherwise not able to remain in school, and what if we could support their education? Maybe some of them eventually would become doctors, female doctors, who could help other women.

That first visit to the villages we identified one girl, Inu, and gave her a scholarship. It costs only $50 per year to support a girl in school, providing her with uniforms, books, supplies, and food. It is now six years later and we are supporting forty-eight girls and one boy from three different villages. We named our foundation after Kiran's father, Madhav Ghimire. We have plans to expand over the coming years until such time that we can grow the next generation of women doctors and professionals (www.ghimirefoundation.org). Inu, the first girls we sponsored, has since graduated from high school and is now attending college where some day she hopes to become a professor. As of this writing, we have just selected our newest scholarship recipients, two six-year-old twin girls who are soon to become orphans after both parents die of AIDS.

✳ ✳ ✳

Changing Relationships

Qualitative research is so much about relationships, with informants as well as with one's mentors and fellow students. It is a collaborative effort in which the interactions with colleagues, supervisors, reviewers, and other students help us to refine our thinking and develop our ideas. I am so privileged to have had such wonderful relationships with the members of my supervisory team who each helped me in different ways.

It is interesting to me how my relationships with my mentors have changed over time. Jeffrey started out being my teacher, then became my colleague. Now we work together with our foundation in my father's name. During these last years, we have laughed together and celebrated our achievements. We also have cried together over the children we want to help.

In Australia, teatime is an important part of the day when all the doctoral students get together to share gossip and talk about our troubles and challenges. We listen to other students complain about their advisors. Some of those advisors could be rather controlling and critical. One day, a friend of mine was having trouble with his supervisor who insisted that he do a comprehensive literature review before collecting data during interviews. My friend, though, was more comfortable doing it the other way. Listening to that dispute helped me clarify my own best method for conducting grounded theory. So many other conversations with students were similarly helpful to me, even if I was only listening to others talk about their projects.

It was during these conversations that I heard about one faculty member who was an expert on grounded theory. He was also a physician so I thought we might have a lot in common. I invited him to join me for tea, and in only a half hour he was able to explain to me what Glaser and Strauss and the other grounded theorists were writing about. I knew I wanted him to join my team and I asked him to do so.

My other mentor, David Plummer, was not available for face-to-face meetings often because he was so busy, but he reviewed my chapters and gave me valuable feedback. He would take a long time to respond to me because he had so many other students. I know he would become annoyed with me because I would ask him for the feedback.

Jeanne was the other member of my team; she had a calming effect on everyone. She was always so supportive and encouraging. She had a way of offering suggestions that seemed to me to be easy to implement. She spent a lot of time with me and was able to navigate the politics within the school. There is always politics in academic life; without Jeanne, I would have been swallowed up by it. She was able to help me get through the ethics approval process. Sometimes there was hurtful gossip and jealousies among the other students, and Jeanne was able to smooth that over. She was the comfort zone for me. I had a very strong connection to her as a woman.

✳ ✳ ✳

I think that Kiran is being both diplomatic and honest talking about the realities of politics in completing any research study. Her supervisory team worked well together because of mutual respect but this is not always the case. Within any academic unit, there are often conflicts that are based on personality and conceptual differences. Students are sometimes caught in the middle of such disputes and end up being hurt by them.

In my own doctoral experience, I had a powerful advisor who was threatening to others in his department. Since they could not go after him directly, I was a vulnerable target. I experienced a lot of suffering, sexual and verbal harassment, and discrimination as a result, even with the protection of my advisor. It sensitized me to just how brutal such skirmishes can be. Even when they are supposed to be about research questions, they can end up really being about retribution for perceived past injustices.

There were times I had to run interference for Kiran and to advocate on her behalf, just as Jeanne and David did. There are power dimensions to all mentor relationships, especially when the advisor is a white, heterosexual male and the student is a minority female from a culture that is patriarchal and hierarchal. I think being able to talk about these issues openly is crucial to working them through. I like to think that, above all else, research advisors have a responsibility to model in our relationships the kind of integrity, respect, and honor that we wish for our students.

✳ ✳ ✳

Editors' Comment

It's All About Relationships

Relationships and rapport *are* qualitative research. Good quality data are outcomes of the level of rapport, intimacy, and trust that exists in the relationship. Let's face it: in conducting these interviews, we ask some of the most personal, intrusive, revealing questions imaginable about sex lives, death, and fear. These subjects are rarely talked about, or at least rarely talked about in an unedited way. In order to encourage participants to discuss such personal matters in a completely honest and authentic manner, you *must* be able to develop the kind of relationship that is open and respectful, in which the participant feels heard and understood.

Just as physicians struggle with this kind of interview that is so different from how they've been trained, so too do social workers, psychologists, counselors, and other helping professionals struggle with making the switch from relationships that are intended to unearth new data to those designed to change people. Qualitative research relationships represent condensed and compressed encounters that elicit the most innermost thoughts and feelings that are disclosed in a few remarkable hours of conversation. This takes both considerable training and practice, which are quite different from what is learned in clinical or other contexts.

Final Thoughts and Implications for Doing Qualitative Research

The dominant biomedical conceptualizations of childbirth with their narrow disease focus inadequately represent the experience of mothers and their families. These models are inadequate because they leave out, or only nominally consider, the social forces and contexts that shape childbirth and women's lives. Unlike what I (Kiran) had learned previously about doing quantitative research, the qualitative framework provided me with the opportunity to understand better the ways that childbirth not only is a biological event, but also is embedded in social context of family, gender, community, culture, medicine, and power. These social phenomena create *scripts*, or shared definitions among birthing women, their families, and the service provider.

The life stories of fifteen informants illustrated the diversity and complexity of culture and traditions that have survived over the ages. Nepal is a multiethnic, multilingual, multicultural, and multireligious country. The communities practice their cultural and religious activities freely and openly. This is, however, true only for male members. In considering the experience of the women, it must be observed that they fall under an overarching patriarchal ideology. From the time of birth, females are repeatedly reminded, in subtle and not so subtle ways, of their inferiority. Even today, women are forced to see themselves as commodities to be bought and sold. Women have no individual identity—socially, religiously, or legally. Access to property and social status is given by their husbands. Opportunities for women to express their views are minimal.

Being invited to participate in a study such as this, in which women were asked, by a compassionate and attentive listener to tell their stories, was a highly unusual opportunity for them, and was also empowering. It is rare that women in Nepal (or elsewhere in this part of the world) are allowed to give voice to their innermost thoughts and feelings.

✳ ✳ ✳

I have been amazed by the powerful ways that qualitative research can have far-reaching influence and impact, not only on the participants in the study, but also for the researcher, her colleagues, and mentors. Learning to do qualitative interviews changed the ways that Kiran practices medicine and relates to her patients and their families. It influenced her to change health policies in rural areas, being far more sensitive to the cultural and gender aspects of the birth experience. Kiran's relationships with members of her family and with her colleagues have become more intimate as well.

As for me? Supervising Kiran's research set me on a different path that has changed my life in so many ways. Kiran challenged many of my most cherished assumptions. Her family has "adopted" me as their American son. I have since returned to Nepal close to a dozen times, having brought over a hundred colleagues during that time to contribute to the work that Kiran and I began some years ago. Such is the power of qualitative research and its long-term impact.

Reference

Glaser, B. G., & Strauss, A. L. (1967). *The discovery of grounded theory: Strategies for qualitative research.* New York: Aldine de Gruyter.

When Serendipity Meets Opportunity 6

*Qualitative Dimensions
of Teacher Perceptions*

LeAnn G. Putney and Connie L. Malin

When I (Connie) entered graduate school for my doctorate, I had been an educator in elementary school settings for more than thirty years. I already had earned two master's degrees—one in education and one in literacy, but I was ready to step up to the doctorate to learn more about students with special needs. I had already taught many students with special needs in my general education classroom, so teaching to different needs and developmental levels was already part of my teaching repertoire.

As a doctoral student, I had experts honing my quantitative skills, encouraging me to rediscover the meanings behind numerical orders and formulas. There was a time when I really believed this should be the crux of my research until I realized that behind every set of numbers was a story waiting to be told. My years of teaching and kid watching in my classroom were an advantage when I started taking qualitative research courses. In the first class with LeAnn Putney, I was able to look beyond the issues that other students raised in terms of validity, reliability, and generalizability in research. For example, I knew that each classroom of students would present a different set of issues and require me to use different strategies if I was going to be an effective teacher. I knew that standardized testing would give me some information about my students, but that my own observations and formal and informal assessments could tell me more about the students than the numbers on the tests.

In the qualitative courses, we were conducting mini research projects. I began to delve into the stories that my students would tell me. We were required to do both observations and interviews. During interviews, people would tell me what they thought I wanted to hear, but their actions in the observations spoke louder than their words in the interviews. The more I worked through the qualitative analysis, the more I came to understand that numbers or self-report alone could only take me so far in my research. Therefore, qualitative research, data collection and analysis, and a triangulation of data became a challenge that I simply could not or would not resist.

✳ ✳ ✳

Teaching graduate students the ins and outs and processes of qualitative research is one of the joys of my career. I (LeAnn) began my career in 1997, and became a qualitative voice in a department of research scholars primarily focused on statistical designs. Over the past ten years, researchers in education have called for more mixed designs or complementary designs to include qualitative methods. I have been called on to serve on committees across the college and university by students who were beginning to ask questions that required qualitative methods beyond statistical analysis.

In my courses on qualitative research, students engage in mini research projects of interest to them, using qualitative design and methods that require active participation in the research process. Not surprisingly, in these courses some students take to the qualitative work as if they had just found a research home while others are somewhat hesitant about the change from the statistical methods they had learned in previous courses.

One of my favorite lessons is on the qualities a qualitative researcher must develop in terms of becoming intuitive, using good communication skills, and having a tolerance for ambiguity. I teach that qualitative research is patterned, not predictive; serendipitous, not controlled; contextualized, not void of context; situated, not universal; purposive, not randomized. Qualitative researchers need to be sensitive to people, conditions, and the data. I also tell students that they must be open to serendipity, to seize the qualitative moment because they cannot always plan what will happen in a study. By the time Connie was approaching her dissertation study, she had already taken three courses from me and was becoming quite adept at conducting small qualitative studies.

Connie exhibited two of the three necessary qualities from the start. Her intuition was keen and her communication skills were already exemplary—not unusual, since she had been a classroom teacher for some thirty years by the time we met. The one characteristic that I knew she still had to hone was her tolerance for ambiguity. I was pretty certain her dissertation process would be the sharpening stone. As students collect, analyze, and interpret qualitative data they often find the process unfolds in unexpected ways. Part of my job as mentor is to assist students in making visible for their committee the strengths, the systematic processes, and the underlying benefits of conducting qualitative research.

At the Crossroads

Having been an educator for more than thirty years, I chose to conduct a study related to the classroom practices of new teachers. At the time I began this study, I knew I had a hard path ahead of me to convince my committee of the benefits of a mixed design. My department consisted of brilliant quantitative researchers who believed that hard data in the form of numbers was the way a study should be formed. They just were not sure of the value of anecdotal evidence in a doctoral dissertation.

My dissertation was to understand how teachers perceived their practices in terms of how appropriate they were for the developmental level of their students. I knew that it would not be enough to merely ask teachers if their practices were appropriate, although I used a questionnaire designed for that purpose. If I really wanted to know what elementary classroom teachers knew about development, I would need to observe them in action in their classroom settings.

I conducted the study in two phases. I used a questionnaire to see whether the teachers understood developmentally appropriate practices and whether they considered themselves to be practitioners of such. I also wanted to see if their training as educators made a difference in what they knew about such practices. The results of the questionnaire potentially would show if any significant difference occurred among three programs: traditional programs outside the local area, the local university traditional program, and the local university alternative program. In the qualitative portion of the research, I observed teachers in their classrooms from each of the three programs during a sixty-minute literacy lesson. I also conducted interviews with the teachers as a member check of my observations.

Throughout my educational career, I have been trained to believe that numbers don't lie. I believed this concept, and saw no problem in using a questionnaire as the first pathway to my research. However, as I progressed through the doctoral program and took many qualitative research classes, I realized that numbers could be manipulated to produce particular outcomes. Along the same lines, I knew that questionnaires result in self-reported data. I found this to be problematic: I wanted to uncover more than surface level self-reported information. Therefore, qualitative research for my project began to take its own form as it began to guide and reformulate what I was seeking.

✳ ✳ ✳

In Connie's design of her study, the observation and interview portion was where the tolerance for ambiguity would become critical. During her proposal defense, I had to be ready to ask the right questions so that Connie could demonstrate her competence in preparing to conduct the research, as well as convince her committee members of the value of the qualitative design.

As can happen, committee members may question why it is necessary to conduct the qualitative portion to begin with, and may try to impose quantitative values on the qualitative process. For example, in Connie's case the committee wanted her to train others to conduct qualitative observations of the video data she collected as to ensure inter-rater reliability of the video data to correspond with her observations in the field. After making the case for why this is not normally done in qualitative studies, we took a different route. We enlisted help of other students from the qualitative class I taught to examine the video data and take field notes to compare with Connie's notes from the field as a form of researcher triangulation.

This procedure resulted in constructing a flexible rubric they could use after watching the video to score the number and type of developmentally appropriate practices viewed. During their training, we cautioned them not to use the rubric as a checklist, but to take field notes from the video, then use the rubric as a form of delineating what the practices were and how often they were sighted.

✳ ✳ ✳

Editors' Comment

Confronting Doubts

Connie's struggle with convincing her committee to accept qualitative research as scientifically legitimate has more to do with a biased and misinformed view of research that is common among those who have been only quantitatively trained. Connie was aware of the need for the depth of description and interpretation qualitative research would offer. Some of history's most significant and influential scientific discoveries have come from using a qualitative, inductive set of principles. For example, Galileo spent time watching the sky and the stars, collecting observational data about patterns and behavior. His analysis led him to a grounded theory that the Earth moves around the sun. A lot of medical discoveries such as penicillin, X-rays, and infection control have been made according to similar inductive qualitative methods. No doubt, qualitative research is quite different in its operating assumptions, philosophy, and procedures, but that is because it is after different forms of explanation as shown by the rest of Connie's story.

✻ ✻ ✻

Another aspect that we encountered was the resistance of recognizing qualitative research as part of the scientific inquiry process. As one committee member noted, qualitative research was interesting because of the anecdotes, but really what could we expect to learn from those stories? Even though they approved her mixed-method design, Connie needed to trust the process of unfolding the nature and interpretation of the qualitative data analysis. I was aware that even though the other members would read her work thoroughly, they might not recognize the value of her journey unless she made it explicitly visible for them. To do so, Connie would have to trust my guidance as well as her own intuition about her interpretations to make the final case for the quality of her work during the dissertation defense.

✻ ✻ ✻

Stepping Stones: Crossing the Path to Qualitative Measures

In my study, I needed to gather information face-to-face in the social setting to verify the information shared on the questionnaire. In addition, the observations and interviews would allow me to identify the meaning that these teachers gave to the practices they initiated with their students. These initial questionnaire data became a basis for the observations and interviews conducted to broaden or enrich the questions being asked. Field notes, head notes, and interviews became vital components of the study, distinguishing between and among teachers. While my committee members approved my proposal to incorporate the qualitative data, many of them remained wary of the utility of my design. As my qualitative mentor, LeAnn, would say, "They are so used to just finding that a significant difference exists. What I hear you saying throughout your defense of the design is that you want to know what difference that difference makes. To do that, you must initiate qualitative inquiry."

OBSERVATIONS

Administering the questionnaire was the quick part of the study and my findings showed that the teachers queried were aware of and regularly used appropriate learning strategies for young children, with no significant differences between those trained in the different teacher education programs. The observations and interviews took me down a path that was much more complex and more interesting than I imagined collecting such data would be. In my review of literature, I had identified practices that I would expect to see in the classrooms. While this information gave me a basis to use for recognizing the differences between developmentally appropriate and traditionally based practices, I duly noted the advice of my mentor: I kept an open mind when conducting the observations by writing descriptive field notes of what I was able to see and hear, and anticipated what might emerge. I waited to make inferences of the data during my analysis after each observation and used my field notes and interview notes as evidence for my inferences.

As I had done in the qualitative class projects, I set myself up in each of the classrooms at a corner desk to be as unobtrusive as possible. I arrived early so that I could look around the room before the students entered. I took note of what kinds of student work were on display, if any. I also looked to see how the room was set up, noting whether seating arrangements were in a more traditional configuration of straight rows or in a manner more conducive to small group work or centers. In most cases, the rooms seemed quite inviting so I expected that I would see teaching practices that were inviting and conducive to learning for young children.

The following field notes are an example of the information gained from an observation completed in a second-grade classroom.

> Students were seated in teams of four to six students facing the teacher as the lesson began. To initiate the lesson, the teacher began by explaining the centers in which the children would be working. One by one, she introduced a listening center, a quiet reading center, a writing center, a partner read center, a homonym center, a word wall center, and a center in which students could work with the teacher. She told the children to listen for a bell to go off and then demonstrated the sound it would make. This would signal the end of the center and the beginning of the rotational process to the next center. The students listened attentively and raised their hands to ask questions for clarification. The students were then dismissed to begin working in small groups at assigned centers. For the next thirty minutes, children could be seen working independently or actively helping each other. Children could also be seen moving around the room, reading to each other, and interacting with the teacher when needed. The teacher was in a corner of the room working with four students. Each of the students in her center was given a word by the teacher, asked to write it on a piece of paper, and then asked to use a dictionary to find the word's meaning. The teacher gave assistance with this by helping the children turn to the correct page and by helping children spell the word correctly. The children were also encouraged to help each other before seeking the teacher's help. As the work continued, the timer went off and the children in the rest of the room switched to their next assigned center. The teacher looked up from what she was doing, but said nothing. (F. N. 6–30–01)

In this particular classroom, the setting caught my eye upon entering. Bright colors, children's work posted, and the development of teams were all evident. The teacher had her desk in a far corner of the room away from the student areas. She used visual and audio cues to keep her students focused. Materials around the room were low enough for students to access independently and students were encouraged to converse with each other while assisting in problem solving. The teacher restated directions as needed. The teacher used hand signals and positive verbal feedback to let the students know she was pleased with what they were doing.

After each observation, I typed up my field notes and began reading and coding them to determine what types of practices were taking place in the classroom settings. I also conducted interviews with each of the teachers and made an audio recording of all interviews for transcription. I transcribed and recorded their responses in a narrative form. In a similar fashion to that of the observation process, I continued coding the interviews. I prepared domain analyses of the transcripts to look for patterns that emerged.

DATA ANALYSIS

In my study, I analyzed the teachers' applications of developmentally appropriate practices in the classrooms. In conducting the observations, two particular elements came to light: (1) ways to teach and (2) the classroom environment. I constructed domains regarding these elements and further analyzed them for relationships of the included terms within each domain, which is referred to as a taxonomy. A taxonomy assists researchers in defining sets of categories within a large group, thus showing relationships of individual elements within a domain. First noted was the instructional methods utilized by teachers at each grade level and within each group. I found some similarities across the grade levels and groups through the initial domain analysis that showed what developmentally appropriate and traditionally based instruction might look like across the groups.

The sample on the following page shows you how this comes to light as I put the data together.

Finally, in my study, I used triangulation of data types to enhance and make visible the participant practices in relation to their perceptions of practice. For example, I compared and contrasted information from the questionnaire, the observations, and the interviews to contribute to the overall credibility of the findings presented. In some cases, I found that what the teachers claimed to do in the interviews did not quite fit what I observed in their classrooms. For example, one theme that I constructed from the interviews was the theme of age-appropriate activities. A typical

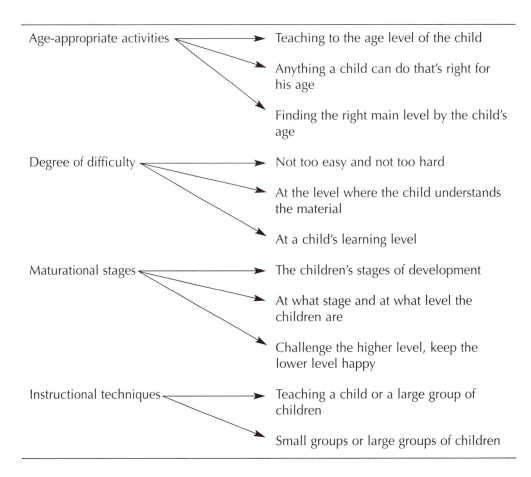

response related to this theme was, "Um, I guess just to make sure that what you're teaching is right for that age level and that you're not doing anything that is too hard or too easy for them." This was an appropriate response for this question from a particular kindergarten teacher. The following shows how observations and interview responses can produce conflicting results.

> When entering this classroom, I immediately observed a child-centered setting filled with color, movement, and age-appropriate materials. When watching this person teach, the words coming from her mouth reiterated that she knew what developmentally appropriate practices were. However, in conducting her classroom, this teacher was not child centered. Instead, she micromanaged and used negative feedback intermingled with a touch of fear for her as the authoritarian figure to control her class. While conducting this observation, I had the distinct displeasure to watch her make a five-year-old girl cry with her cutting remarks. This truly was an incident of knowing what to say and do, but not doing what was appropriate in the classroom.

An example of how the data from observations and interviews can be congruent came from a different teacher's response. When I asked her what age-appropriate teaching meant to her she replied, "Anything a child can do with simple explanation from the instructor that is right for the age and does not exceed the ability level," and "I believe it is basically right for the child's age and finding the right main level the student is working on." This kindergarten teacher did what she said should be done. Her classroom was filled with color, activity, independent work, and the celebration of individuality and success. Her remarks encouraged children to interact, to ask questions, and to voice their own opinions while problem solving their way through the ocean food chain. Role-playing and creativity were highly valued and rewarded in this classroom. What this teacher claimed to do in her interviews was actually played out in the classroom setting. Therefore, my interpretations were confirmed by more than one instrument measuring the same thing (Miles & Huberman, 1994).

Note the example below of the data triangulation.

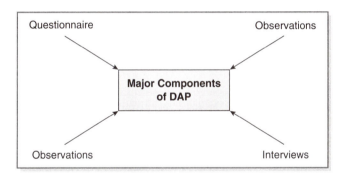

＊ ＊ ＊

Triangulation is a somewhat contested notion in qualitative research. I have found, however, that when students make visuals of their qualitative data it helps the committee members to see the systematicity of the work. They are so used to seeing charts and graphs that seeing a huge pool of text without any visuals seems to dredge up the statistical concepts that usually do not apply in the same way to qualitative studies. Using a form of triangulation can make visible that the subjectivity inherent in qualitative design is no less credible than the numbers produced in other designs. Indeed, in Connie's case her committee members recognized the work produced in her visuals and in her juxtapositioning of different types of data. This became a compelling strategy in the research design.

＊ ＊ ＊

What became most interesting to me in this study was that the statistical analysis of the questionnaire data showed that no significance surfaced in the between-subjects effects for the questionnaires. This might have been considered a problem since most quantitative studies presume a difference to exist among the subjects being studied. However, given that this was a mixed design study, I found the qualitative portion to reveal a rather surprising difference among the three groups of teachers that could not have been realized through mere self-report data.

Editors' Comment

The Language of Research

Note that Connie is using the language of quantitative research in describing the findings from the survey data by discussing "no differences between teachers," "significantly more likely to," and "teachers were noted to score highly." These are measurement terms associated with a research paradigm that seeks to quantify and predict, as opposed to exploring and describing, experiences. Since Connie was ambitious enough to use a mixed-method design, she had to reconcile what specific questions were going to be addressed by the qualitative and quantitative components.

Beginning students often confuse the different paradigms and use terms inappropriately because they belong to a particular methodology incompatible with the application. For example, in qualitative research we talk about *informants* or *participants* as opposed to *subjects* or *respondents* (note the more active role in the former). Another example is that quantitative methods speak about *controlling variables*, *measuring outcomes*, *predicting results*, and *demonstrating associations between variables*, whereas qualitative methods use language such as *describing themes*, *presenting typologies*, *exploring phenomena*, *recounting stories*, *sharing discourses*, and *describing human experiences*. Even more pronounced is the language used for describing results. One is numerical and graphical, presenting data as aggregate numbers, whereas the other showcases data in the form of text and associated with individual experiences. As you can see from this study, the qualitative tells a different and more complex story than the quantitative data could.

✳ ✳ ✳

While the questionnaire and interviews suggested no differences between the teachers in terms of what they understood developmentally appropriate practices to be, the observations revealed that the teachers from different programs showed a practical difference in how they approached the children in their classrooms. Teachers in Group One, who were from out-of-state traditional programs, spent a large portion of their time disciplining children and using extrinsic rewards to keep children on task. Their students spent a large portion of the lessons following teacher directions, listening, and attempting to intake the information being given by their teachers. Although centers were used, children were not free to interact with their peers in a social nature because the teachers needed to have quiet to work with the small groups they had pulled aside.

✳ ✳ ✳

In Group Two, teachers from the local university traditional program monitored children's behaviors but spent less direct time in vocalizing the disciplinary actions than did their colleagues in Group One. Children in these lessons began with large group instruction, but in most cases moved to work with peers or independently from the teacher before the completion of the lesson. Further observations showed these teachers to be strong in guiding the students to learn through individual assistance and attention. However, it is here we find a lack of socialization and more teacher-directed assistance when the child has problems. These teachers also scored high in building the child's internal motivation rather than using an external reward system. Again, this is an interesting twist to the observation process; the teachers used a great deal of verbal praise and positive comments, but they also had team point systems on the board and matched students' behaviors with team behaviors for rewards to be issued later in the day or the week.

Teachers from Group Three, the local nontraditional program, took an overall more child-centered approach. The teachers spent a large portion of their time facilitating learning for the students. They were very strong in guiding the students to learn with individual assistance and attention and in building the child's internal motivation rather than using an external reward system. They also provided opportunities for students to interact with each other in an effort to do some peer instruction or clarification of misunderstood concepts or directions. These teachers acted as guides to assist children to learn. They used individual assistance and attention, providing opportunities for students to interact with each other through the use of small groups and center work. Children were free to speak with peers and to move about the room in an attempt to continue working on something individually or in another small group as their classmates completed a task assigned by the teacher.

As demonstrated by the differences in the classrooms upon observing the social setting, using a questionnaire as the only indicator of teachers' developmentally appropriate or traditionally based perceptions and applications would have led to skewed conclusions without the incorporation of the observations and the interviews. It was evident that the interplay between the teachers and students in each classroom, combined with the qualitative interview information became a valuable asset to the study. Sifting through the layers of information, watching and listening, and then comparing and contrasting the shared information brought forth the most valuable information in the study.

✳ ✳ ✳

During the data presentation at her dissertation defense, Connie first recounted the quantitative work that showed "no significant differences" among the three groups of teachers. I had advised her to prepare a case in point of the qualitative data regarding the literacy centers, illustrating a dramatic difference in the ways in which the teachers approached the classroom practices with their students. It was at that point that the committee members realized that without the qualitative portion of her study not much could be revealed. With the qualitative portion, however, she demonstrated the practical differences in the teachers' approaches to their students as well as the differences between outcomes of the programs in which they were prepared as teachers. When her committee members noted that the qualitative portion became the study, we knew that they had seen the value of the qualitative work and they appreciated the contribution the qualitative research made.

The Road Next Taken

So, now the dissertation is history and the knowledge gained is embedded in my brain. Qualitative research has become secondary nature to what I do and how I approach my career. Currently I serve as the Chief Educational Officer of a public K–12 charter school. Daily, almost minute by minute, I am called upon to make disciplinary, academic, and staff decisions that affect the school and its effectiveness. I watch the eyes and body language of the people in front of me, listen to what comes out of their discourse, and then observe their behaviors as they interact with other students or adults. It is evident that all is not as it seems. I have learned to look past the obvious, ask the hard questions, and read all the signs before making decisions that will have a long-lasting effect. Qualitative methods for collecting and analyzing data work well for my administrative duties and serve the school well in establishing policy based on data, hard evidence, and feedback from multiple sources.

Editors' Comment

Making Sense of the World

One of the most delightful outcomes of qualitative research training is that its legacy is the way it prepares the researcher to be a more reflective, analytic professional and human being. This method teaches you to be inquisitive, to ask complex questions, to deconstruct meaning in behavior, and, most importantly, to make sense of your own experiences. The same procedures that helped you to investigate a research study are just as valuable in approaching any problem or issue. For example, as a result of conducting this study Connie now views the classrooms under her supervision through ethnographic eyes. This has changed significantly the way she operates as a teacher-educator and as an administrator in her K–12 charter school.

Just as interesting are the ways qualitative research training changes all of your relationships. Since you learn to become more skilled at building trust and intimacy during interviews, you become far more sensitive and responsive in other conversations. You learn to become more curious about why people do the things they do, you learn to suspend judgment, to quiet your critical voice, to become more responsive to others, and to enrich all your friendships and family relationships.

I find myself using domains and taxonomies to construct overarching themes for working with parents, teachers, support staff, and students. I find myself relying on my powers of observation to probe beneath the surface of what is happening in the school. I watch to see if people's actions relay the same message as their words. I conduct interviews on a regular basis, although not in a formal sense. I find that when I let kids tell their story about an incident it builds empathy and trust, and lets them know that they are all going to have the chance to tell their side of the story. One thing I learned for certain from my qualitative courses is that multiple realities exist and must be examined and juxtaposed against each other so that all sides are considered. One of the primary characteristics of a qualitative researcher is to be a good listener, and I find that honing my listening ear was of great benefit to me as a school administrator. I find that as much as I truly enjoyed qualitative research as a graduate student, it has become an integral part of my daily life to help me understand what is happening in my school through the eyes of all involved.

✳ ✳ ✳

What Connie's story demonstrates is the value in conducting research that follows the questions you want to answer. Her mixed design was quite appropriate for the research questions she asked, and her approach to justify her work was to show explicitly how the qualitative data revealed what the statistics could not—how people make sense of their real-world experiences in relation to what they learned through their educational programs. While the call for mixed or complementary methods in research has become more readily accepted than when Connie completed her dissertation, having to justify the qualitative methods portion is still a reality for some graduate students as they work their way through the process of their dissertation or thesis studies.

For students who wish to conduct qualitative research, my advice is to find a strong advocate who can assist you with the methods design and analysis, but who can also help you to work your way through the process of constructing a valid and valued research design. I am delighted that Connie did not give up on the process of conducting a study reliant on qualitative design because the relationship we forged through her dissertation journey resulted in the work we are doing today. She did develop that tolerance for ambiguity and it served us well as we worked together to open a public charter school, a school in which she is now the administrator and I am the governing body president. We learned to build on each other's strengths and we use our differences in complementary ways.

I can see how Connie uses the qualitative methods even today in her meetings with students, teachers, and parents as she encourages them to talk while she takes in what they are saying and observes how they are responding to her and to each other. Fortuitously, the utility of the rubric Connie developed in her dissertation has proven itself later in her journey in her role as school administrator. The rubric gives her a method for observing teachers beyond a standardized checklist to determine how well the teachers are putting into practice the type of teaching that relates to the mission and vision of the school in which she now works.

In my classes, Connie learned to observe through ethnographic eyes—that is, observing an ongoing situation to see who is doing or saying what, with or to whom, for what purposes, under what conditions, with what consequences (Frank, 1999). By using these skills in her daily work at the charter school, Connie can better understand people's motives and can move toward resolution of an issue because she can get to the heart of the meaning making that is happening among the people in the setting. As students in my classes tell me, once they learn to look at the world through ethnographic eyes, it never looks the same to them again. My response to them is to smile and say, "Good—that means that I am doing my job."

References

Frank, C. (1999). *Ethnographic eyes: A teacher's guide to classroom observation.* Portsmouth, NH: Heinemann.

Miles, M. B., & Huberman, A. M. (1994). *Qualitative data analysis.* Thousand Oaks, CA: Sage Publications.

Online Dating and Mating 7

Methodological and Personal Reflections on Our Journey

Danielle Couch and Pranee Liamputtong

While driving home one night, listening to a mainstream, commercial radio station, I (Danielle) heard an advertisement for an online dating website. I was curious. When I arrived home, I found the website, registered, set up my personal profile, and began my first forays into the world of online dating. I was soon receiving contacts from other members of the website. I was astounded by the spontaneity of it all and the ability to interact with so many people that I could potentially meet in person. This particular website was an adult site, which meant that it was sexually focused, with members listing their sexual preferences along with basic demographic details. These sexographic details included sexuality, relationship status, sexual interests such as spanking (light or hard), oral sex (giving or receiving), anal sex (giving or receiving), one-on-one sex, group sex, erotic picture swapping, erotic email, and numerous other options. Details also included whether the member was registered as a single person, or part of a couple or group, and whether the member's interests were in other members who were male, female, transgender, single, couples, or groups. Members could also nominate safe sex preferences from a choice of always, sometimes, or never practice safe sex.

After becoming familiar with this website, I soon discovered another major online dating website that was more about dating and less about sex. I was working in public health and completing my master's of public health at that time. These sites and other similar sites I found myself or read about in the media started me thinking about the potential health impacts of online dating and the resultant sexual interactions that could come of the dating. I had been contemplating what I would do for my minor thesis as part of my master's and now I knew—my research topic would be online dating and mating.

Editors' Comment

Outside the Boundaries

Danielle's research demonstrates only one of the ways that technology has opened up new avenues for accessing human experience, especially the ways that people interact with one another. Qualitative studies can now be undertaken exploring text messages, blogs, photographs, online videos, graphics, and other media—all collected via cyberspace. You have opportunities to think way outside the boundaries of what we have normally conceived as data.

I (Danielle) knew I wanted to undertake a qualitative study, and the variety of methods and orientation of this type of research for focusing on individuals' experiences really appealed to me. Coupled with the fact that much of my day-to-day work involved churning through quantitative data, I was keen to have a new research experience and to extend my understandings. My next step was to find an appropriate supervisor. I took the obvious steps, trawling through the university website trying to identify an appropriate supervisor from the various staff members' listed research interests. I wanted someone who had an interest in the Internet or sexuality, or both; an interest in online research; and someone who was a qualitative expert. It turned out that I found a perfect match in Pranee Liamputtong, someone who shared my interest in online methods of investigation.

✳ ✳ ✳

I (Pranee) knew a few people who had used online dating as a method for meeting a potential partner. They seemed to enjoy their journeys, and some of them had successfully met their long-term partners through Internet dating, but I have also heard about the negative aspects of this method. Then it occurred to me that this way of meeting people could also be used as a way for us, as researchers, to elicit information from potential research participants. I started to read literature on doing research online, and that was the beginning of my attempt to write a book on online research.

When I started working on my book on research in cyberspace (Liamputtong, 2006b), I was keen to have someone working with me on this topic. None of my students at that time had an interest in pursuing their research in this new and innovative field, however. Going into a photocopying room one morning, a form that had been left on the copy machine caught my eye. It was a form regarding a research topic filled out by Danielle. It was something to do with online research. That was fantastic and I was thrilled to see such an attempt from a student.

❊ ❊ ❊

Honing the Idea and Proposal

Discussing my thoughts with Pranee, we decided to undertake a qualitative research project that involved analysis of a selection of personal profiles on the adult online dating website, with a particular focus on the health-related content, or lack thereof, within individuals' profiles. I also thought that this would be a relatively easy way to do the research—sampling the profiles seemed much easier than actually endeavoring to engage with people online from a research context. Undertaking the research in this way would be expedient, also—I could complete the required amount of work within a relatively short time frame. This research was to be the minor thesis as part of my master's. That is, it was meant to be a project worth the credit for about three subjects. I was keen to do the project, finish it, and graduate with my degree, presumably ready for bigger and better things.

Unfortunately, after scoping this idea, developing the research proposal, and submitting the ethics application, the website we were interested in using changed its terms and conditions to explicitly prohibit the use of its content for study and research purposes, and so my ethics application was rejected. This was disappointing, as I had put a lot of thought and effort into developing my research proposal and ethics application. It also meant that my proposed timeline was going to be pushed out. As a result, there was a good chance I would not finish my degree within my hoped-for time frame. I am sure many researchers would say that having to go through the ethics approval process a couple of times for a project can assist in further developing and targeting a project. That's true— and it certainly helps you make sure you have dotted your "i's" and crossed your "t's," too! In retrospect, to pass this ethics hurdle it might have been useful if I had broadened the scope of potential websites from which to sample profiles. This might have required me to reorient my proposal to be more globally focused than local, but it also might have allowed me to identify sexually focused websites that had content more freely accessible. Although it would have been a completely different research project, I am glad I undertook the one I did. Having people share their real, lived experiences of online dating made me feel very privileged.

Around this time, I also noticed that individuals had started posting warnings within their personal dating profiles, with these warnings targeted at researchers from a particular university stating they would take legal action if any details from their profiles were used for research purposes. We were not able to determine what the research was that was so offending and affronting to many of the website's members, but it made clear the need to investigate online dating and sexual behaviors using a different method, one that gave those being studied the opportunity to be involved in a far more participatory manner.

Editors' Comment

Preparation and the Review of Sources

No research commences with data collection. A question always begins with a search for what else has been written about a subject. It is only after extensive review of what is already known that you begin to formulate your own ideas about where to go next. This often includes a review of literature, as well as searches on the Internet, conversations with experts in the field, biographical studies, popular media, and cultural artifacts such as photographs, films, advertising, and historical archives.

This background locates a context for the study and provides important clues as to where researchers can focus their own efforts. This is a time-consuming exercise because of the requirement that your study include sources that are most relevant. Yet as opposed to quantitative studies where such reviews are supposed to be comprehensive and exhaustive, completely defining the parameters of the research question, qualitative studies use the existing literature as data that form part of an analytic process that is itself questioned as the study progresses. Just as the review informs your procedures and process, so too do subsequent results lead you back into other facets that you hadn't considered previously. This recursive or cyclical process continues until you are reasonably confident that you have covered the territory.

Through my personal use of online dating websites, we came to realize that it was common practice among website users to move away from the website to freely available chat programs such as MSN (or Windows) Messenger or Yahoo! Messenger, which allow users to chat in real-time (synchronously) online via text (and increasingly via voice and video). Moving communications away from the website did not necessarily mean that a date would eventuate between contacts or even that there would be extensive chat between them. It did allow, however, a way to circumvent the fees related to communicating through fee-based online dating websites and to avoid the clunky private chat options offered by the site. Using online chat can feel just like having a conversation with someone, although it involves a lot of keystrokes rather than talking. I was already a regular user of chat programs. Like many people, I had found them a useful method for keeping in contact with family and friends, and for liaising with work colleagues when working offsite.

Conversation with Pranee about emerging online research methods led to the idea of using chat as a method to explore how people were using online dating, their engagement with those they met online and offline, particularly in a sexual context, and how they thought about online dating in relation to risk and safety. It seemed appropriate to do so, because it was a method of communication that many online daters were already comfortable with and using regularly for dating purposes. At that time recognition of the Internet as a useful tool for exploring HIV risk behaviors was also emerging, with particular relevance to isolated and hard-to-reach groups (Davis, Bolding, Hart, Sherr, & Elford, 2004; Davis, Hart, Bolding, Sherr, & Elford, 2006; Elford, Bolding, Davis, Sherr, & Hart, 2004; Liamputtong, 2007; Lombardo & Gil let, 2006; Ross, Rosser, & Stanton, 2004). Therefore, the second rendition of the research proposal and ethics submission was based on undertaking online in-depth interviews, conducted via chat, to explore the website members' experiences of online dating.

Discussing the methods with Pranee and her encouragement that I conduct online interviews allowed me to reconceptualize my project and figure out how I could still investigate an area of interest to me. At first, I found the thought of interviewing a little confronting; I had wanted to be the silent researcher, staying in the background and researching without engaging. Soon after I started data collection via the interviews, I was thrilled that we had decided to use this method. I was able to take my research a step farther—I engaged and interacted with the participants of my study. It was challenging, and at times confronting, especially when my participants turned my questions back on me. An example of this was when a participant, Nathan, was telling me about one of his autoerotic practices and some of his other sexual practices. He then started asking me how it made me feel—was I sexually reacting to what he was telling me? I was discomforted in the dialogue because I was trying to be a professional researcher, but he was asking me questions that were trying to push me into a sexual role rather than the role of researcher.

Speaker	*Dialogue*
Nathan	i guess there is another thing that may shock you or you may be turned on by. . . .
Danielle	ok . . .
Nathan	well i guess you know i love toys . . .
Danielle	yes, you've told me about that. :)

(Continued)

(Continued)

Speaker	Dialogue
Nathan	it sounds gay and all but i assure you im 110% straight . . . when im really horney there is a dildo i have that has a suction cap on it and when in the shower i sometime stick it on the wall and masturbate while fucking myself with it . . . it is good when i climax as it hits the prostate.
Danielle	wow. suction cap. that's cool. i didn't know you could get them.
Danielle	as i said to you my knowledge of toys is limited . . .
Nathan	did that sound bad to u?
Danielle	no, it didn't sound bad at all
Danielle	are you worried it sounds bad as in gay?
Nathan	yeah so what do u think of it then
Danielle	sorry, are you trying to get a sexual reaction out of me or do you want my honest opinion?
Nathan	honest opinion
Danielle	well i reckon it sounds like a pretty cool way of pleasuring yourself.
Danielle	i don't think it's "gay" in any sense. lots of guys are into anal penetration of some kind or another
Nathan	ok
Danielle	or anal play: fingering, rimming.
Danielle	i mean you men have the prostate gland accessible from there
Danielle	makes sense that it feels good.
Nathan	:)
Nathan	ok
Nathan	does it turn u on? or are you not bothered by it?
Danielle	i'm not at all bothered by it

Nathan continued to be curious about my response to what he was telling me, by asking me again if our interview dialogue made me horny.

Speaker	Dialogue
Nathan	so does any of this make you horny or are you oblivious to it all?
Danielle	well I am definitely oblivious when i'm in this mode. i'm not thinking about what you tell me in a personal sexual context. thinking more about how it might or might not fit with what others have told me, whether there is anything from a public health point of view i should be thinking about and following up. b/c at the end of the day, i have to think about it from that point of view, rather than
Danielle	personal sexual gratification. that's not where i'm at when i'm interviewing
Danielle	kinda wearing a different hat!

I found these questions challenging, but I was also mindful that Nathan was exposing himself and may have been feeling exposed and vulnerable or "horny" by what he was sharing with me, and he was genuinely curious as to how I was engaging with our dialogue. I was torn between whether my participant might be sexually harassing me with his questions or whether it was his right to do so, because I was asking and expecting him to answer sexually explicit questions about his own life. I was glad I was conducting these interviews online: I could sit in the comfort of my study, while Nathan was in his own home. It made me feel much safer than I would have felt if I had encountered such dialogue face to face. This conversation with Nathan really confirmed for me that participants are not passive recipients of our research agenda—they are individuals who can and do choose to engage with us as researchers and individuals. If I think participatory research is important then shouldn't I see their desire to engage as ultimately their right? They have the right to expect from us what we expect from them, and it is our role to decide how we will manage this interaction. This situation made clear to me that I have not yet reconciled with myself what my stance is on research participant versus research subject. Interactions such as these gave me much more from the project intellectually, professionally, and personally than I could have initially foreseen. I hope that as I become a more experienced researcher my feelings and responses to these situations become easier to understand. But perhaps that is naïve.

My finalized research proposal noted my project would be qualitative and would explore the following questions:

- How do people who use online dating think about risk and safety in relation to their online dating contacts and interactions?

- How do people experience engagement and interaction with those they meet, both online and offline, particularly in a sexual context?
- What public health risks and opportunities does online dating present?

These questions were driven by my personal experiences, readings, and formal study in public health. I had thought about risk and safety in my own use of online dating, and I knew some users of online dating were sexually very active. I had knowledge of the epidemiology of sexually transmitted infections and I had done some reading on the Internet as a channel for facilitating sexual interaction soon after meeting online.

Methodology: Chat Interviews

* * *

Data collection in the study took place via in-depth online chat interviews. Chat can be defined as "real-time communication between two users via computer. Once a chat has been initiated, either user can enter text by typing on the keyboard, and the entered text will appear on the other user's monitor" (Webopedia, 2007). These were text-based real-time interviews, where we typed questions to the participant and the participant typed responses. Each interview was conducted as a private chat—that is, only the participant being interviewed and Danielle were present in the chat space where the in-depth interview took place.

Conducting the in-depth interviews online via chat software offered some benefits and challenges. Sex and sexual behaviors are largely private activities. In addition, there are often religious, social, moral, and cultural norms and taboos surrounding the discussion of sexual behavior, which can influence how and who is willing to participate in sex research (Fenton, Johnson, McManus, & Erens, 2001; Wang & Ross, 2002). The use of online chat interviews provided the possibility for participants to respond more freely, without feeling constrained by what might be regarded as risky or deviant behaviors (Markham, 1998). It offered a method of collecting data that allowed the participant to maintain confidentiality and privacy. It also may have assisted in ensuring the data collected best represented the actual sexual interests, activities, and behaviors the participants were seeking and living through online dating. It also meant that the project was not constrained by geography or time (Liamputtong, 2006c; Liamputtong & Ezzy, 2005).

Editors' Comment

Types of Interviews

To state the obvious, there are many different kinds of possible interviews. They can take place face to face, on the phone, in focus groups, via teleconferencing, or on the Internet and electronic media. So, how do you decide which format is optimal?

Ideally, the choice of type of interview should be made based on what is likely to produce the richest, most informative data, but in reality researchers often do what is most expedient and convenient. In this study, however, Danielle specifically selected chat rooms as opposed to any other possibility because of the more-ready access to what she wanted to explore. Research is often driven by pragmatic realities of what you can do and can afford to do within the time and space allocated. Whatever choice you make as to how and where you find your sample and what kind of data collection you do, you must provide a defensible rationale for this decision, one that is supported by the literature you have reviewed.

✳ ✳ ✳

Similar to other online research methods, interviewing using chat online may present some difficulties (Liamputtong, 2006b; Mann & Stewart, 2000; Whitehead, 2007). Dialogue is not always linear and word-play such as jest, sarcasm, or the use of metaphors can be ambiguous (Davis et al., 2004). To minimize this possible ambiguity, it was important for me to seek clarification from participants about their comments and remarks. It is not possible to see a participant's face when conducting the interview, or to gauge their facial expressions (Liamputtong, 2006c). This may result in the interviewer missing nuances within the dialogue, although Davis and colleagues (2004) argue that online interviewing is its own distinctive social practice and should not be simply compared to or equated with face-to-face interviewing. Chat allows the sharing of feelings and expressions by using emoticons or acronyms, and through the text that is typed. Users also can personalize the way in which their text appears in chat, changing the font type, size, and color. In some chat programs, users can display an image file, which can be a personal photo, further personalizing their chat self-presentation (Mann & Stewart, 2000).

Learning to interview online presented some challenges. I read some literature about the process before and during the data collection period because I needed to be up to date with my methodology. At the same time, I was heavily guided by my own use of online chat, in the same way that if I were to interview by telephone many of my actions relating to what is appropriate on the telephone would be guided by years of use and familiarity. Because I had used online dating and chat to talk to fellow online daters before starting the research project, I had been immersed in the field and was familiar with most of the chat acronyms I encountered in the interviews. If I had not had this previous online dating exposure, the interview process would have been more difficult.

I did need to learn to be patient. Because the interviews were text based, it took participants longer to articulate their responses via text, compared to responding orally. Some participants were multitasking while being interviewed, so this meant they could take a while to respond. I soon learned that staring at a chat box waiting for a reply could be frustrating and not conducive to keeping me in the right frame of mind for interviewing. To get around this, I would have a spreadsheet for interview notes open on my computer which I could add to, or I would just complete other administrative tasks I needed to do, or even tidy up my desk while pondering the participant's most recent response and what my next question might be.

Occasionally, I did need to follow up a response to clarify what participants had meant, perhaps because their text response contained typographical errors or because the response had become out of order with my questions, or if I just wanted to be 100 percent clear on meaning.

Methodological Issues: Some Challenges

In addition to the issue I faced with my ethics submission and needing to refocus the project, I encountered a number of methodological issues and challenges along the way. These included how best to recruit participants, how to collect consent online, and if and how to end the data collection. I was faced also with unplanned media attention around online dating and sex in the midst of my data collection. Despite thinking I had planned my project well, these issues did arise; through dialogue with Pranee, reading literature, and active problem solving I was able to manage them, however.

RECRUITING—PLANNED AND REAL

I wanted to interview people who were using online dating and focus on any sexual experiences they might have as a result of their online dating, so I chose to use snowball sampling as the main sampling method. Snowball sampling is the method of recruitment in which the researcher asks his or her initial research participants to suggest others who might be willing to participate in the research. It is regarded as a useful sampling strategy for participants who may be hard to reach directly, but who may be well networked (Liamputtong, 2007; Liamputtong & Ezzy, 2005). Looking back, this was appropriate for the project, because at the time there was some stigma surrounding the use of online dating websites.

I recruited participants through snowball sampling from contacts I had made through my personal use of online dating websites. I also recruited participants through contacts of my contacts. On several occasions, when I had finished interviewing a participant she was able to suggest one of her own contacts who might participate. Establishing a positive and respectful rapport with the participants was vital to the success of gaining further contacts to interview.

In order to broaden opportunities for participation, I had also hoped to place an advertisement about the research, giving information on how to participate, on the community notice boards of the adult online dating website. This was what we had planned to use:

> Using the Internet to meet people? We would like to hear from you.
>
> Want to share your experiences?
>
> Hello,
>
> As a fellow online dater and _____ user, I am interested in exploring sexual behavior and online dating as part of my thesis.
>
> The research project will aim to examine the use of the Internet and online adult dating to meet sexual partners, and to gain insights into the sexual interests and behaviors of people using the Internet to meet sexual partners.
>
> I am very keen to hear the thoughts of other people who use online dating, and I would like to undertake *confidential* online interviews with anyone interested in being involved. The interview would take place via chat software (e.g., MSN Messenger).
>
> I will provide an information sheet and a consent form that outline the project and your potential involvement. You will be able to opt out of the interview at any point.
>
> I hope that the interview process will be insightful for all parties involved, so that we all get something out of the experience.
>
> If you would like to be involved or would like further information, please contact me at *onlineresearch@optusnet.com.au*.
>
> Thanks,
>
> Danielle

The advertisement was submitted to the website, but it was unfortunately rejected with no explanation provided. The advertisement was submitted after the media frenzy that accompanied the disappearance of Maria Korp and the subsequent trial. This was a case of a woman who was strangled and kept in a car boot for four days, who died about six months later, without recovering from her coma. The case and the media frenzy surrounding it were associated with online dating and the Internet as methods for meeting sexual partners. Much of the media about this case focused on the sex or swingers' website with which Maria Korp was allegedly involved. This was the site where I wanted to recruit potential participants—the same site that had explicitly prohibited use of its content for research purposes, and the same site where a number of users had already been upset by other researchers (as noted previously). Thus, although disappointing, it was not too surprising that the website managers were not amenable to me using their site to recruit participants.

Occasionally, the research may not proceed as planned. Research takes place within social, cultural, and political contexts and it involves others (Liamputtong, 2007). Things may become problematic. Unfortunately, when this happens we may have to change our research plans and directions, or worse, we may have to abandon it. The Korp case mentioned above is a good example of an unforeseen event that can have an unexpected impact on a research project. Fortunately, we only needed to change the way we recruited potential participants.

In an attempt to recruit more potential participants, on a couple of occasions, I changed my online handle to reflect my desire to interview people. A *handle* is a nickname that an individual chooses to use when appearing online in chat. It may be similar to the user's email address, or it may be completely different. It is common for people regularly to change their handle depending on how they feel and what they want to express at a particular time. For example, in MSN Messenger chat I use the email address spectraelectra@hotmail.com. My handle changes regularly and has included some even flippant handles:

- Miss Spectra
- Studious Spectra
- Spectra Is Sleeping
- Domestic Goddess

For specifically recruiting people to interview for this project, I used the handles noted below:

- Let's talk about sex and online dating.
- Anyone want to talk about online dating and sex???
- I'm looking for people to interview.

Changing my handle to reflect that I wanted to interview people attracted three people that I ultimately interviewed: they responded to my handle and asked what I was doing, then opted in to participate after I told them about the project and allowing them to view the information and consent form.

> **Editors' Comment**
>
> **Sampling Choices**
>
> The one thing you can be certain about with qualitative sampling is that the numbers are usually small when compared to quantitative studies. Furthermore, the sample selected is not considered to be statistically representative of the larger population. Remember that the goal of qualitative research is not to prove, to predict, or to generalize to large groups of people based on what is supposed to be a representative sample of that population. Rather the intent is to recruit those individuals who are in the best position to provide meaningful data about the phenomenon.
>
> There is a range of techniques, including snowball sampling (the choice in this study), purposeful sampling (cases selected because of their specific characteristics), theoretical sampling (cases of greatest relevance), and convenience sampling (those who are most available). In order to make an informed choice as to which is best for your own study, you first have to clarify what you most want to discover and what resources are available.

There were a few participants who initially indicated interest in participating but could not start an interview at the time they indicated interest. In order to interview these people, I waited until I saw them next online, when I also was going to be online for a few hours (long enough for an interview), and I would ask them if they still wanted to be interviewed and if now was a good time. For a couple of people, I had to ask them several times, which worried me. I did not want them to think I was harassing them. I was mindful that they were probably online for leisure and meeting my research needs was not their main priority. I also did not want to ask them too frequently in case this turned them off from participating, so being patient until when I felt was the right time to ask again meant my data collection took longer than I initially foresaw.

CONSENT ONLINE?

Another practicality I had to work through was how to acquire consent in an online environment. The standard ethics procedure was to have the participant read, understand, and sign a consent form prior to the beginning of an interview. This would obviously not work in an online environment—sending someone an electronic consent form and then expecting them to post back a signed copy was impractical, and would not fit with how people use chat technology (see Liamputtong, 2006a; Mann & Stewart, 2000). To manage this, I planned to use the file transfer capability available in the chat programs to send the information and consent form. If this was not possible, I could email the form. When the potential participant had reviewed the form, I asked him to advise his consent in the chat window or via email.

Once the study had commenced, I found that some people to whom I emailed the consent form would consent via return email and others would open a chat when we were next online concurrently and advise via chat that they consented to participate. Being concurrently online with the potential participants when the consent form was sent allowed potential participants to ask any questions they might have and clarify issues of confidentiality and how long the interview might take. In the instance below, we also were able to answer questions and concerns of the partner of the potential participant.

Epstein Rev Page 230Memo, 06/03/2004

Asked Serena to participate. I have emailed her the consent form. She will check it out and let me know. Might have some other contacts too. Have spent quite a bit of time explaining the process to her as I am very keen to have her support and participation, as I think she is very well networked in the scene. Her husband also had a question re why there were no set questions. I endeavored to explain and have also sent a website link that is quite theoretical, but should hopefully demonstrate that we are not making up this research style!!!

The chat software has conversation history functionality, so when consent was provided there was a written record of the consent. The conversation history also provided the interview transcripts for the project.

RECOGNIZING THE CONTEXT OF THE METHOD

Because online research is fairly new and there is no set handbook on how to do it, it was important to read literature about how others had conducted their research online, how they tackled any problems they encountered, and to reflect consciously on the research context and how this would affect the data collection. This required thought both before starting and in the midst of interviewing and data collection.

Most of us are comfortable with how to use a telephone or how to hold a face-to-face discussion, and how these communication mediums might be used in research. Online interviewing is different from those methods, and less familiar to many people. Because of this, the interview methods and techniques need to be adapted to the situation.

When conducting this research online, it was important to think about why and how people use technology and, in particular, chat, so that I could be an effective and appropriate interviewer. Chat is convenient;

when chatting online a person is generally in her own home and she can be doing any number of other things on her computer at the same time as chatting or being interviewed. That is, she might be reading emails, chatting with several other people, and paying her household bills online. Typing takes longer than talking, so there are chat- and Web-specific acronyms and emoticons that have arisen to help make typing faster (Liamputtong, 2006c).

PEOPLE MULTITASKING WHILE BEING INTERVIEWED

I was made acutely aware of one of my participants multitasking when I was conducting an interview. When I had my first opportunity to interview Serena, I was keen to grasp the chance when it arose, because at that point in the research I had not had the chance to interview many women. My memo below notes the context of the interview and my initial concerns about it.

> Memo, 25/04/2004
>
> I have asked Serena again if she would like to participate and she is keen, so I have commenced the interview. She has told me she is in four chats and has a guy masturbating on webcam for her at the moment, so she might be a little slow in responding. I was originally introduced to Serena via one of my online dating contacts. I have been keen to interview her for awhile as I would like more female participants. Just not certain how well the interview will go if she is really distracted. . . . A pro or a con—she can multitask while being interviewed and so can I, but if she is doing something more interesting in another window, the responses to me might suffer.

LEARNING TO SLOW DOWN AND WAIT FOR RESPONSES

Markham (1998, p. 70) notes, "[B]ecause writing takes much longer than talking, being a good interviewer means being patient." Typing takes longer than speaking, and so responses take longer to iterate. As an online interviewer, I needed to be aware that my participants could be multitasking during the interview. The three memos below from different interviews and relating to different participants indicate how each interview is unique and also how I, as a researcher, learned to be aware of the context and conduct the interviews in a manner that suited the context.

Need to remember to slow down. Takes time to read the information sheet and consent form! Seems to be quite hard to get detailed responses. . . . Am I asking the wrong questions? Is my topic boring??? Need to be careful how I phrase things re safe sex. don't prompt or put value judgments in there. (Memo, 7/11/2004)

Really hard to provide feedback or just encourage continuation of the interview without entering the conversation. If I just stick with "Yes," "Aha," or "I see" as responses it makes the interview seem stilted and the medium is all about chat!!! and conversation = interaction 2-ways. Yet I am conscious of trying not to lead the interview or to put too much of "me" into it. (Memo, 17/2/2005)

Jeff starting telling me about his experiences in general chat, so I jumped in and asked if I could interview him as he was telling me things I would ask!!! He's a good interviewee, just keeps going with the flow, I don't need to prompt him much. Or maybe it's just "cause I'm getting more relaxed at this and giving them time to ruminate rather than jumping in with next question every few seconds!!! Have managed to go a bit sideways in our interview realizing we know some of the same ppl. the internet is a small, small place. or maybe it's melbourne that's small!!! I love researching online. Listening to pulp fiction soundtrack whilst interviewing, getting up and having a dance every now and then, in between making a cuppa! Interview topics finished, but we are continuing to chat about a whole range of things. family, pets etc. It is amazing the rapport and r/ships you build with ppl online. and what you end up sharing. (Memo, 29/03/2005)

WHAT TO DO ONCE THE INTERVIEW IS OVER

Having people added to my chat contact list for this research project raised the question of what to do after the interview was done. To remove someone from a contact list, I would need to block her (which means she could no longer see me when I was online). For this research, I left that option with the participants. My experience of blocking was that it tends to be only done to one's online contacts when there has been rudeness or offense. I thought blocking participants after their interview was completed would seem rude. Participants always had the power to block me, but I was not going to block them—I left this in their control. This has resulted in some people proactively following up on the state of the research and offering to introduce contacts. Others continued to be visible when online, but did not initiate any further dialogue. Remaining available also allowed participants to follow up any concerns they might have had. For example, some time after an interview one participant was concerned about his gender, age, and location being revealed in the research; he believed it would make him identifiable, even though I had ensured this confidentiality prior to his consenting to participate in this study. I was able to talk through this issue in this postinterview chat so that he felt comfortable with the process and his anonymity.

Throughout the research all participants continued to appear sporadically online in the chat contact list, so I felt reassured that they were comfortable with my presence, the research, and their role in it. Of course, if someone stopped appearing online in the chat list, I would have no way of knowing if that person had blocked me or was simply spending less time or no time using the chat program.

This also provided me with the opportunity to ask quick follow-up questions when I was undertaking the data analysis and gave participants the opportunity to ask further questions about the research process and experience. Many of the participants demonstrated a genuine interest in the research: they initiated postinterview chats with me to update me on their experiences or to introduce me to their contacts who might be available for interview. They could introduce me by inviting another person into their chat. This was a great method because it helped to provide me with credentials in the eyes of possible participants.

Editors' Comment

Exiting the Field

The fieldwork process includes a number of distinct stages—preparation, entering the field, establishing solid relationships, learning the ropes, and exiting the field after you are done. Danielle makes the important point that exiting the field does not simply mean leaving behind what you started. There is quite a lot of work involved in closing the research relationship. You must make sure you delivered what was promised to the participants. Were the products of the research kept accessible to the participants, as well as safe from unauthorized scrutiny? Were the participants satisfied with their experience? Was there any unintentional harm that occurred, either to the informants or to others within that community?

So much time and effort on the part of researchers is devoted to gaining access to participants, recruiting their participation, and working under pressure to find those who will provide what you are looking for. It is just as important that you invest time to develop appropriate strategies for terminating the relationship so that it is a positive experience for everyone involved.

When the participants updated me on their experiences, I was careful to ask if they were telling me this *off the record* or *on the record*; that is, I again sought their consent to use what they are telling me in my research. My experiences of chat were that people and relationships could become very intimate and familiar, so I wanted to make sure I was not taking advantage of any familiarity or friendship that these people might have felt with me.

I did not leave the field when I completed the interviews. It has been noted that there are at least three ways by which researchers can leave the field: withdraw by cutting relations quickly and completely, withdraw gradually, or never withdraw completely (Minichiello, Aroni, Timewell, & Alexander, 1995; see also Liamputtong, 2007). My perception and understanding of courteous use of chat meant that I could not leave the field quickly and completely.

A Continuing Journey

The project allowed me to develop my research skills, to gain real research experiences, and to intellectualize these experiences and the research process in the real world. I have begun to understand how people in academia work, and particularly to understand the need to undertake research in their everyday life. It has opened my eyes to an array of other research opportunities and topics that would be worthwhile to explore. It has also allowed me to understand that there are many different ways of researching and knowing. Conducting interviews made me reflect on the participatory role of research and to critically reflect on the researcher versus the researched, and the roles each can play in the research process.

Working with Pranee was a joy. I consider myself very lucky to have found a supervisor who had an avid interest in my area of study, who I got along with on personal level, and with whom I could establish a working relationship that worked well for both us. The project allowed us both to develop further our interest in online research, to publish in the area, and to consider other possible research projects.

Our collaboration has led to having three papers written; two have been published in peer-reviewed journals. Pranee also invited me to collaborate with her on a chapter in a book she was editing (Couch & Liamputtong, 2006) and to participate in this chapter. We are working up an additional project, entitled "Marketing the Self," where we will explore personal advertisements in Australian newspapers, something that Pranee has been interested in doing for some time, but for which she has not had time to do herself. Pranee put together a grant proposal for a collaborative project with the Australian Research Centre in Sex, Health and Society, La Trobe University, which has been successful and is extending our initial online dating and sexual health research. Another grant proposal is in the pipeline, which if successful will further add to our growing research in this area. I am also exploring ideas for doctoral work that would continue to develop my online research skills. Pranee has happily accepted to be my supervisor.

My initial research idea has expanded and grown beyond what I could have originally envisaged, which has only been possible because Pranee and I have been able to have such a complementary relationship.

✳ ✳ ✳

Working with Danielle was also a great joy for me. Danielle is a very diligent student who is dead keen on everything I suggest. She would get on with the tasks she had to perform without reluctance or complaints (as far as I know). I like Danielle's open personality; she did not exhibit any ambiguity or doubt in working with me and did what she was meant to do. This was the reason why we got along so well with each other. I would love to have her as my student and colleague at any point in my life. As Danielle has mentioned above, we have started working on another project due to my success in securing funding from the university. With the help of Danielle and in collaboration with the Australian Research Centre in Sex, Health and Society, I have recently submitted a research grant application to the Victorian Health Promotion Foundation, a project that extends Danielle's initial research to the wider Victorian population. It is also likely that we will continue to expand our online dating project to cover Australian people in the near future. So, from working with Danielle as a supervisor, we have now begun to work as a team. Our good relationship will continue to grow.

❊ ❊ ❊

Dealing With Issues: Learning Tips

- Find a supervisor with whom you get along well, and with whom you share personal and academic interests.

- Check the supervisor's interest and personality from a university website and publication lists.

- Have a clear agreement about the outcome of your research, such as publications arising from the project and authorship. Deal with any disagreement or ambiguity early.

- If you are not very familiar with the methodology or other issues, ask your supervisor for advice.

- During the candidature, discuss ideas regularly with your supervisor. Find a way to do this that works best for both of you. This might be regular email updates, regular face-to-face meetings, a phone conversation, or a mix of all.

- When you do meet with your supervisor, do some preparation beforehand. It does not need to be as formal as having an agenda but you should have a clear idea of what you want to discuss. This might include what current issues you are facing, how you want the supervisor to help, how you think you can help yourself, new ideas or possibilities, or an update on timelines and deliverables. Make clear your expectations of your supervisor and make sure your supervisor makes clear his expectations of you. Your relationship should be professional.

- Continue to show your interest and express your ideas to attract the interest of your supervisor.

- Do not resist suggestions from your supervisor. Her attempts do not mean to cause any harm but rather mean to enhance your career prospective.

- Do not blame your supervisor if things go wrong.

References

Couch, D., & Liamputtong, P. (2006). Dating and mating online: Some research experiences. In P. Liamputtong (Ed.), *Health research in cyberspace: Methodological, practical and personal issues.* New York: Nova Science Publishers.

Davis, M., Bolding, G., Hart, G., Sherr, L., & Elford, J. (2004). Reflecting on the experience of interviewing online: Perspectives from the Internet and HIV study in London. *AIDS Care, 16,* 944–952.

Davis, M., Hart, G., Bolding, G., Sherr, L., & Elford, J. (2006). Sex and the Internet: Gay men, risk reduction and serostatus. *Culture, Health & Sexuality, 8,* 161–174.

Elford, J., Bolding, G., Davis, M., Sherr, L., & Hart, G. (2004). The Internet and HIV study: Design and methods. *BMC Public Health, 4,* 39–50.

Fenton, K. A., Johnson, A. M., McManus, S., & Erens, B. (2001). Measuring sexual behaviour: Methodological challenges in survey research. *Sexually Transmitted Infections, 77,* 84–92.

Liamputtong, P. (2006a). Cyber research: Focusing on methodology. In P. Liamputtong (Ed.), *Health research in cyberspace: Methodological, practical and personal issues.* New York: Nova Science Publishers.

Liamputtong, P. (Ed.). (2006b). *Health research in cyberspace: Methodological, practical and personal issues.* New York: Nova Science Publishers.

Liamputtong, P. (2006c). Qualitative cyber research: An introduction. In P. Liamputtong (Ed.), *Health research in cyberspace: Methodological, practical and personal issues.* New York: Nova Science Publishers.

Liamputtong, P. (2007). *Researching the vulnerable: A guide to sensitive research methods.* London: Sage Publications.

Liamputtong, P., & Ezzy, D. (2005). *Qualitative research methods* (2nd ed.). South Melbourne: Oxford University Press.

Lombardo, A. P., & Gillet, J. (2006). Online HIV research: Assessing three case study methodologies. In P. Liamputtong (Ed.), *Health research in cyberspace: Methodological, practical and personal issues.* New York: Nova Science Publishers.

Mann, C., & Stewart, F. (2000). *Internet communication and qualitative research: A handbook for researching online.* London: Sage Publications.

Markham, A. (1998). *Life online: Researching real experience in virtual space.* Walnut Creek, CA: Altamira Press.

Minichiello, V., Aroni, R., Timewell, E., & Alexander, L. (1995). *In-depth interviewing.* Melbourne: Longman.

Ross, M. W., Rosser, B. R. S., & Stanton, J. (2004). Beliefs about cybersex and Internet-mediated sex of Latino men who have Internet sex with men: Relationships with sexual practices in cybersex and in real life. *AIDS Care, 16*, 1002–1011.

Wang, Q., & Ross, M. W. (2002). Differences between chat room and email sampling approaches in Chinese men who have sex with men. *AIDS Education and Prevention, 14*, 361–366.

Webopedia. (2007). Webopedia: The only online dictionary and search engine you need for computer and Internet technology definitions. Jupiter Media Corporation. Accessed July 25, 2007, at http://www.webopedia.com.

Whitehead, L. C. (2007). Methodological and ethical issues in Internet-mediated research in the field of health: An integrated review of the literature. *Social Science and Medicine, 65*, 782–791.

Student, Supervisor, Researcher, Researched 8

Relationships and the Qualitative Research Journey

Wendy Hu and Carol Grbich

The Context: A Story of Three Clinics

My (Wendy's) story is about relationships, between student and supervisors, and between researcher and the researched. It is about how shifts in these relationships through shifts in my position in relation to others generated insights. The story begins with my long-standing interest in medical uncertainty. Differences in medical opinion, often to the point of rupturing collegiality and professional etiquette, are well known within the medical community, although they are usually sanitized for public debate. Despite a logical connection, doctors in one clinical specialty may refuse to refer patients to another. An example might be oncologists not referring patients to palliative care specialists when treatments no longer work, although publicly they appear to have complementary roles. The basis for such differences is a failure of science. When scientific knowledge and method cannot provide cures and answers, other factors come into play, such as the clinician's personal biases, prior experiences, and institutional cultures and histories.

From my experience as a family physician working in child health, I knew that there were three specialist clinics in the city where I practiced that had entirely different approaches to food allergy in children. In itself, this condition is a controversial health risk over which prominent experts have publicly differed (Colver, 2006; Hourihane, 2006). Like other risks such as bovine spongiform encephalopathy (BSE, or mad cow disease), the numerically remote risk of fatal reactions from foods such as peanuts in food-allergic children, estimated to be 1 in 16.7 million children per year (Macdougall, Cant, & Colver, 2002), was not proportional to the degree of community concern, public policymaking, and media attention—or so it seemed to me, with my medical training. In addition, the three clinics appeared to be an ideal and convenient setting to conduct research into what happens when doctors disagree. My aim was phenomenological, to understand the meaning of people's experiences, but also pragmatic, to determine if there was sufficient commonality for consensus to occur between the warring clinicians and bewildered families.

As the research encompassed professional attitudes and in situ organizational practice, it was planned as a multistage study incorporating ethnographic methods. Ethnographic researchers seek to understand the values and practices of communities from the perspective of its members, and do this by entering and becoming part of the group (van der Geest & Finkler, 2004). The researcher plays a crucial role in that she must forge relationships with members of the group, and effectively become an insider. While this rapprochement lends itself to data collection, it may become difficult for the researcher to later distance herself and become an outsider in order to analyze the data.

To introduce myself to all the participants on their own terms, I initially met with all the clinicians (doctors, nurses, dieticians, and technicians) at the three clinics and gained their agreement to conduct in-depth interviews to garner their views on food allergy risk. As a clinician with an interest in psychosocial counseling, I was familiar with interviews or consultations where I listened and guided, rather than constantly proffering advice, as doctors tend to do. For this research, though, I had to learn to talk even less than usual and to put aside prior notions of time. In effect, for the period of the interview or observation, my time dissolved and became time as experienced by the research participants. Aside from practical considerations such as clinic opening hours and fatigue, the interview or observation would last as long as the participant was comfortable with the process. Listening to my own recordings, while disconcerting, was an invaluable way to improve my sensitivity to the participants' response in relation to my questions and prompts, as well as the conscious use of silence and pauses to provoke reflection in less-talkative participants. Being open to the participants' experience, which included time as they experienced it, contributed to the richness of the data collected. Following the interviews, I became a participant observer in the clinics; this term acknowledges that the observer, by virtue of his presence, will become a participant in or influence the activities of the group, despite his best efforts to be unobtrusive. Families with food-allergic children were randomly recruited from the waiting room, and observed throughout their clinic visit. Consultations with these families were audio-recorded. After the clinic visit, I interviewed the parents of these families to hear their perspective. Follow-up interviews and observations (for example, when families returned for follow-up appointments) with additional focus groups conducted with parents from food-allergy consumer groups, were continued over a fourteen-month period. This period proved critical, because it allowed relationships to develop in a way that would not have been possible with a cross-sectional study design.

As the principal data collector, transcriber, analyst, and report writer, I became immersed in the worlds of researcher and participants. Without such immersion and reiteration, it would not have been possible to understand the perspectives of the individuals in my study, because they differed to the point of conflict. At other times, though, I had to disengage myself in order to reflect on and critically examine what I now understood, but from the position of the others. This was not as odd as it sounds. As a family physician, I would constantly mediate between the multiple perspectives of my patient, her family, and different medical specialists. My professional role was to evaluate dispassionately all viewpoints, but to remain true to my patient. Here, doctor and patient were replaced by researcher and the researched. Similarly, it was a relationship in constant flux. Analogies can be drawn here with the etic and emic stances. In the former, the researcher attempts to understand the values and meanings held by a community or social group from an external, objective perspective. In the latter, group values and meanings are examined from within the group, as if the researcher were a member of the group. Both offer valid but different perspectives on the reality experienced by the group. So here, at times my stance was detached, minimized by adopting the scientific researcher's etic stance; at other times I was drawn in by the need to gain a richer understanding and adopted an insider's or emic stance. Because individuals' viewpoints differed considerably from one to the other, holding an emic stance in itself required contradictory shifts from one participant to the next, as well as requiring me to be conscious of which stance I had adopted. Further complicating this were my own values, assumptions, and experiences, which inevitably colored the insights I gained from the research.

Relationships: Student and Supervisors

Developing in parallel to the relationships between the participants and me were the relationships between my supervisors and me, and their relationship to the research. These relationships predated and now continue after the story recounted here, and their evolution profoundly affected my research experience. Before I began my doctoral work, a recent graduate gave me this advice: supervisors, she said, have different strengths and play different roles in the process. In her case, one of her supervisors, a male high in the medical hierarchy, could open doors and command resources, while her other supervisor, a female, provided encouragement and was a personal mentor. This was apposite; as an older female candidate with children, I wished to have the understanding of a female academic who was familiar with the tensions between career fulfillment and domestic demands. At the same time, as a doctor I was well aware of and needed an antidote to the achievement-oriented and positivistic nature of my profession.

✳ ✳ ✳

My (Carol's) view of being a supervisor is that there is a delicate dance to be performed and the key is to understand when a quickstep, an underwater ballet, or a combination of the two is appropriate. My involvement with an individual project can vary at any one time from distant assessor to highly involved participant. In this study, Wendy's complex design and the large qualitative database she was collecting meant that high participation was needed and appropriate. When I was a doctoral student in the 1980s, someone put an illustrated map with a marked pathway on the wall of the students' tearoom. This map apparently represented the journey of the doctoral student. The map was titled "Pilgrim's Progress." Comments and crosses on the map located in the Slough of Despond (a deep bog situated in the center but at the base of the map) indicated that this was an oft-inhabited location. I try to prevent students getting to this inauspicious place but when I see them teetering on the brink I weigh in firmly, dealing out support, timelines, encouragement, praise, etc., while becoming an enthusiastic article reviewer, comparative analyzer, and a guide through troubled waters to the safety of the shore. Wendy bypassed the Slough of Despond largely through persistence, hard work, and determination, leaving me the more collegial role of supporting, guiding, reassuring, and mentoring. Supervisors need to be able to get inside a student's head if they are to be successful mentors so that they can sense when to back off, when to gently tread water while supporting the ailing student, and when to pull out all stops and indicate that the time for excuses is over and progress is essential.

The supervisor-doctoral student relationship is the closest of all teacher-student relationships. It combines the excitement and passion for a topic and style of research with the nurturing skills of a parent or friend. The years spent together (often many years) are precious. Although the annual hundreds of undergraduates will quickly be forgotten, doctoral students will never be forgotten. They become respected friends and form the next generation of colleagues.

✳ ✳ ✳

And thus it was in my case. One supervisor was a respected senior opinion leader in the field of allergy. He engineered introductions to clinic and departmental heads—essential for gaining entry into closed medical communities (Pope, 2005)—and informed me of developments and opportunities in the field. Although open to interview methods, he was uncertain about the nature of qualitative research and tended to seek confirmation that the research was being performed in the correct way. Accordingly another supervisor was needed, one who had a deep knowledge of qualitative research, the ability to reflect on questions of medical epistemology—"how doctors think"—and the experience to guide a novice researcher. The complementarity of this dual supervisory arrangement was particularly evident with data analysis. When reviewing transcripts of clinicians' talk concerning the risks, the medical supervisor would focus on *objective uncertainty*, defined as uncertainty arising from limited information or insufficient evidence to justify a premise. He was disturbed when clinicians made statements and decisions that were presented to families as incontrovertible fact, despite not being widely accepted practice. For example, families were told that they must avoid foods labeled with "may contain traces of nut," or that they should undergo a challenge where the child is deliberately given a food to see if he or she will react, when neither is universally recommended. He was also concerned about nonmedical clinicians providing information that was not sanctioned by the medical hierarchy to families. His interpretation of the text centered on what he viewed as matters of fact and on who should rightfully deliver information.

As an experienced qualitative researcher, my other supervisor rigorously reviewed the text, identified instances and events, and linked them to the participants' construal of risk, always referring to the data to support or refute the analysis as it emerged. Her analysis centered on parental constructions of risk and their subjective experience of uncertainty consequent to the doctor's advice and actions. For this parent-centered approach, a technical knowledge of allergy and medicine was not necessary. Indeed, such knowledge could potentially hamper understanding by tending to judge laypeople as wrong, or as misperceiving the risks. Conversely, without content knowledge uncertainty expressed through the absence of or erroneous information provision would not necessarily have been identified. Both supervisors' constructions of uncertainty, which clearly related to their epistemological and professional stances, were immensely useful to the research and illustrate the absurdity of seeking inter-rater reliability to validate interpretive research.

THE SUPERVISOR AS EXPERT?

✳ ✳ ✳

One of the things I (Carol) recall as a doctoral student myself was concern that my area of research was not an area of expertise (or even a topic of great interest) to any of my supervisors. Early on, I asked my main supervisor his view on this and he responded robustly "Any academic worth his salt can supervise any doctoral thesis—it is primarily a process." I both agree and disagree. I have never supervised a thesis in my original area of expertise and I have successfully supervised students in a huge variety of topics across several disciplines. But I still maintain that if in-depth knowledge is lacking, then intellectual curiosity and real interest in the topic are essential if the excitement of hunting, gathering, and discovering new knowledge is to be developed and maintained between supervisor and student.

✳ ✳ ✳

However, there was a twist in this otherwise neat tale of complementarity. The medical supervisor was not only a facilitator and technical expert, but also a research participant, a protagonist in the story of the three clinics, on whom I was to turn my critical analyst's gaze. Could the student-supervisor relationship be satisfactorily reconciled with that of the researcher-participant? Could findings that were critical of the supervisor's practice or potentially identifiable be freely discussed with him? I addressed this quandary in several ways. First, being a mature-aged student whose background and professional identity arose from another field of medicine released me from constraints that I would have felt if I had been a younger doctor who was aspiring to gain entry into the specialist allergy field; specialist training is often an apprenticeship that prizes allegiance and loyalty (Bosk, 1979). Moreover, presenting my results to him was a test of the rigor of my approach and my capacity, as a developing researcher, to defend my work. In effect, they were participant checks of the most scrutinizing kind.

Editors' Comment

Participants as Experts

In qualitative research, the real expert is the participant. This is a marked departure from the traditional hierarchical paradigm in which the scholar or the *supervisor* (the one with enhanced vision) is considered the ultimate holder of knowledge. While it is true that the mentors have advanced expertise and experience at a conceptual level, and the researcher is grounded in the existing literature and data collection, participants are considered experts in their own experiences because they are the only ones who hold that knowledge. This suggests a position of humility and openness on the part of the researcher to be maximally receptive to what participants can offer. For those who come from a medical background, it is especially challenging to surrender what they believe they already know so they can access new knowledge that may be beyond their current understanding.

Second, while this supervisor reviewed texts, I did not present to him any texts that concerned him or his patients. For those texts that were presented, all identifying details were scrupulously removed. Finally, I was fortunate in that while he was very certain about his point of view, he was not averse to considering alternative viewpoints. In fact, some of these different viewpoints proved illuminating for his practice. Underpinning this dialogue, however, was the sound and continuous support of my mentoring supervisor. By being removed geographically and professionally from the research setting and from the participants, she and I could converse freely about findings, speculate on alternative interpretations, and critique doctors' actions without fear of offense or loss of confidentiality. These opportunities to explore and imagine were critical to the production of analytic insights. In one sense, my student-supervisor relationships mirrored the dynamic etic-emic relationships between researcher and participants. The medical supervisor was an epistemological outsider to the research methodology and the constructions of other participants, but, simultaneously, he was an insider who could allow physical access to the clinics, and interpretive access to his technical knowledge and views as a participant. The mentoring supervisor was an insider to the theoretical approach of the research and my personal needs for emotional and intellectual support, but an outsider to the scientific technicalities and to the participants, thus preserving their anonymity and enabling critical reflection on their practices.

✳ ✳ ✳

SUPERVISION BY DISTANCE

Wendy is the first doctoral student I have supervised from a distance. I have always avoided this situation but I accepted her because she had another supervisor in her own state. Nevertheless, I had some initial qualms as to how we would manage, especially through the collection and management of a large qualitative database for which my input would be essential.

But my fears were groundless. Wendy and I met at conferences or when visiting each other's states and spent time on the thesis. We emailed often, and put aside regular times for telephone conversations of a minimum of one hour each (one hour on the thesis, and the rest on personal issues at home and at work that might be influencing progress). Large blocks of transcripts and observational notes were either posted by snail mail or downloaded for comparative analysis. These arrangements worked well and made up for the lack of face-to-face communication. One of the limitations for me of being an interstate supervisor was that I had no contact with the other supervisor: apart from the formal letter of invitation, no other communication ever occurred between us. As a result, the round table discussions and bouncing around of ideas was missing. Perhaps in this situation, where the two main supervisors were poles apart in terms of both discipline and research methods, this was a good thing. For me it meant that I dealt only with Wendy so my role was simple and clear, but it meant that Wendy had to be very skilled at balancing two very different perspectives on her work and in taking responsibility for her own decisions. This scenario certainly was an improvement on one of my previous doctoral student's regular meetings where so many disciplines and research styles were collected around the table that consensus was almost impossible. In that case, the student experienced considerable confusion at times while representatives of different disciplines fought old boundary wars and struggled to understand different research methods.

✹ ✹ ✹

THE CLINICIAN PARTICIPANTS

A key barrier to ethnographic and other forms of research in medical settings that do not follow a biomedical paradigm is the necessity for such research to be accepted by medical professionals (Miller & Crabtree, 1994). My project made sense to me, but convincing my medical colleagues of its validity was rather more difficult. Although my medical supervisor could open doors, the process of stepping through them was not as simple as the metaphor suggests. Similar to research conducted on elites such as judges and corporate leaders (Grbich, 1999), trust had to be nurtured. This began with a series of preliminary meetings, essential to gaining the support of the clinic directors who were key protagonists in the story. My intention was to be the nonaligned and naïve researcher who was merely aiming to understand doctors' practices through observation. Although I was based at one of the clinics, my nonalignment was accepted. For example, I did not request to attend nor was I invited to the joint clinic meetings, which had been organized in order to promote exchange between the groups. Nevertheless, after these meetings, I would be regaled by participants from all three clinics about the disagreements that had occurred.

Doubtless, my nonspecialist medical background and knowledge of professional etiquette and hierarchy helped, as did the topicality of the subject. Each clinic group recognized the difficulties that their disparate approaches had created, especially when parents sought second opinions. Nevertheless, I had to argue my case, defend the validity and intellectual rigor of my approach, explain why recruitment to the point of statistical significance was not required, and how I would redress bias. These arguments were also demanded by the three institutional review boards (IRBs) governing research at the respective clinics. The IRBs varied in their familiarity with qualitative research. The IRBs also stipulated that local staff were to be included as coinvestigators in any research projects, however. By inviting the clinic directors to be coinvestigators, their endorsement was formalized, substantiating the informal negotiations that had taken place. The relationship between these senior doctors and me was thus not only that of researcher-participant, but also that of researcher-collaborator and colleague. Without their endorsement, it is likely that there would have been more reluctance from the other clinicians about participating in the study.

The next stage in the researcher-participant relationship emerged with the initial interviews. I would allow the participants to take the lead—in the case of the often extremely articulate medical opinion leaders there was little choice but to do so—and I substantiated their trust in me and my research by offering them a transcript or summary of the interview for their approval. Only one medical clinician requested a transcript; the others received a summary and none of the doctors suggested changes or offered comments on the summary. This could be interpreted as a tacit approval of the procedure, or, as is likely, the view that the research was inconsequential (repeatedly referred to by even supportive participants as soft, compared to the hard science of laboratory experiments) and harmless. This harmlessness has been reported by other medical ethnographers such as Pope (2005), who described being viewed as a mascot by doctors. This agreed with my experience, which recalled being a medical student again. In the consulting rooms I was a nonthreatening extra in the performance that is clinical work—present but peripheral, not intrusive but somewhat in the way. Nevertheless, medical students are also privileged observers; they have rights of entry to normally private clinical settings without any of the responsibilities required of clinicians. In this case, my responsibilities were as a qualitative researcher, but my research methods were a curiosity to the participants. In contrast to clinical trials, the research created little extra work for the participants, apart from accommodating my presence and answering my questions. Paradoxically, this impression of insignificance and harmlessness improved access to the research setting.

To varying degrees, another type of researcher-participant relationship emerged with all the clinicians, one that had more potential to alter research findings. This was what Sarangi and Candlin (2003) have described as the *evaluator* role. In response to my presence, medical clinicians may have altered their practice to conform to norms or socially desirable practices. A few doctors did appear to play to the audience, which at times included hospital visitors and students, by addressing rhetorical questions to the observers. For example, one doctor would turn to the students and ask them questions about what "parents were most worried about," referring to the parents in the third person as if to demonstrate that he was addressing their concerns. All the clinicians were aware that the study was being conducted across the three clinics, and this may have intensified such justificatory and defensive maneuvers. With a longer field study, these participants may have further acclimatized to being observed; a few appeared more relaxed on subsequent observations. All the doctors were explicitly asked at the end of the study about ways in which the research had changed their practice. Nearly all replied that it had not led to any changes and that the observed practices were typical.

Atkinson argues that length of time in the field precludes any sustained and deliberate alteration of behavior to a socially desired practice (Atkinson & Pugsley, 2005). Contrary to this argument, I found that the evaluator relationship did not necessarily lessen with time, but shifted so that the in situ interviews began to be used by doctors as an opportunity to reflect on their practice and to entertain alternative strategies. Rather than consultations normalizing over time, they may have been subtly altered by the development of my role as a confessor. These postconsultation interviews illustrated how my medical background did influence data collection; the doctors would structure the account as an informal case presentation between colleagues, use medical terminology, and take for granted that I shared their practice values. Because these values were not necessarily obvious, I had to again become the naïve researcher and ask the doctors to explain their assumptions.

At the end of the study, the evaluator relationship overtly reappeared when I presented results at clinical meetings at each of the clinics. The audience's responses were used to interrogate and further develop the findings for final write-up. To sum, the researcher-clinician participant relationship shifted through different forms as I changed from the naïve researcher, colleague, mascot, evaluator, confessor, and evaluator again, with each role I played influencing the course of the research in different ways.

THE PARENT PARTICIPANTS

Similarly, to parent participants I was initially the neutral researcher, with the aim of hearing about their views and experiences in dealing with food allergy. In contrast to the clinician participants, recruiting parents to the study was straightforward. There were few refusals, and no parent or young child appeared to be concerned or expressed any unease about consultations being recorded. Many parents would start to volunteer their experiences while still in the waiting room. In the consulting room, my presence and the parents' perception of my alignment with them may therefore have subtly altered power differentials between parent and doctor, because there was a researcher to bear witness. For example, parents would occasionally address their remarks to me, particularly if the doctor was writing or apparently not attending to the parent. To counter such effects, I would physically place myself outside the consultation circle created by the doctor, her desk, and the family, and interact with the child while discreetly observing proceedings.

Editors' Comment

Before and After the Formal Interview

The interview actually has three distinct parts: (1) The preinterview consists of all the background work and preparation that takes place before the first formal meeting. The researcher is still collecting valuable information during these preliminary interactions. (2) The interview itself involves the time actually spent within the planned structure. (3) The postinterview takes place after the recorder has been turned off, when the session is over, yet when some of the best material can emerge. Many researchers report that it was only after the interview was supposedly concluded that new opportunities arose, new disclosures were shared, and revealing and surprising data emerged. For instance, in one study of nursing home residents investigating what led them to their present situations, one of the participants was somewhat reticent during the recorded interview. It was only after the researcher packed his bags that the woman blurted out that her daughter "is a real bitch." This revealed an underlying pattern of collusion between the family and the medical staff that became a key finding in the study.

Most researchers will transcribe their interviews diligently but fail to record the informal interactions that take place around and through the informal interactions. We strongly recommend that you log all such interactions and consider them as potentially valuable data.

Accompanying the family throughout their clinic visit smoothed the conduct of the postconsultation interview because I had shared, through my presence, their clinic experiences. In many cases, we were able to conduct interviews via telephone because a personal connection had already been established. Most parents were candid about negative experiences with doctors. For these conversations, I could draw on my experience as a mother with a child with a chronic illness seeking advice from pediatric specialists, and the frustrations that this situation can bring. It was in my role as a mother that I conducted the informal talk between the parents and me before and after the interviews. I brought other personal qualities to the researcher-parent participant relationship. Because I am a person of Asian origin, parents of similar origin would draw on shared cultural understandings to explain their views on food and medical care. Conversely, perhaps not wishing to offend, some parents of European background were hesitant when citing Asian food as being untrustworthy and likely to contain peanut and other allergenic contaminants. My being a woman may have resulted in mothers recounting difficulties with their male partners in caring for the allergy. Their male partners did not share with me in that way, and all participating fathers supported the care provided by their female partners. Because mothers rather than fathers usually bring children to consultations with doctors, perhaps the fathers in this study represented a subgroup who was more involved in childcare.

All researchers, particularly where participants experience much uncertainty, are likely to be seen as an information resource (Sarangi & Candlin, 2003). I was careful to point out to all parents at the beginning of the study that I was not an expert in food allergy. With the exception of one family, who saw the interview as an opportunity to find out the information they had missed, I was not questioned about allergy. To minimize the effect of such questions on interviews, I would defer answering them until the end of the interview, or direct parents to clinic-approved information sources. In contrast, if I attempted to offer information to consumer organization parents when a factual question had been raised, I would often be corrected or given alternative information. A recurrent theme with these parents was the tension between their need to be acknowledged as experts in their child's condition and expressing their uncertainty within the security of their consumer group. As a parent who did not have a food-allergic child, I had not earned this insider status.

As with the clinician participants, trust increased over time, particularly after the initial interview summaries were returned and participants saw that a genuine attempt had been made to faithfully depict their views. In contrast to the doctor participants who did not do so, parents would return comments on the summaries because they wished to have a correct representation of their views. For several, the summary represented a validation of their experiences; their story had been documented and could be retained for future memory, so I was their historian.

The process of reflection during these first interviews also seemed to help parents to clarify their concerns and formulate questions, which would then be asked at subsequent clinic visits. My presence during these visits may have also emboldened parents to ask these questions. This development was an expression of my roles in bearing witness and being a confessor, described by Sarangi as the "befriender role" (Sarangi & Candlin, 2003), in the same way that parents reported bringing a friend or relative to consultations as a support person. At times, this role had a quasitherapeutic effect. Several families in the study had been extremely distressed by their clinic experiences and needed to talk through them, afterwards expressing gratitude to me for the opportunity to do so.

Far more troubling were situations where I felt compelled to transcend the befriender relationship by intervening for therapeutic reasons. Researchers have an ethical obligation to protect research participants against harm, and in cases where there was imminent harm my training and experience as a clinician could not be put aside. I would exercise my clinical judgment, cease being the detached researcher, and consciously interfere with the course of events. For example, parents would relate actions that were potentially harmful to their child, by testing, at home, whether their child could eat suspected foods, including nuts. While on face this might seem a clear case requiring intervention, in food allergy little is certain. The same food may cause different reactions on separate occasions, and my judgment could have easily erred on the side of over-precaution or negligence. Where there was a confirmed report of such experimentation, I would voice my concerns at the end of the interview, suggest follow-up at the clinic, and, with parental knowledge, contact the nurse educator to initiate follow-up. In one such case, the parent denied to the nurse that he had given his child nuts, although he had repeatedly and unequivocally stated so to me, and he did not return for follow-up. These instances create considerable quandaries for ethnographic researchers, and particularly for me as a clinician.

Although debates concerning the impact of ethnographers entering a community are not new to anthropology, such research is relatively novel in clinical settings and has created new dilemmas (Hoeyer, Dahlager, & Lynöe, 2005). For example, are the researcher's obligations to the partici-pant different if the research is observational rather than interventional, such as the clinical trial of a pharmacological agent? Are these obligations different if the researcher is medically qualified? Can the researcher claim ignorance, interference with the phenomenon under study, or a non-therapeutic role to justify nonintervention?

Editors' Comment

Ethical Obligations

Researchers must consider carefully the ethical ramifications of their behavior and the impact of their research. These include assessing the potential harm that could occur, issues of confidentiality and privacy, legal duties to protect the community welfare, being deceptive or manipulative, or otherwise compromising the safety and well-being of participants. Although all studies have been approved ahead of time by ethics com-mittees, there is an obligation to continually monitor the effects of what you do. More than other forms of research, qualitative studies can be particularly intrusive and provocative. As the process of your study naturally evolves, so too will the anticipated ethical challenges change in light of adjustments you make in method and procedures.

In another family recruited early in the study, the mother described tremendous family upheaval and conflict as a result of the strict precau-tionary measures advised by the allergist. These included removing all foods labeled "may contain traces," not only from the child's diet, but also from the entire family and any households or places that the child visited, including the childcare center. At a second interview at the end of the study, she reported that she had sought another opinion and her child's allergy had been shown to have resolved itself, with a complete lifting of restrictions and resolution of family conflict. Because I had been immersed in the practices of the clinic that she had first attended, I had not realized that its recommendations were so extreme. If the family had been recruited at the end of the study, would it have been justifiable to advise the family to seek another opinion? If I had been their family physician I would have had no hesitation in doing so, but as a researcher such an action would imply a very different relationship to what is usually encouraged in research.

RELATIONSHIPS: A PERSONAL JOURNEY

Over time, and particularly after observing consultations and listening to parents' stories, I began to better understand parents' concerns, and that it was not only a lack of science but also problematic relations between doctors and parents that were the cause of doctors failing to understand the parental perspective, and parents being dissatisfied with medical advice. It was not, as one doctor stated at the beginning of the study, that there was a "lot of [parental] psychopathology," but rather as one medically trained parent laughingly said, none of the clinics deserved a booby prize. I also realized that the fundamental issue was not misperceptions of risk, as clinicians at each clinic tended to think of those at other clinics, or as doctors thought of parents. Instead, the situation was far better conceptualized as differing responses to uncertainty. Nevertheless, a significant proportion of parental uncertainty was avoidable, and was caused by lack of information provision. This information was available, if one knew where to look. The omission was on the part of the doctors, who were ostensibly experts in the condition. These insights further shifted my alignment toward the parents' predicament.

However, to have adopted a single perspective with an unvarying researcher-participant relationship would have diminished my analysis of how uncertainty is created, maintained, and disseminated. For example, as a medically trained evaluator I may be more aware of cues indicating that the doctor is hedging or bluffing, which may not be apparent to a nonmedically trained observer. Conversely, as a colleague who has implicitly assumed practice norms I may be unable to identify uncertainties experienced by parents, thus requiring the shift to being a naïve researcher, or parental historian. As a resource, I was able to recognize situations where parents were unaware of information that was important to their child's care. If I had only been a witness, the parents' story may have been unremarkable because it was internally coherent and consistent.

Editors' Comment

Negotiations in the Mentor Relationship

Sometimes you have to "fire" a mentor, or at least negotiate changes in supervision because of the ways that a qualitative study changes from the original plan. Because such relationships are hierarchical and unequal in power, students may sometimes believe that their needs and interests are not being met. Either inadvertently or deliberately, a student may be encouraged (cajoled) to pursue avenues that are more consistent with the mentor's interests. Yet all interpersonal disagreements or incompatibilities are interactive effects—meaning both participants have a role and responsibility in the unsatisfactory outcome. That is why open communication is so critical so you can express thoughts and feelings openly, and hopefully negotiate a resolution. In some cases, you may want to request a neutral party to help find common ground. Sometimes it may be best for both parties to part ways and for the student to build a more collaborative alliance with another mentor. Naturally, there are political implications to such a choice that must be considered.

Similarly, my relationships with my supervisors, in addition to making the research possible, added depth to the research findings. Informational uncertainties can be identified objectively and reproducibly from the text, but uncertainty is also subjectively experienced, with objective and subjective uncertainties not necessarily following each other. One example is where both doctor and parent, through lack of discussion in the consultation, are unaware of significant gaps in parental knowledge, with both being satisfied with the consultation and believing that all important concerns have been addressed.

Conceptualizing the research journey as a succession of changing relationships, each described by different roles, encouraged a critical and reflexive approach to data analysis and to interpreting my own responses to the findings. This approach allowed me to shift perspectives while still being personally immersed in the research. Rather than being invalidated by bias, as would be claimed by positivists, different biases led to additional insights. My intermediate personae, as a doctor but not an allergist, and as a parent but not of a food-allergic child, allowed me to enter and interpret the participants' respective worlds in particular ways. This bias is arguably less than the unthinking use of a quantitative survey instrument, no matter how statistically valid the findings. In my research journey, I learned to nurture, build, and maintain relationships; to appreciate the time and persistence required; and to explore the complexities induced by shifts in both my own stance and that of others. Although this particular journey has now ended, the experience has proved invaluable in my current journey as an academic: in my daily relations with staff, interactions with academic colleagues, and collaborations with researchers. Relationships, and the ability to examine them critically, are crucial for the success of any social endeavor.

Learning Tips

- Reflexivity demands that researchers consider the effect of their stance on the conduct of the research and its findings. This can be facilitated by reflecting on the different relationships that develop during a research study.

- Different roles and relationships can be adopted consciously and actively to generate new insights.

- Initiating, building, and maintaining relationships takes time and persistent effort, but is essential for research that is unfamiliar or alien to prospective participants.

References

Atkinson, P., & Pugsley, L. (2005). Making sense of ethnography and medical education. *Medical Education, 39,* 228–234.

Bosk, C. (1979). *Forgive and remember: Managing medical failure.* Chicago: Chicago University Press.

Colver, A. (2006). Are the dangers of childhood food allergy exaggerated? *British Medical Journal, 333,* 494–496.

Grbich, C. (1999). *Qualitative research in health: An introduction.* St. Leonards, Australia: Allen & Unwin.

Hoeyer, K., Dahlager, L., & Lynöe, N. (2005). Conflicting notions of research ethics: The mutually challenging traditions of social scientists and medical researchers. *Social Science and Medicine, 61,* 1741–1749.

Hourihane, J. O. (2006). Are the dangers of childhood food allergy exaggerated? *British Medical Journal, 333,* 496–498.

Macdougall, C. F., Cant, A. J., & Colver, A. F. (2002). How dangerous is food allergy in childhood? The incidence of severe and fatal allergic reactions across the UK and Ireland. Comment. *Archives of Disease in Childhood, 86,* 236–239.

Miller, W., & Crabtree, B. (1994). Clinical research. In N. Denzin and Y. Lincoln (Eds.), *Handbook of qualitative research* (pp. 340–349). Thousand Oaks, CA: Sage Publications.

Pope, C. (2005). Conducting ethnography in medical settings. *Medical Education, 39,* 1180–1187.

Sarangi, S., & Candlin, C. (2003). Trading between reflexivity and relevance: New challenges for applied linguistics. *Applied Linguistics, 24,* 271–285.

van der Geest, S., & Finkler, K. (2004). Hospital ethnography: Introduction. *Social Science and Medicine, 59,* 1995–2001.

Exploring the Meaning and Function of Music in the Lives of Older People

Terrence Hays and Victor Minichiello

I n this day and age, it would be difficult to escape the presence of music in our lives. Music is everywhere: in advertisements, in entertainment, in elevators, in waiting rooms, when refueling the car at service stations, in films and television, at sporting events, and in religious rituals. Prerecorded music is available on radio, compact discs, tapes, videos, iPods, and TV.

My (Terrence's) qualitative study grew from a personal interest in wanting to understand the psychosocial function of music in people's lives. Prior to starting my postgraduate studies, I had trained as a music educator with a strong background in music performance. I have two grand pianos in my home, give concerts overseas, and play music nearly every day. I am a passionate musician. It was from my experience of performing that I became interested in knowing more about the ways people use music in their lives. In particular, what was the function and meaning of music in people's lives? One important person who inspired my curiosity was Mildred. Mildred described music in her life as giving her meaningfulness. She had been a piano teacher all her life, and although having retired from teaching in her late sixties, she told me (at the age of ninety-eight years) that playing the piano each day provided her with a purpose, so that "each day is worth living." Mildred plays and practices the piano as often as she can and draws much pleasure from music. At the age of ninety-seven, she climbed the Sydney Harbour Bridge; on her ninety-eighth birthday she parachuted from a plane. Today, Mildred is one hundred and five years old and still going strong.

So, why is music important to people? After meeting Mildred, I realized that music must have special meaning and function for many older people, regardless of whether they are musicians or just enthusiastic listeners. To explore fully the complexity and depth of this question, it became clear that I needed to talk to older people to discover how music influenced and shaped their lives. Thus, my study had to have a qualitative framework. I had previously read much about the use of music as therapy for people of all ages. By researching older people, I hoped it would be possible to explore how music facilitates a dimension in people's lives that goes beyond entertainment and to explore the possibility that music might also influence concepts of identity, health, and well-being.

The Research Project

How do people use music in their lives? What is the function and meaning people assign to music in their lives? As a musician, this seemed to be straightforward. My instinct also told me that this experience was not restricted to trained professionals, however. After all, many people who are not musically trained can often be extremely passionate about music and spend much of their time listening to music, attending concerts, and reading about music history.

The study specifically focused on the role music played in the emotional, social, intellectual, and spiritual well-being for older people. The informants were drawn from various backgrounds. They included older people who had no training in music, those who had some training, and those who had been professional musicians. It was their life stories that became the focus of my study.

✳ ✳ ✳

The initial supervision sessions with Terrence focused on the use of music as therapy and how music could be used to improve the lives of seniors. I (Victor) asked Terrence to read the sociological literature related to identity so that he could begin to think about the wider application of music in people's lives. I asked that he not assume that music can only have a positive influence. We spoke about how in some cases music can be associated with violence, suicide, and drugs, for example. These discussions opened up his study beyond what was reported in the gerontology literature, where the focus was on music as therapy, particularly for the frail aged.

✳ ✳ ✳

Beginning the Research Journey

As a music educator and musician, I (Terrence) came to this research study with no training in sociology and limited training in research methods. The only undergraduate training that gave me some preparatory skills for undertaking this qualitative research project was a unit in social psychology where I had studied humanistic psychology and practiced listening skills. To this end, the project at the time seemed daunting. Not only did I need to interview people and collect data, but I also needed to become familiar with the literature that focused on music as therapy, well-being, gerontology, and life-long learning. I also needed to assemble the literature review in a meaningful way and make critical commentary as it related to my project.

✻ ✻ ✻

The key word here is critical. *Giving students articles to read or pointing them in the right direction for their literature searches is the easy part. Helping students to read critically at a conceptual and methodological level and to locate their research as an original contribution to the literature is much more difficult. I recall Terrence struggling with this issue. How could he possibly be critical about these highly published professors he was reading for guidance? Many supervision sessions focused on teaching Terrence to think critically about what was not said in the literature, to phrase his questions from a different angle, and to challenge his own thinking or what others had written. These were the what if, why not, and why questions. Music is not always good, not experienced in the same way by all, and could have different relevance depending on what is going on in a person's life. It is not static or a given objective entity. Eventually, Terrence discovered that he did have an original angle and something new to say. He gained confidence in his ability to think like a researcher and to acknowledge himself as one of the experts in the field.*

✻ ✻ ✻

Reviewing the literature for this study required reading in the areas of psychology, gerontology, sociology, and music therapy. This was because the study crossed the areas of aging, the psychosocial literature of music and learning, and the sociology literature that focused on self and identity. By reading in these areas, I was able to understand possible connections the data collection might involve, and to be able to make some preparatory links between the fields. For example, by studying the gerontology literature alongside the psychosocial, musicology, and sociology literature, it was reasonable for me to assume that music facilitated a sense of well-being, and that it might also influence perceptions of identity, self-esteem, and health for older people. This could only be tested out by talking to people and getting their stories, however. At the same time, collecting data in terms of meaningful conversations means suspending one's own belief and rigorously checking and crosschecking the data.

FINDING A THEORETICAL FRAMEWORK

At the outset, my mentors stated that my study needed to be placed within the context of a theoretical perspective. In other words, was the study to focus on a symbolic interactionist perspective, using a hermeneutic perspective, a grounded theory perspective, or a phenomenological or phenomenographical approach? The answers to this question came with time and resulted from much reading on qualitative theoretical frameworks as well as long discussions with my supervisors as my data collection progressed.

Editors' Comment

Phenomenology

Phenomenology is among the most popular but also among the most challenging qualitative methods. Terrence chose that approach because he wanted to understand the inner experiences of older people in terms of how music lives within them. Unlike an approach such as grounded theory in which the data are broken into smaller units in order to understand the intrinsic connections of ideas, phenomenology seeks a bigger picture as a focus of explanation. The literature of this paradigm is especially difficult to grasp, the concepts are presented in complex language, and the methodology is not clearly specified. Nevertheless, this approach is particularly well suited when you want to understand how people experience the world.

If I used a phenomenology methodology, the data collection would have focused on the diversity of the personal experience of music in people's lives. In considering a phenomenographical perspective, I would have been mapping the experience from each individual involved in the study. What was clear from the outset was the data collected would only be rich if it were older people's personal accounts of the function and meaning of music in their lives. It would be the diversity of the experience from a range of participants that would allow me to unravel and explore the complexity of the topic.

The theoretical perspective I chose to underpin my study was symbolic interactionism, using a grounded theory methodology. I chose this theory because music, while having an objective component (that is, sounds that can be heard and measured on scientific instruments), also contains subjective significance and meaning for people, and facilitates ways for people to construct meaning in their lives. The meaning is different for each individual and is directly related to her life experiences and emotional needs. The study would therefore try to explore these subjective meanings and interpretations and provide important insights into how people live and interact in the world. More importantly, by studying the subjective experiences of the meaning of music we might gain insights into the person's self. For example, the study showed how music could connect older persons to people who may no longer be living, validate memories, give meaning to life, and facilitate a greater sense of spirituality.

The conceptual framework I used to guide the analysis of the data was based on the self acting as an agent capable of using symbols to help define his experiences. The study framed music as a symbol used by people to give meaning to experiences and emotions. The interview scheduled included open-ended questions and focused on the participants' life experience. In the interviews, I asked the informants to reflect on the importance of music in their daily lives and what they perceived were the benefits of being engaged in music, whether it was making or listening to music.

The idea of using grounded theory to order my thinking around the data made sense to me after I read Strauss and Corbin (1998). This textbook gave me a solid foundation for understanding and applying the grounded theory methodology to identify themes and concepts in my data. Not only was my thinking less clouded, but also I was able to gain confidence that my data analysis was on track. I finally had a system that allowed me to shape my text into manageable data pieces that I could explain to others. There was another benefit, as well: A grounded theory approach also meant the data could be collected to inform new insights on aging and the psychosocial importance of music in people's live. Ultimately, I opted to take a cross perspective that included both grounded theory methodological principles to guide data collection and phenomenology to capture the depth of the lived personal experience and explore the diversity of the meaning and function that music might have for many older people.

✻ ✻ ✻

I recall well the debate Terrence was having with his theoretical framework. He had one supervisor who was a strong advocate of phenomenology. Conversely, I had a strong preference for interpretivism and believed that the focus of Terrence's study should be on discovering a new theory about how older people use music. It was clear that Terrence preferred understanding the lived experience of how the informants were expressing their use of music in their everyday lives. A phenomenology perspective provided him with a useful platform to collect his data and create his line of analysis. It was interesting to see the struggle here because he wanted to be guided by his supervisors. It was only after he had made up his own mind that he was able to proceed with his study and write up his results in a confident manner. This highlights the importance for researchers to understand what conceptual traditions they are going to work with and to understand how this decision will influence and shape their research. This is not an easy decision because there are many theoretical traditions from which to select, and supervisors have their own preferred ways of thinking.

✻ ✻ ✻

THE METHODOLOGY

At the outset, I was encouraged by my supervisors to read the literature on aging, music psychology, music therapy, and the sociology of the self. The reason for choosing these areas of literature was clear. As a researcher, I figured that it would be the intersections between these foci that would help me to better understand the extent of the possible meaning and importance of music in the lives of older people. This literature provided an initial preparation before going into the field.

After studying the literature, my supervisors encouraged me to immerse myself in data collection—in other words, to start talking with people and to start exploring the complexity and depth of the music experience for older people. Before embarking on my in-depth interviews, I began with two initial focus group interviews where I met with two groups of people to ask them about music in their lives. The plan was to do some preliminary data collection and analysis of the data, which would better equip me to undertake the in-depth interviewing. I then prepared an interview schedule that listed some of the key topic areas that might help facilitate the focus group participants in terms of open discussion. While this was a good fallback position, it limited the discussion and had the potential to concentrate on the findings from the literature.

DATA COLLECTION AND WORKING IN THE FIELD

At the outset of the study, I needed to address the parameters of data collection. Whom exactly should I be interviewing? Should I be following up with people who had musical training or those with little or no musical background? How many people should I interview? Where should I start and with whom? I decided the best way to explore some of the main themes of the meaning and function of music would be to conduct two focus groups interviews. These two groups would help me identify topics for discussion later during the one-on-one in-depth interviews.

The first focus group was a heterogeneous group that consisted of two men and five women who had varied backgrounds, affiliations, and exposure to music. The term *heterogeneous* meant that the participants had no particular common traits and would potentially bring together people with various backgrounds. The second group was a homogeneous group of eight older people who self-identified as amateur musicians actively involved with music in their life. By *homogeneous*, the group was identified having a common unity, which in this case was their collective participation in a choir. By arranging the focus groups along these two types of grouping, I was able to explore from the outset the different perspectives older people have on music. These focus groups were instrumental in my study. They gave me confidence to move forward with collecting data via the in-depth interviews because I was able to better understand whom I wanted to interview and why I wanted to interview them. For example, I discovered that there was little reason to pursue interviewing people who had little or no interest in music, and to pursue interviewing people who self-identified as people who were passionate about music in their lives.

This use of focus groups is common in the early stages of qualitative research. In my particular study, the focus group interview helped me realize that music was not necessarily important to all older people, nor would my study speak for all older people. This revelation then meant that I would need to think carefully about how I recruited participants. My participants would need to be people for whom music was important and meaningful. It is for this reason that I decided to adopt the qualitative approach of recruitment referred in the literature as *snowballing*. This technique involves asking an initial group of informants to refer the researcher to other people in their networks.

The first focus group discussion was purposely organized with a homogeneous group of eight people. This group was made up of people who shared a common bond of belonging—in this case, belonging to the same choir. I assumed that these eight people might also be enthusiastic about the topic and have interesting thoughts to share with me as the researcher. The second group was a heterogeneous group of eight people comprising older people from a community center who did not necessarily have any musical background nor assumed common experiences of music in their lives.

The qualitative research literature suggests that eight people are the optimum number of people for these type of interviews (Minichiello, Aroni, & Hays, 2008), which is why I chose that number. It is also important that each person be allowed time to speak and to contribute to the collective nature of the discussion. While the qualitative research literature makes this point, learning to master successful focus group interviews in the real world takes time and skill. I experienced this firsthand when I discovered in one of my groups two dominant people who had little regard for hearing anyone's voice but their own. This required skill and assertiveness in getting others to open up and speak, and keeping some control of the dominating participants in the group.

The data collection followed an inductive course of action, whereby the data were collected at intervals to allow me to review the process. This included both the focus group interviews and the in-depth interviews in three sequential field excursions. Staggering the data collection allowed me to review the emerging themes and perspectives from the participants, and then to take it back for focus and inclusion in the next round of interviews. This was important in terms of developing a grounded theory approach to the study. It was also important for the validity of the study to take the findings back to a final validity-checking group to see if they agreed with my findings and write-up of the data. This not only was reality checking, but also allowed me to be inclusive of the participants who freely gave their time to the study.

While this inductive approach worked like clockwork for me in this particular study, from previous experience I discovered that if you do not take time to stop, examine, and learn from the data during the time of collection, your study can quickly become flawed in terms of methodology and data collection. Waiting until the end of data collection to discover that you have missed vital clues and leads also means that the research can lack depth and be limited in the breadth of its outcomes.

Conducting in-depth interviews and analyzing the data following each stage of the data-collection process provided me the opportunity for closer examination of the data and for the collecting of more in-depth personal accounts of the meaning of music in the subsequent interviews. This process of integrating data collection with analysis also resulted in three modes of inquiry happening at the same time: (1) induction, which allowed me to follow an idea or concept that presented itself in the data, (2) deduction, and (3) verification, where I could identify keys concepts and seek further clarification, description, and detail of issues and topics that emerged through the in-depth interview. For example, when the participants spoke about music facilitating a sense of connection in their lives, some said music had a direct influence on their choice of lifestyle while others said it was about people and the sharing of their lives, while others used music as a way of connecting with beauty and aesthetics. This was especially the case for Noreen, ninety-three years old, who said she was no longer able to take long walks on the beach or go to places where she could see "breath-taking sunsets." For other participants, music was described as facilitating a connection with spirituality and the "inner self"; for many, there was strong connection with memories including friends, family, and loved ones.

The Interview Process

Like most novice researchers, I read my literature and carefully honed my research question. After all, I wanted ultimately to contribute to scholarly knowledge in the field of psychosocial musicology. Whether this would be in the form of a book or a series of articles in refereed journals remained to be seen. After preparing a detailed critical review of the literature, I launched into development of an interview guide to capture the essence of my research focus. The following types of questions formed the basis of my preliminary interview schedule:

- "Does music play an important role in your life?"
- "How is music essential to your sense of well-being and health?"
- "What particular ways do you use music in your life?"
- "What are the ways you think music directly or indirectly affects you?"
- "Have the ways you use music in your life changed over the years?"
- "Do you use music as a way of expressing yourself?"
- "Do you see music as an essential part of your identity?"
- "Which of your life experiences do you associate with music?"

Editors' Comment

Publishing Findings

From the outset, Terrence consulted with his mentors about publishing opportunities for his research. After all, most people who undertake studies are interested in having an audience larger than just their mentors and family members. You have a responsibility to disseminate the findings to a wider audience who can profit from what you found if you are going to invest time and energy to conduct a study to advance knowledge. In Terrence's case, after completing his literature review he wrote a critical review (yes, he mastered the art of reading critically in the field) in collaboration with Victor and another expert in the field. This review described how music was investigated as a research phenomenon; it was published in *Journal of Aging and Identity* (Hays, Bright, & Minichiello, 2002). The article provided a research agenda for other researchers to consider. He then published the results of his thesis once it was marked, in two prominent international journals in the field, *Ageing and Society* (Hays & Minichiello, 2005a) and *Psychology of Music* (Hays & Minichiello, 2005b).

These were the burning questions that needed answers. However, as I progressed through my first round of interviews I discovered that I was hearing fairly concise responses. I discovered upon showing my transcripts to my supervisor that I was making some major mistakes as an interviewer with regard to data collection. First, when I looked closely at the interview schedule I noticed the questions were narrowly focused in terms of asking discrete questions to which there were limited answers. For example, in response to the question, "Does music play an important role in your life?," people would say yes, then I would struggle with trying to expand on that answer with a detailed description. Another example was the question, "Do you use music as a way of expressing yourself"? Again, the informants struggled with the question because they were not sure exactly what I was getting at or what answer would be appropriate. In this case, a better question would have been open ended: "Tell me about music and how it is part of you and your life." When I used this question, it resulted in diverse answers from informants and life stories of the meaning and function of music for these older people.

Second, after careful consideration I realized that the questions posed in the early round of interviews seemed to be more concerned with confirming the findings of the literature. On reflection, I realized these were more attuned to a quantitative approach than exploring the depths of the individual experience. The lesson for me was to stop asking closed questions like, "Is music important in your life?" and instead to ask more open-ended questions like, "Tell me about the importance of music in your life." From this technique of using more open questions I could deliberately use a funneling approach to focus on the life experiences of the informants. This also meant relaxing a little more during my interviews and actively listening to their stories. Doing this meant I could begin collecting more interesting and richer data.

I remember one particular informant teaching me this lesson in the early stages of my data collection. His name was Donald. He had been a professional musician all his life, and had also held senior administrative positions in tertiary education. At the age of eighty-seven he was still teaching. When I arrived to interview him, he said to me, "I don't know what I can tell you about my life and music, but how about I lead off and you can save whatever questions you have to ask me at the end." (In other words, don't interrupt me!) At the time this was somewhat confronting to me. After all, this was my study and I thought I was the one in control in terms of the interview—not my informant. So I began by asking Donald, "Tell me about music in your life," to which he responded with a detailed account of his life history, and the meaning and function of music in his life. This proved to be one of the most beneficial moments of learning for me as a researcher. In later interviews, I then would say to the participant at the beginning of the interview, "Tell me about music in your life," or I would ask, "What is your life story in terms of music?"

When reading the literature on conducting qualitative research I was constantly reminded about the need to suspend my own prejudices and presuppositions about the research topic and the data I was collecting. This sounds easy enough. During the interviews, I tried carefully not to lead the informant. We all come to our research with an informed background knowledge, enthusiasm, and life experience, however, that often provides the drive and incentive for us to keep persevering with the study.

The most important aspect of interviewing and suspending one's own assumptions is to listen carefully to the informant's story and to be attentive to detail in terms of getting his or her story right. This means closely following the dialogue and noting particular aspects of the story that need expanding and further follow-up. You should never assume that you know what was meant by a throwaway line such as, "Music is a religious experience to me," particularly if you agree. It was with this in mind that I learned my second major lesson of conducting interviews. After looking at the initial transcripts from interviews, I discovered to my horror that the weighting of discussion between the informant and me was almost equal. So who was actually being interviewed? Why was my voice so prominent? The lesson was clear: I needed to spend more time listening and not allow myself to become carried away with enthusiastic discussion that muddied the data, as well as possibly leading the informant.

Ideally, a transcript should look something like the following where the interviewer is occasionally speaking and the informant is providing the in-depth story.

Researcher: How important was music in terms of your personal development, do you think?

Informant: Oh, very important, because although my mother was very sporty and actually taught gymnastics both to children and adults, I wasn't. I wasn't interested in it. And so music was always a main interest, and it was something by which I was able to be recognized, you know, get some sort of recognition as having some sort of value as a person both at school and later on as well. Then I went to a music camp. I think I'd just turned fifteen, and that was a very fortunate, it was wonderful one, because that was the one where Hepsibah came down and played. And I actually, in later years, met her again and mentioned that to her, and sort of got a, not exactly a friendship, but a friendly acquaintance. Whenever she came I would go backstage and I'd talk to her, even though she was normally a very shy person. So again, you know, it opened all sorts of doors for me.

Researcher: How has music been important in terms of connecting with people for you?

Informant: Most of my friends just find it hard to find the time. But most of my friends have been in sort of musical areas. My first wife was a musician. My current is not, although she quite enjoys it, but I met her through music in Germany.

Researcher: What are some ways that music's been important to you?

Informant: I guess with me, I mean, it's quite an emotional thing as well with me. And partly related to my background, and the strange thing with not having a father, and subsequently I did have a stepfather, but that was a problematic relationship because he was actually very ill and he had spent a couple of years in a concentration camp. He got very bad diabetes, and in those days they couldn't treat it that well, so it was not surprising he also had personality disorders. And that was a very sad situation. But, for me it's provided the nearest thing to any kind of a grounding or a stability. . . . It just seems so extraordinary to me, you know, things like Mozart, which is my greatest, you know, I really love Mozart. But any of the geniuses, and you listen to that and you think, my God, you know, there is something that's outside the normal human experience. Maybe there is something like a god, or whatever, behind it. There is obviously something that's beyond what we can normally understand. And music opens that world to me.

These interviews were informal and purposely organized with the participants to be held in their homes. From my perspective as a researcher, this ensured that they would be less likely to be distracted by other people or commitments in the workplace. The home environment also made the participants more relaxed and in control of the interview process. From my perspective, they were more focused in the telling of their life story and there was not the need to keep to a strict time schedule. For example, two of my informants were interviewed in their work setting and both were only able to give me limited time. This meant that time for reflection and follow-up during the interview was extremely limited. I was acutely aware the clock was ticking and they both needed to get back to their tasks at hand.

While having good listening skills is important in doing in-depth interviews, there are other important skills necessary to collect solid data. These include not rushing the participants to respond. They need time to pull their thoughts together and to find the words to express themselves. Therefore, thinking time is essential for quality responses. For example, as a novice researcher in the early stages of interviewing participants, whenever there was a gap in the conversation I would quickly move to the next focused question in my interviewing guide. This was a huge mistake. If only I had been patient and given the participant more reflection time, I would have collected an interesting life story that contributed significantly to my study. Instead, I consciously moved them from their train of thought and lost the thread of the discussion.

Editors' Comment

Questioning Skills

People who don't understand qualitative research well often ask, How difficult could it be to ask a few questions and record what people say? After all, surveys have a hundred questions rather than a handful.

Learning to become a skilled research interviewer takes years of practice. Most likely, you should start right away. Although you'll likely get some training in this area, the most important things to keep in mind are these: (1) Start from the general and move to the specific. (2) Let the participant's voice dominate the conversation. (3) Crosscheck things you hear with alternative lines of inquiry. (4) Paraphrase what you think you've heard and understood. (5) If you have a solid relationship, play devil's advocate with provocative inquiry. One of the best ways to improve your skills is to practice doing an interview with an expert observing who can critique the session and provide valuable feedback.

Another important lesson I learned in the field while collecting data was not to rush to turn off the recorder at the end of the interview. If you do, always be ready to quickly switch it back on. The reason for suggesting this action is based on personal experience where much of my best data came from people who, thinking the interview was finished, relaxed and then provided extra interesting commentary. It was always when I had turned off the voice recorder that this interesting and poignant commentary came forward. If the recorder is already turned off and put away, it is highly unlikely you will capture this commentary. An example of this happening was in my interview with Margaret. Her life story was focused on her experiences of being a nun. It was only after turning off the recorder that she disclosed that, while she had a talent for singing, she had purposely been forbidden to study music because her superiors thought "indulging in music" was considered too dangerous for her spiritual development as a nun.

During the interviews, specific music genres were not discussed nor were the informants asked to identify any particular style that they preferred, such as classical, folk, pop, easy listening, country, and so on. This was purposely done to lessen any possible interpretation of bias on the part of the researcher and to maximize the depth of response from the individual. It became clear, however, that the people who were most passionate about music in their lives tended to be focused on classical music. It is also interesting to note that many informants said they enjoyed their retirement because they now were able "to find time to indulge," including spending more time on music activities.

The analysis focused on thematic discovery from the transcripts recorded through the interviews with the informants. This included themes around identity, well-being, connection, spirituality, and the benefits of music. This was achieved using the methodological principles of open and axial coding described by Strauss and Corbin (1998). There were four rounds of interviews; within each round, data collection centered on emerging themes, issues or ideas grounded in the data. The process involved identifying relevant thematic codes by a constant examination of themes and crosschecking these through referencing to individual transcripts and as a collective data set. While reading the transcripts of each interview I examined each line of the text; in a column on the right-hand side of the text I noted what each participant was focusing on in her story. This became my open coding, whereby I developed a table of 176 emerging themes. Of course, many of these themes were interrelated. For example, most participants spoke of a sense of spirituality that music provided in their lives. This theme emerged even though many of the participants prefaced their comments about music and spirituality by saying that they did not see themselves as religious people, yet music facilitated this connection for them. As the interviews progressed, I sought clarification on this aspect of the data and how people gave meaning to spirituality. For example, some participants spoke about music providing a transcendental experience for them, others said it provided a direct link with aesthetics in their life, and still others said that music contributed significantly to both their private and collective spiritual experiences.

Editors' Comment

Identifying Themes

Each qualitative methodology has different names for the data analysis procedure. Grounded theory, for example, requires that the researcher code data, often using computer programs to help with the process. In phenomenology, the process may involve identifying themes. To complicate matters further, contemporary researchers often combine the best features of different approaches to arrive at an optimal strategy that best facilitates their analysis. In Terrence's case, he used a phenomenological approach to his topic but adapted grounded theory's coding principles to help him make sense of themes.

When analyzing the data, I also validated the coding categories by asking my supervisors to read some of the transcripts and to double-check my open coding categories. While it might seem that this study was a study of the psychosocial aspects of music within a gerontology context, it was also a study that produced interesting data and commentary on self, life-long learning, health, and spirituality. The findings revealed that music has the potential to provide older people with ways of understanding and developing their self-identity, of connecting with others, of maintaining well-being, and of experiencing and expressing spirituality. The results demonstrated ways that music could contribute to positive aging by providing ways for people to maintain positive self-esteem, feel competent, remain independent, and avoid feelings of isolation or loneliness.

Editors' Comment

Coding Procedures

There are lots of guides that are designed to help you analyze qualitative data. There are books, computer programs, and highly structured manuals on this subject. The choices can be arranged on a continuum from the most technical (axial coding) to the most intuitive (putting slips of paper in a shoebox). Regardless of your preferred style and what is most appropriate for your study, you will follow a systematic process that can be explained and defended to others. This is the core business of your research, the culminating activity that is designed to make and create meaning from the raw data.

* * *

I recall the interview Terrence conducted that I observed. It was in the early stages of the study and I wanted to ensure that Terrence was conducting quality in-depth qualitative interviews. I had read some of his early transcripts and was concerned that he was too committed to his interview guide questions, and was not allowing the informants to go where they wanted to go, or that he was recursive in his questioning style. I recall the gentleman well. He was keen to tell his story. Terrence and I had a coaching session prior to arriving at the informant's apartment. The apartment was well decorated and full of pictures of his family. I was impressed with Terrence's sensitivity to this man. He allowed him to tell his story and used good probes. Unlike his previous interviews, he was more open to following up issues that the informant was keen to discuss and go with the flow, so to speak. That is, the interview had a more natural flavor to it. It was more of a conversation with the informant leading the interview and Terrence asking probing questions to gain a better understanding of how music was helping this man enjoy his life and combat some of his loneliness. It was clear from this interview that the theme of how music was used by older people to connect with their memories would be one of the major findings of this study. I left this interview confident that Terrence had a good understanding of how to conduct interviews that would now provide him with depth of data and a unique study.

* * *

Conclusion and Main Lesson Learned

The main point I would like to leave you with as you begin your own journey into qualitative research is to not be afraid of making mistakes. From my own learning experience, it became clear that undertaking an extensive research project requires good organization skills and reflective thinking in terms of practice, methodology, and theoretical framework. I believe qualitative researchers need to be open to the fact that their projects will evolve and the nature of the question might change. To effectively undertake this type of project requires an enquiring mind and a person who can learn from his mistakes and make informed decisions about research design. When you achieve this in your development as a researcher, you will experience a personal feeling of achievement and reward.

A final comment. Undertaking a research project that involves getting in the shoes of people or their minds involves some risk taking. It involves reflective thinking and being open to new leads that may take you on paths that are totally unexpected, unpredictable, and possibly confronting. The lesson here is to be open to this experience and direction. Be diligent to explore all the truths and realities out there.

References

Hays, T., Bright, R., & Minichiello, V. (2002). The contribution of music to positive aging: A review. *Journal of Aging and Identity, 7,* 165–176.

Hays, T., & Minichiello, V. (2005a). The contribution of music to quality of life in older people: An Australian qualitative study. *Ageing and Society, 25,* 261–278.

Hays, T., & Minichiello, V. (2005b). The meaning of music in the lives of older people: A qualitative study. *Psychology of Music, 33,* 37–51.

Minichiello, V., Aroni, R., & Hays, T. (2008). *In-depth interviewing* (3rd ed.). Sydney: Pearson/Prentice Hall.

Strauss, A., & Corbin, J. (1998). *Basics of qualitative research: Techniques and procedures for developing grounded theory.* Thousand Oaks, CA: Sage Publications.

Through My Eyes 10

Conducting Research as a Vision-Impaired Researcher

*Theresa Smith-Ruig and
Alison Sheridan*

W hen the notion of writing this chapter was first presented to me, initially I (Theresa) thought, "Hey, no problem. I can write about my experiences as a research student." In practice, however, having to write with such honesty and frankness has been more than a little daunting. It has meant that I have had to take time to reflect on and revisit many of the experiences in which I believed I was unqualified to do academic research, and which intimidated me.

My research study explored the career development of men and women in the accounting profession in Australia. The research led to the development of a metaphor to describe the career development of my research participants. The metaphor was based on a road map that conceptualized the career journey of the people interviewed. I have used this journey metaphor in this chapter to describe my own experiences of completing my research.

Initially, I was a little naïve about the challenges of completing a doctoral-level research study. When I returned to the university to commence my studies, many other academics talked of the "agony" ahead of me. I remember thinking, naïvely, how bad can it be?

Initially I did not encounter any problems and everything appeared to be in control as I completed my literature review, and outlined my proposed study and the means by which I would conduct it. Then, shortly into the data collection stage, I began to encounter some road bumps and hazards. The journey no longer seemed straightforward. From then on during the process,

I experienced many highs and lows. I became acutely aware of those early dire predictions by other academics. One of the major challenges I faced during the research journey was based on my vision impairment and how this impairment influenced choices I made about the nature of the study and the manner in which it was conducted. The following provides a brief background on what it means to conduct research as a vision-impaired person.

My Background

At the age of ten, I suddenly began to lose my sight. I was diagnosed with a condition known as bilateral retinal detachments, which meant the part of the eye known as the retina was tearing in both my eyes. It is unusual for the condition to occur in both eyes. There was no medical reason to explain the onset; it was simply bad luck. I underwent many operations over the coming years to treat the condition, but none was successful in repairing the damage. Since then my eyesight has gradually deteriorated, and it continues to do so today.

When I first started to lose my sight, many of my family and friends thought I faced a challenging life ahead. Despite being a relatively intelligent student throughout high school, not everyone believed I would ever attend university. Going on to university, completing my undergraduate degree, and receiving both First Class Honors and the University Medal were proud milestones in my life.

I have always been determined throughout my life to show that my vision impairment would not be a barrier, but merely a challenge that could be overcome. So when the notion of completing a doctoral program was first proposed to me, I thought, "Yes! Another challenge, another opportunity to prove I can do it."

Editors' Comment

Locating the Researcher

Notice how Theresa is locating herself as a researcher. Her choice to do this study and the way she chose to approach it are partially explained by her own experiences losing her sight. This personal motive is evident in many of the other chapters you've read, as well. Yet, the sanitized view of how and why research is undertaken gives the distinct impression that scholars are only motivated by professional aims; the researcher's authentic voice is marginalized or silenced altogether. In the real world, there must be considerable dialogue between students and their mentors about the role of personal agendas, their legitimate resources, as well as their limitations.

We often encourage our students to write about what led them to their particular research topic, owning their personal motives and interest so that the reader understands the context for what will follow. Notice how we modeled this behavior in the first chapter of the book, informing you about our research journeys.

So how does a vision-impaired person study and conduct research, I hear you ask. I have no vision in my right eye, and very limited vision in my left eye. I can distinguish light from dark, and everything else is just blurred shapes and shadows. To study and work I use specialized screen-reading software (JAWS) on my computer. It consists of a synthesized voice that reads out the text on my screen. It tells me the keys I press on the keyboard and reads back a word document or Internet page to me, as long as the content is only text. When I started to lose my sight, I took a typing course in primary school. As a result, I have acquired a highly accurate and extremely fast typing speed over the years. A limitation of the speech software on my computer is that it is unable to recognize and read graphics, tables, diagrams, and illustrations. This drawback is one of the challenges I faced during my journey.

✳ ✳ ✳

Theresa's capacity to tackle a research project had been obvious to me (Alison) in my earlier role as mentor of her honors thesis. She'd done a sound piece of qualitative research exploring the experiences of vision-impaired people in the law profession. When she began her doctoral program, she spent time adapting her honors thesis to submit as a refereed journal article (Smith, 2002) without disrupting the progress of her literature review.

In managing the feedback on her various draft chapters, an arrangement evolved that suited us. My normal method of providing feedback is to write comments over the hard copy of the drafts, and then the student and I meet to discuss the feedback. For her honors thesis, I had written my notes on sticky paper and attached them to her drafts, and a colleague of hers read them out to her. She would then work on them, and let me know what she had done. For her doctoral work, we tried the track changes tool for me to provide my comments, but that wasn't ideal, not only because it was time consuming for me, but also because I found that the comments I wrote by hand didn't work well in the track change format. Often I draw lines linking points, highlighting inconsistencies, pointing to the common themes that may be able to be reduced to one point, and this just doesn't make as much sense through the track change tool. Her other supervisor had similar concerns and arrived at the solution of us recording our comments on tapes as we read through the drafts. Attaching simple instructions to identify where on the page we were commenting and what our feedback was allowed us to develop a much more constructive approach. It was less time consuming for us and more accessible to her, and, more importantly, I found I was able to replicate verbally the sorts of comments that I would have normally handwritten and that I hadn't been able to convey with track changes. It was through this reflection on how I negotiated communication with Theresa that I realized that such negotiation happens with all my doctoral students. I don't have exactly the same communication with each student, because they all have different styles. Together we work out which processes work and which don't. I have found that the discussion around what we each expect helps to minimize misunderstandings.

❊ ❊ ❊

I found my supervisors' recorded comments to be a very effective tool for providing feedback to me. Listening to their comments on tape about suggested changes and amendments was like having a detailed conversation with them. It enabled them to clearly outline their suggestions in a detailed and expansive manner. They would provide comments regarding structure, grammar, the logic of my arguments, and issues I needed to expand on further. Any points that were not clear from their recorded comments I was able to follow up directly with them. Most valuably, the recording meant I had constructive comments to refer back to constantly when I was alone and making revisions; as if they were in the room with me. Perhaps, in contrast, the quality and quantity of feedback would not be as detailed if it were only marked down on a hard copy of the thesis.

Thanks to the increasing electronic environment in which we now live and work, the challenges of dealing with a highly visualized world have improved. Many journals are now available electronically on the Internet, which enabled me to conduct a literature review with few difficulties. There were, however, a couple of challenges. The first was accessing journal articles and books that were not available electronically. This meant I spent many long and laborious hours scanning the printed material on to my computer, which the computer then read back to me via the speech software. Some books could take half a day to scan, and the quality was not always accurate. This problem was frustrating for me. Although I scanned countless books and articles, there was so much more material I should have read. I became somewhat selective in my literature review because I favored electronic sources over printed material.

❊ ❊ ❊

From my experience as a supervisor, I have often found that students are too hard on themselves as they work through their research journey. While it is important they hold themselves to high standards, they often need to be reminded that perfection is unattainable. Theresa's literature review was an example of her being too hard on herself. All students have to do some form of screening to manage their literature review. In many cases, they do it unreflexively, reflecting their paradigm biases. In Theresa's case, she was aware of what she was doing—because of her constraints—and her expectations about the literature review were, as with many students, almost impossible. As her supervisor, I was confident she was covering the terrain very well and so did not share her concerns. All of her examiners commented very positively on the quality and breadth of her literature review.

❊ ❊ ❊

The other major limitation I faced was the inability to scan and understand diagrams or models. Many of the researchers in the career development field developed complex and sometimes very abstract diagrams to illustrate their theories. While this is useful for the majority of the population without sight impairment, it meant I was missing out on one key component of my research. Such theorists used the diagrams or models to summarize their career theories to make it easier to understand. Others developed their diagrams based on metaphors that were derived from the research participants' conceptualization of career, or were researcher derived. Metaphors are a common means by which researchers in the field describe and conceptualize career development. Some of these diagrams I could understand, because they were based on an image I could visualize. For example, Powell and Mainiero (1992) developed the "cross currents in the river of time" metaphor to illustrate the currents that act as push and pull factors in women's career development. This diagram was based on a physical feature (riverbanks and currents) that I could readily visualize and understand.

Other researchers, however, often used complex diagrams or flow charts to illustrate their theories, which were too abstract for me to appreciate. I look back now and wonder why I just didn't ask my supervisor to describe the diagrams to me, but that is probably where my pride comes in. I have always been an independent person, not wanting to ask others for help. I like to be able to complete a task myself. As a lesson for other doctoral students, it is important to recognize that you may have limitations. It is okay to ask for assistance or guidance when necessary.

The other lesson is that diagrams are useful for summarizing, illustrating, or conceptualizing qualitative data. One of the characteristics of qualitative research is the large volume of written data collected and presented in a thesis. In contrast, people conducting quantitative research can present their data using charts, graphs, or other graphical representations, thereby providing a concise snapshot of their findings. If possible and where relevant, it is useful for qualitative researchers to translate or summarize their extensive written data into a diagram or model that captures the essence of their findings.

The Study

I undertook a doctoral program to explore the topic of career development. I completed a Bachelor of Commerce majoring in finance, marketing, and human resource management. Following graduation, I worked in the banking sector. Given this background, I was interested in researching the career experiences of men and women in the finance profession. I have always viewed myself as somewhat ambitious, wanting to excel at everything.

Researching the career experiences of men and women in the finance industry would give me an insight into how I, too, might have a successful career. So choosing the topic of my doctoral was relatively easy.

My research topic was exploring the career experiences of men and women in the accounting profession in Australia. The aim of the research was to enhance our understanding of how men and women in the accounting profession in Australia conceptualize their own sense of career and career success, and how this shapes their career development and behavior in the organization and in their personal lives. To control for differences in occupational contexts, the sample was restricted to individuals employed in the accounting profession.

Research Design

The major decision all researchers face concerns which paradigm they will use to conduct the research: qualitative or quantitative. Despite being very competent at mathematics, I quickly decided that qualitative research would be my preferred avenue. This decision was based on a number of factors. One of the major motivations for choosing qualitative research methods was based on my vision impairment. I associated quantitative research with designing and distributing surveys and questionnaires to a large sample size. While I could recognize the benefits of such a methodological instrument, there would be inherent difficulties for me. As a vision-impaired person, how could I read all those printed responses to the survey or questionnaire? It would have meant relying on someone else to record and input my data into a relevant software program. This point raised another issue: would my screen-reading software be compatible with statistical packages? While I knew JAWS worked with programs such as SPSS, I was aware that it was a difficult program to learn and use for vision-impaired people.

Although my vision impairment played an influencing role in choosing a qualitative design, I also strongly believed it was best suited to the type of research I was conducting. A qualitative method (through the use of semi-structured interviews) would provide a highly personalized and rich detailed exploration of the career development of participants. Previous researchers had successfully used both interviews and story telling as an effective means of researching careers (Arthur, Inkson, & Pringle, 1999; Cochran, 1990; Cohen & Mallon, 2001; Marshall, 1989, 1995; White, Cox, & Cooper, 1992). Importantly for my purposes, interviews enable the researcher to understand the world from the subject's point of view (Kvale, 1993).

The interview questions were open ended, allowing participants considerable scope for their responses. The questions were developed through my understanding of the relevant career development literature and based on my three key research objectives. I sought to fill the gaps in our existing knowledge of career development as experienced by those in the accounting profession. I conducted a pilot test of the interview questions with three colleagues (including my two supervisors) to determine whether my questions enabled all the key issues to be explored; to assess the logic and flow of the interview; and to gauge the reaction of the interviewees. The pilot test confirmed that the interview schedule was appropriately structured and that no amendments were considered necessary.

The use of interviews allowed me to explore and understand the range of feelings, attitudes, and motivations expressed by each participant, creating an individualized account of their career development. Previous researchers had made similar comments on the benefits of interviews in careers research, so I was pleased to discover that my interviews yielded similar outcomes. I believe that a quantitative design involving surveys would not have produced such a wealth of information from respondents. The participants were encouraged to expand on their responses, enabling me to explore the context surrounding their career decisions. The interviews ranged in length from 30 to 120 minutes.

The Sample

The sample included thirty men and twenty-nine women employed in a range of organizations, including universities, chartered firms, the corporate sector, the not-for-profit sector, and sole practice. Participants included part-time and full-time employees, employed at various levels within an organization.

The actual process of targeting participants for the research was more difficult than I had anticipated. In the textbooks, this is generally treated as a straightforward process. You make a decision about the sampling process you will use and then you get on with it. In practice, I found it wasn't that straightforward. Purposive, convenience, and snowball sampling techniques were used to obtain the sample. Initially, I targeted a series of organizations in an attempt to recruit some of their staff (purposive and convenience sampling). I targeted local firms due to their smaller size and proximity, as well as large professional services firms and multinationals. Approaching accounting firms and large multinationals did not prove very successful. This became quite a frustrating part of the data collection phase. When I feared that sample selection was coming to a standstill, I resorted to snowball sampling, where I asked participants to identify other potential respondents.

✳ ✳ ✳

One of the reviewers for the chapter queried our use of the word sample here, rather than participants. The reviewer's query made it obvious to us how we had slipped, unconsciously, into employing language associated with scientific research, as though this legitimized the qualitative approach taken. While there was never any claim that the sample was generalizable, the words used to describe how participants were selected—the sampling process—tend to inflate the process in a way that can, in some ways, be seen as reinforcing a hierarchy of research methods. As the more experienced researcher, I should have picked up on this slip and challenged Theresa on it, but I had overlooked the value-laden nature of the term. It is a salient reminder not to fall into such traps.

Editors' Comment

Finding Your Participants

Whenever you consult any such set of instructions, whether they relate to qualitative research or tell you how to program an electronic device, you often find that circumstances are more challenging and complex than what was advertised. It was one of the universals of doing this kind of research that finding participants is going to be difficult for one reason or another. People are concerned about their privacy. They don't wish to be inconvenienced. They volunteer but don't follow through. For example, you can't access prisoners without permission of a gatekeeper, and you can't go to the phone book and get a comprehensive list of sex workers to interview. You have to think like a detective in order to solve the mystery of where people are located—and you won't find definitive clues in this or any other textbook.

✳ ✳ ✳

After nearly twelve months of data collection, I had completed thirty-eight interviews. I had projected this would be a sufficient sample size for my research and breathed a great sigh of relief. On the one hand, I found the interview process to be quite informative, inspiring, stimulating, and emotional. On the other hand, though, I found it draining because some interviews had to be rescheduled when participants were unavailable. Other interviews had to be conducted at night or on weekends because their work schedules were too busy. I remember one interview especially well: it was with a female partner of one of the major professional service firms in Australia. She conducted the interview with her four-year-old daughter (who was unwell at the time) on her lap. Another female participant juggled talking to me on the phone while watching over her two-year-old twins. Such juggling was commonplace for the women because balancing work and family commitments was a daily challenge in their lives. For me, it brought home the reality of their circumstances, and provided me with extra insight into their lives that would have been absent if impersonal questionnaires or surveys were used in the study. The career and life stories of the participants were very personalized as they talked about the high and low points of their careers. Some stories were quite inspiring as participants told of how they had to overcome significant challenges in their lives to achieve success, such as an abusive childhood or marriage, the serious illness of a newborn child, or the negative treatment received by some females in their male-dominated workplaces. The experiences of the participants made me reflect on my own life and how it compared and contrasted with theirs. The most depressing stories related to those participants who were obviously experiencing considerable stress, anxiety, and depression over the lack of a good work-family balance. I was surprised, given that on the surface these participants could be viewed as very successful: they received high salaries and were employed at the most senior levels of their organization. It reinforced my own misconceptions of what success really means. The key lesson for me was that the interview is an extremely powerful tool for understanding and exploring the personal and emotional experiences of participants.

After some initial resistance on my part (because I believed I had enough data) my supervisors persuaded me to conduct additional interviews to add more weight to my data and the quality of the research. The aim was to reach saturation in the data collection phase, something they weren't convinced had yet happened. With the help of a colleague, I approached the state arm of a national accounting body. This yielded another twenty-one participants. I encountered more stories, some inspiring and some depressing. When I had completed the additional interviews, I could see how they provided additional depth to my study.

✳ ✳ ✳

People differ in their approaches to work, life, and, of course, their research. Doctoral programs vary both across and within countries. Different programs offer a range of periods of candidature for their research components and different mixes of coursework and research components. The program in which students choose to enroll may reflect a keen self-awareness as to what would best suit them, or they may unreflexively enroll in what is, in their context, the normal *program. How students respond to the different requirements may reflect a range of factors—their personality, where they are in their life-cycle, perhaps some critical incidents in their lives—and cannot be taken as a given. While some students complete on time (whatever their period of candidature), others require extended periods. Despite what many may perceive as a stumbling block—a vision impairment—Theresa was able to enroll in and complete a three-year doctoral program where the thesis was the sole output. As must be clear from her story so far, Theresa is a doer. Her focus on her research throughout the three years of her doctoral candidature, even while she was visiting surgeons to explore (what ultimately were unsuccessful) options for improving her sight, was inspirational.*

✳ ✳ ✳

Conducting the Interviews

All the interviews were audiotaped and transcribed by me. Initially, the aim was to conduct all the interviews face to face. In practice, though, only twelve were conducted in person and the remaining forty-seven by phone. There were a number of reasons for this outcome. First, given that the sample was located throughout Australia it became difficult to coordinate and organize interviews in person due to cost, scheduling, and convenience. Second, while I was able to travel interstate independently to conduct some of the interviews, it was much easier to avoid the logistical problems of travel and use phone interviews. While I recognize the inconsistency in the interview method (some face to face, some by phone), I believe that participants were equally comfortable answering questions either way.

In addition to the interview, I also directed a short demographic questionnaire to participants. Initially, I handed this questionnaire to the participants during the face-to-face interview and they completed it and returned it to me by mail. I then scanned the questionnaire to ascertain the participant's responses. This proved difficult, because the quality of the scanning was not accurate. I had to have someone else read back the responses to me. Following the first brief round of five interviews, I then chose to ask the questions from the demographic survey during the interview itself. This enabled me to audiotape the answers, which I later transcribed with the rest of the interview. There were only seventeen questions in the demographic questionnaire, so it was not time consuming or difficult to include them in the interview. In fact, I believe that the basic demographic questions that I asked at the commencement of the interview provided an icebreaker and a means of gently transitioning the participant into the more detailed interview questions.

Data Analysis

The research was conducted using an interpretive and grounded theory approach. In contrast to positivist researchers who develop hypotheses that they seek to confirm or disconfirm, a grounded theory approach commences with an area of study that allows relevant theoretical constructs to emerge from the research process. The theory is formulated through iterative analysis of data, and through the development of core concepts whose interrelationships are explored in order to generate an explanatory theoretical framework (Glaser & Strauss, 1967).

In the case of my research, I followed a number of steps in the grounded theory process. First, I presented and discussed the existing theories of career development. Second, I identified a range of possible factors found to influence career development. I used these core themes to guide the data collection during the interview phase. An important feature of the grounded theory approach, however, is that it allows for new salient issues to emerge from the data collection stage. This is known as an inductive approach. The flexible nature of the semistructured interviews allowed respondents to identify any additional factors they considered important in their career development. Third, the grounded theory approach allowed a theory or general framework to emerge from the iterative analysis of the data. In this case, the career stories of respondents were used to develop a framework that described the stages through which men and women progress in their career. The final step involved analyzing the interview data and comparing and contrasting it to existing theories. An important feature of the grounded approach is the emphasis on understanding the world of the actors as they have consciously or unconsciously constructed it, and to provide the foundations for developing a theory that will serve as a future basis for explanation (Glaser & Strauss, 1967). Similarly, interpretive studies allow the researcher to understand and describe meaningful social action or phenomena in specific contexts (Denzin & Lincoln, 2002). In the case of this research, the social action under investigation was the issue of career development. The specific context chosen for analysis was that of the accounting profession in Australia.

I found choosing a methodology extremely confusing and difficult. It took some time for me to understand the range of approaches available. To help clarify the choice, I studied the methodologies used by other researchers in the career development field. It ranged across the continuum, from positivistic to interpretive or phenomenological approaches. Given my previous comments about quantitative research, I favored the interpretive studies. I believed such research would yield a much richer form of data, particularly through the use of interviews. My suggestion for other students is to read many texts and articles on how to conduct research and the various methodologies available.

Although my research did not strictly adhere to the steps of grounded theory, I followed the Strauss and Corbin (1990, 1998) approach to grounded theory in the data collection and analysis. There were several key steps in my data analysis. First, each interview was audiotaped, then transcribed. Second, each interview was content analyzed and coded for emerging themes. These themes related to my three key research objectives: how men and women discussed the concept of career and success; the role that various personal, interpersonal, and organizational factors had on career; and the nature of personal career development. For example, specific themes included balancing work and family, mentoring, networking, career management practices, and language used to describe career experiences. In general, the process of data analysis was characterized by a constant comparative method to compare specific codes, concepts, themes, and patterns of relationships generated from the interview data. Specifically, each interview was individually coded. Then common responses from all the participants relating to a particular theme (such as mentoring) were grouped together, compared, and contrasted. The analysis also involved comparing the comments of the male to the female participants, of those employed in firms versus those employed in larger firms, and regional organizations versus city-based firms. I identified a range of factors that influence the career development of the male and female participants. This information, combined with the existing literature, was used to develop a framework to describe the career stages through which men and women progress in their career.

I chose to transcribe all the interviews myself because it allowed me to become better informed about what participants said during the interview. I usually tried to transcribe the interviews immediately after they were conducted, which reinforced their particular narratives in my mind. I carried out the content analysis and coding of the data in Microsoft Word by listening to the transcribed interviews. I made a deliberate decision not to use a qualitative software program to analyze the data because, as I have said previously, I believed there may be too many challenges in learning how to use JAWS and the software program. I had much more control over and a more in-depth knowledge of the interviews by constantly rereading and combing the transcripts for relevant themes. Each participant interview had its own Word file. I then compared each of the responses to similar questions among the participants from the same organization, and then across all fifty-nine participants. I also analyzed the data by sex to determine any similarities and differences in the results. Within the transcribed files, I would mark particular responses with codes relating to relevant themes, such as the work mentor or network. The search function in Word allowed me to come back later and search for these codes, which I had typed in the document. The search function also allowed me to search for repetitive words and phrases in the transcripts. In addition, each participant was given a number; I used that number in developing a Microsoft Excel spreadsheet that summarized all their demographic details and brief work histories. The process of coding and organizing the data was quite involved, but I soon became intimately aware of the participants' background and stories. I had grown up with and become quite used to using a computer for accessing and reading information and not relying on printed text so I was probably more efficient and certainly more comfortable using Word than I would have been using a qualitative software program.

✳ ✳ ✳

Theresa's decision to develop her own systems for handling her data rather than using qualitative software raises an interesting point more generally about the handling of data. While there is no doubt that the development of qualitative software such as NVivo has transformed the handling of data (Richards, 2005), enabling greater efficiencies, especially for large data sets, they are simply tools. This is often overlooked in the reification of the software. In Theresa's case, such tools are not particularly useful because they have been designed as visual packages. For Theresa, whose experience has been such that her skills at processing information have been enhanced in other ways (Ahmedi, Raz, Pianka, Malach, & Zohary, 2003), such tools to enhance the efficiency of handling data are not required. For instance, her memory for detail is phenomenal. I have seen her give numerous presentations without a single note and be word perfect in the presentation of the argument that is depicted in words on overheads. There is no doubt that her own tool for handling the interview data—through Word—was as rigorous as if she had used a software package such as NVivo.

✳ ✳ ✳

My Model for Career Development

As mentioned earlier, in my literature review of existing theories on career development I came across many diagrams and models that other researchers used to conceptualize their theory. I found it difficult and often impossible to visualize these models and diagrams because they were often too abstract or complex for me to meaningfully comprehend. While I could not visualize the diagrams, it did not affect my level of understanding of the theories: some theorists often describe the diagrams within the text of their publications. During the write-up of my results, my supervisors suggested that perhaps I needed to represent my theory using a model, something I hadn't been considering. When faced with the idea, though, I realized that it made sense (as explained earlier).

✳ ✳ ✳

It is at this point that I as a supervisor feel most remiss. Despite having supervised Theresa in her honors thesis and teaching her in her undergraduate Human Resource Management unit, I hadn't ever reflected on the visual dimensions of the materials with which she was engaging. I was unaware that she wasn't processing the models liberally sprinkled through much of the human resource literature in the same way I did.

✳ ✳ ✳

So I, too, chose to develop a model that could be used to illustrate the nature of career development of my participants. It was this aspect of the doctoral program that initially posed a particular challenge for me as a vision-impaired researcher. I was faced with the challenge of how to represent my own theory in a meaningful way that I could visualize and that I could use to permit a wider audience to visualize.

My supervisors and I discussed this challenge at length. They even discussed the problem with colleagues at other universities. At first we thought I could develop a diagram and then trace it so I would have a tactile image to perceive, but the challenge would remain of developing that specific diagram. As a means of working through this problem, my supervisor suggested I read literature relating to the use of metaphors to explain phenomena. Lakoff and Johnson (1980) argue that metaphors are pervasive in everyday life—not just in language, but also in thought and action. One of the first theorists to use metaphors was Morgan (1983). He states that metaphors are "a basic structural form of experience through which human beings engage, organize, and understand their world" (Morgan, 1983, p. 601). He uses metaphors as a means of describing and analyzing organizations. For example, he describes the metaphor of an organization as a "machine," "organism," "political system," "brain," and as an "instrument of domination." Similarly, Oswick and Montgomery (1999) argue that metaphors enable perceptions, attitudes, and feelings to be uncovered and articulated. Morgan acknowledges that there are strengths and weaknesses in using metaphors: "The strengths rest in the insights created through the metaphor. The limitations rest in the fact that no metaphor ever captures the totality of experience to which it is applied. In creating one set of insights it excludes others" (Morgan, 1996, p. 232). When I was reading over one of the interview transcripts, a phrase leapt out at me. A participant said, "Career is not a destination, it is a journey." From this comment, I realized that many of the participants in my research used similar language to describe aspects of their careers and they all related to journey metaphors. Words and terms such as *parallel routes, crossroads, turning point, career path, propelled, plateau,* and *travel* all reinforce the notion of a road-map metaphor. The metaphor of driving along a highway with alternative roads, roundabouts, and exits was also something I could readily understand and visualize, and concluded that it would best illustrate the various pathways followed by participants in the study.

Editors' Comment

Patience With the Data Analysis

The leaps of awareness that Theresa describes are indicative of the data analysis process. There is always a struggle in the beginning to organize and make sense of the vast body of information that you have gathered, much less digested. The insight process that is often so much a part of learning occurs when the researcher is able to incrementally—or suddenly—recognize key themes that begin to order and link discrepant threads together into a more cohesive pattern.

It often takes a degree of patience and tolerance for ambiguity to live with the uncertainty, to manage your frustration, and to trust the process that, given sufficient time, reflection, and convergent thinking, greater understanding will often emerge. Fair warning, however: sometimes this is the point at which students and researchers abandon their projects because they can't tolerate the ongoing uncertainty or because they sense they've run out of time.

Once I decided on the metaphor, my supervisor's partner (who had graphic design skills) produced road-map graphics for my dissertation. I explained how the metaphor diagram should look, based on my understanding of physical objects like highways, roundabouts, exits, and so on. While I was unable to draw the diagrams myself, I was able to explain easily how they should be depicted. He transposed an image from a street directory to illustrate the complex journey metaphor. Although this was a complex diagram, I could remember as a child looking at maps and even at a street directory, so I could easily visualize the diagram.

The metaphor of a road map provided a useful and novel means of understanding and illustrating the fluidity of career paths for the sample. The benefit of such a metaphor is that it recognizes there are multiple factors influencing the career development of men and women, factors that often mean their career paths are neither linear nor stable. The limitation of the road-map metaphor is that it is only two-dimensional and does not capture the personal motivations of the participants. Furthermore, it cannot fully reflect the idiosyncratic nature of the participants' careers. Since a metaphor cannot capture the totality of experience, it is acknowledged that this metaphor is not generalizable to other accounting professionals or individuals in the broader community, but merely reflects the men and women interviewed in my research. The metaphor, however, could be used in future research to test its applicability to other demographic or occupational contexts.

A lesson for all of us in my struggles to develop a diagram is that people process information in different ways. We all have issues that may shape our conceptualization or interpretation of events. As Denzin and Lincoln (2002, p. 12) argue, our interpretations are often filtered by language, gender, social class, and race and ethnicity, and we act on these interpretations "rather than what is."

I look back now and conclude that if I had not been faced with the challenge of developing a meaningful diagram, I might have missed the common metaphoric language that was woven throughout the transcripts. The metaphor of a road map or journey is a useful means for anyone to examine his own life and experiences. I can examine my own life and think about the potholes and plateaus in my life and even apply it to the doctoral journey. At times, you cruise along at speed, experiencing no hazards, while at other times you are forced to change gears and take different directions to avoid as challenges arise along the way. You may even lose track of where you are going, but that is when you need to pull over on the journey and take a brief rest to reenergize and even redirect your path.

For example, as a doctoral student I was required to read extensive literature, critique it, and develop my own opinions and path for conducting research. In the early months of my doctoral program, I found this a very confronting and daunting task. How could I, a twenty-four-year-old student with limited work experience and academic qualifications critique other researchers who had clearly marked their position in academic research? I saw my supervisors as extremely wise and well-experienced "real academics" whose world I thought I would never be qualified to join. These feelings of self-doubt extended throughout much of the doctoral process, despite all the endless journal articles and books I read. It was not until I was in the final stages of writing my thesis that I was somehow transformed into a "real academic." I had reached a major crossroads in the doctoral journey. The metamorphosis had obviously been occurring for some time, but it was not until I faced the major dilemma of my doctoral experience that I suddenly realized I finally had the confidence and ability to make a major decision about my thesis.

To explain briefly, in what I thought would be a final draft of my thesis before publication, my supervisors had read the thesis and, for the first time, disagreed on how I had been presenting and discussing the data from my research. I had used elements of the grounded theory approach in analyzing my data and the disagreement centered on how true I had remained to grounded theory. One supervisor thought I should not refer to my data in a quantitative sense. For example, I often stated that 12 percent of participants said this, or 50 percent said that. The debate was whether I should present my data in such a quantitative manner. Both supervisors seemed to be well justified in their differing positions, but for me it just meant an agony of indecision and uncertainty. While it was quite traumatic at the time, this was the crossroads in my academic research career, when I was finally required to make a decision as to what I believed would be appropriate.

I spoke to a number of colleagues in an attempt to resolve the dilemma, and reread countless books and articles on grounded theory methodology. I had to stop and think about which paradigm I based my research on and what implications that had for presenting the data. I realized that my research was qualitative and the strength rested in the unique personal stories of participants. While it was useful to highlight whether a minority or majority of participants had similar experiences, it was not necessary to quantify the data to the extent I had been doing. I realized that although there are specific rules and conditions relating to the range of research methodologies, each researcher can have her own interpretation about how those specifics are played out in a research project.

Once I had finally made the decision on which approach to adopt and made the necessary changes to my thesis, I realized my journey from an inexperienced doctoral student to a confident academic researcher was complete. I finally possessed the courage and confidence to make my own decision and to be comfortable holding a different view from that of a supervisor, now colleague, who I had put on such a high pedestal.

In summary, while the journey may be arduous, the process of conducting research provides you with many lessons about not just academia, but also about life. Research teaches you patience and a tolerance for change (the ability to change direction when the research process has stalled or requires new thinking), critical thinking (the ability to critique how other researchers have carried out their study or refute their findings), empathy and insight into the human experience (particularly in the case of my research), and the confidence to back your own ideas or arguments. As the blind and deaf American author and educator Helen Keller (1880–1968) said, "Life is a succession of lessons which must be lived to be understood."

References

Ahmedi, A., Raz, N., Pianka, P., Malach, R., & Zohary, E. (2003). Early "visual" cortex activation correlates with superior verbal memory performance in the blind. *Nature Neuroscience, 6*, 758–766.

Arthur, M. B., Inkson, K., & Pringle, J. K. (1999). *The new careers: Individual action and economic change.* London: Sage Publications.

Cochran, L. (1990). Narrative as a paradigm for careers research. In R. A. Young & W. A. Borgen (Eds.), *Methodological approaches to the study of careers* (pp. 71–86). New York: Praeger Publishers.

Cohen, L., & Mallon, M. (2001). My brilliant career?: Using stories as a methodological tool in careers research. *International Studies of Management & Organization, 31*, 48–68.

Denzin, N. K., & Lincoln, Y. S. (Eds.). (2002). *Handbook of qualitative research.* Thousand Oaks, CA: Sage Publications.

Glaser, B. G., & Strauss, A. L. (1967). *The discovery of grounded theory: Strategies for qualitative research.* New York: Aldine de Gruyter.

Kvale, S. (1993). *Interviews: An introduction to qualitative research interviewing.* London: Sage Publications.

Lakoff, G., & Johnson, M. (1980). *Metaphors we live by.* Chicago: University of Chicago Press.

Marshall, J. (1989). Re-visioning career concepts: A feminist invitation. In M. B. Arthur, D. T. Hall, & B. S. Lawrence, *Handbook of career theory* (pp. 275–291). Cambridge: Cambridge University Press.

Marshall, J. (1995). *Women managers moving on: Exploring career and life choices.* London: Routledge.

Morgan, G. (1983). More on metaphor: Why we cannot control tropes in administrative science. *Administrative Science Quarterly, 27,* 601–607.

Morgan, G. (1996). An afterword: Is there anything more to be said about metaphor? In D. Grant & C. Oswick, *Metaphor and organizations* (pp. 227–240). London: Sage Publications.

Oswick, C., & Montgomery, J. (1999). Images of an organization: The use of metaphor in a multinational company. *Journal of Organizational Change Management, 12,* 501.

Powell, G. N., & Mainiero, L. A. (1992). Cross-currents in the river of time: Conceptualizing the complexities of women's careers. *Journal of Management, 18,* 215–238.

Richards, L. (2005). *Handling qualitative data: A practical guide.* London: Sage Publications.

Smith, T. (2002). Diversity and disability: Exploring the experiences of blind and vision-impaired people in the workplace. *Equal Opportunities International, 21,* 59–72.

Strauss, A., & Corbin, J. (1990). *Basics of qualitative research: Grounded theory procedures and techniques.* Newbury Park, CA: Sage Publications.

Strauss, A. L., & Corbin, J. (1998). *Basics of qualitative research: Techniques and procedures for developing grounded theory* (2nd ed.). Thousand Oaks, CA: Sage Publications.

White, B., Cox, C., & Cooper, C. L. (1992). *Women's career development: A study of high flyers.* Oxford: Blackwell Business.

Encounters With Comforting Uncertainties

11

Understanding Unobtrusive Methods

John Scott and Raymond Donovan

Introduction: The Journey Ends

I (John) had decided to quit graduate school. I remember the moment well: the month, where I was, the time of day, the weather. I can recall even minor details of that day now, despite so many other days and moments since then having faded from memory. Quitting school (or anything else) can be a relief, even pleasurable, but it hardly compares with the experience of completing an arduous journey.

My moment of doubt came in 1998. As it happened, I persisted with my studies. A few days later I was back to writing my research project and three years later I graduated. It would be easy to put this achievement down to my individual capacities and character, but, as a budding social scientist, I realize that there was much more than that to writing a thesis. One of the most important things is the interaction that occurs between student and supervisor. This interaction is complex and cannot be reduced to a formula to be applied with disregard to the varied contexts in which research projects are conducted.

Looking back on the interaction between my supervisor and me, it was a positive, even life-changing experience, but there were moments when I doubted his capacity or questioned his advice. The capacity for doubt is an important part of the process of conducting a research project. This work involves confronting uncertainties—of the self, the other, and valued truths—and embracing these uncertainties. I want to discuss these aspects of doing a research project further, but first, in a qualitative fashion, let me provide some context to my experiences.

Context of the Journey

I began my research journey following a period working as a project officer for a large regional medical advocacy group based in New South Wales, Australia. My work had largely involved collecting information on the health status of marginalized and at-risk young people and their use of primary health-care services. I had adopted an ethnographic approach to this work and had collected data from health professionals, social workers, and the youth themselves, using a combination of interviews, focus groups, and observatory methods. In the process, I had become familiar with the use of a range of qualitative methods. The process had led me to become disillusioned with qualitative methods, however. While these methods had appeared useful in solving apparent problems associated with so-called problem youth, I had come to question how these problems were defined. I became interested in how those who were trying to solve problems associated with these youth had created the problems. I had also become interested in how meanings were socially derived and maintained. The questions I was asking tended to not be so much who, what, where, or why, but rather, "How had current meanings associated with young people come to be?" The research I had been doing seemed to me to represent a retreat into the present, and did not appear to concern itself with longer-term social processes.

This was the context in which I commenced my research. My supervisor, who had a background in hermeneutics, historiography, phenomenology, and interpretive sociology, seemed the right person to guide me on the journey I sought to undertake. In their broadest sense, these research traditions had argued that understandings of human behavior must account for the meanings that people give to their own actions and those of others, the emphasis here being on social interaction and interpretation. This theoretical tradition is regularly contrasted with positions, often referred to as *structuralist*, that view social life as governed by systems that are external to and independent of social actors. In contrast, interpretive traditions tend to be highly contextual in their approach and have regularly highlighted the often malleable and shifting patterns of social life. While I was interested in interpretive theoretical traditions, my knowledge of them was limited: these perspectives had been neglected in my undergraduate studies or skimmed over in my texts, in favor of theoretical traditions that promised a broader and more-encompassing account of social life.

The Research Problem

My research was concerned with prostitution and public health in nineteenth- and twentieth-century Britain and New South Wales. The topic addressed two of my key research interests: (1) the sociology of health and illness, and (2) the sociology of crime and deviance. Prostitution appeared at the junction of these two topical areas, prostitutes being a deviant and criminalized population who had been regularly subjected to public health controls. It was apparent to me that the way in which prostitutes had been defined as deviant had changed over time, as had the way in which they had been regulated. I sought to document these changes. While the historical period I would focus on was not immediately evident, initial surveys of the literature made it apparent that key changes in our understandings of prostitution had emerged in more modern times, following the Enlightenment. I spent the first year reading and taking notes on the extensive body of literature concerned with prostitution and moral delinquency. The first thing I noted with regard to the literature was that it was largely psychosocial and tended to pathologize prostitutes as so-called problem populations who posed a public health threat to the general (that is, healthy) community. The literature had also categorized prostitutes into specific subgroupings that were evaluated and hierarchically positioned according to the degree to which they were found to present an epidemiological threat to the community. It was apparent to me that the way in which prostitution was problematized was constantly changing. There had been a broad shift historically from religious to scientific methods of understanding prostitution. I wanted to understand this shift and explore how this shift had influenced the way in which prostitution was regulated.

It is tempting to think of prostitution as a historical constant, particularly given the current tendency to associate prostitution with sexual behavior and economic exchange. Prostitution has regularly been portrayed as a biological and social certainty. Rather than being some stable anthropological entity, I wanted to conceptualize prostitution as the name given to a historical construct of recent origin and temporary significance. I wanted to argue that prostitution has been rendered socially problematic in recent times. This was hardly a unique position, but my commentary would differ from others in its insistence that prostitution had not always been a social problem.

While prostitution had invariably been problematic, it had only recently been rendered socially problematic. The conditions had not always existed for prostitution to be understood as socially problematic. In previous periods, prostitution may have been problematized according to moral, spiritual, or ethical frameworks (see Benjamin & Masters, 1964; Bullough, 1964). As a social problem, though, prostitution had been constituted in a unique and specific manner. Moreover, I wanted to explore how our contemporary understanding of prostitution had been framed historically. Particular persons had been authorized to speak about prostitution and speak on behalf of prostitutes, and specific methods had developed to manage prostitution. Prostitutes may have been punished in the past, but the rationale and ends of punishment were quite different from those that obtain today. It seemed to me that rather than the term *punishment*, the term *protection* best reflects current objectives of social control systems in the management of prostitution.

In the past two hundred years, social control had been concerned with the protection, cure, reformation, and rehabilitation of the prostitute. For example, a common goal of authorities and reformers has been to sanitize prostitution and render the prostitute a so-called hygienic subject. Prostitution had been governed as a public health issue, with certain classes of prostitute having been classified as diseased and dangerous or at risk of contracting a disease. Public health had amplified the significance of prostitution—not by severing the links between prostitute and community, but by expanding, multiplying, and reinforcing them.

Editors' Comment

Theory-Driven Research

John is beginning his study with a very solid theoretical base that informs his decisions on what to investigate and how best to contribute new knowledge. While this isn't an absolute requirement for beginning qualitative researchers, it does demonstrate what is possible for those researchers who have a more thorough grounding in the conceptual literature. That's why John makes it clear that his research agenda was not just about simply describing participant experiences (e.g., narrative analysis and phenomenology), but rather to make significant contributions to the literature on the causes of prostitution.

As I immersed myself in the literature, what struck me was the way in which it was rooted in a particular cultural moment. Scientists and historians do not present theory-free, objective facts, but rather frame data according to sociocultural concepts. The selection procedure of the historian is not transparent. Much of the earlier social scientific literature had dated quickly (see Sanger, 1939). The questions asked seemed to lack contemporary relevance. Nevertheless, common assumptions remained embedded in the literature that guided the types of questions asked by researchers. While couched in an objective language, time had exposed latent moralism below the surface of many of the early studies of prostitution. I wanted to adopt a methodological approach that would save my own research from a similar fate.

Social scientific studies of prostitution were variously grounded in a qualitative or quantitative methodology. Time had also shown many of the methods used to be blatantly flawed. I suspected that research into prostitution had not always produced truths, but that participants had told researchers what they wanted to hear. An example of this was the way in which prostitutes had variously defined themselves as victims of social systems or predatory populations. For instance, early studies define male prostitutes as young heterosexual victims of predatory homosexuals, while later research predominantly reports male sex workers to be gay identified men, servicing an often-straight clientele (Scott, 2003). Moreover, generalizations were often constructed through research conducted with prostitutes who were the most marginalized, and thus the most visible in what was a broad and varied cohort. I suspected that there were deep conceptual and methodological flaws in much of the social scientific work on prostitution. What was to be done about this? I decided I wanted to explore how contemporary ideas associated with prostitution had come about and how they had been justified and rationalized, while identifying gaps and limits in current thinking associated with prostitution.

I was not much interested in solving problems associated with prostitution. What concerned me instead was how prostitution was constructed as a social problem. Was prostitution inherently problematic? How had perceptions of prostitution changed over time? Moreover, in tackling these questions I become interested in ways in which prostitution had been regulated and managed, both in the contemporary period and historically. My objective was not to establish facts or truths, but to examine how facts and truths had been established. I was not seeking to adopt a vocational or professional approach to problems of prostitution, in which the objective is to improve immediate practices of social regulation. I wanted to develop a critical and analytical approach that delved into deeper philosophical issues by questioning whether current understandings of prostitution and attempts to regulate it were validated. My research fell within that minor research tradition concerned with *problem analysis* as opposed to *problem solving* (see Schnieder, 1985). I was interested in how language produces phenomena, and not in how it exposes them. I was interested in how the data were formulated and used for practical ends, and not in the accuracy of the data produced. I was interested in the way in which people who have spoken about and written about prostitution had organized and given meaning to their work in the context of specific sociocultural frameworks. I wanted to explore the layer of cultural meanings that sat beneath the scientific façade of the texts I encountered. My broader objective was to strengthen conceptualization and theory building—to generate new concepts and broaden perspectives. Unobtrusive methods, sometimes referred to as nonreactive methods, seemed ideal for this purpose (Lee, 2000; Webb, Campbell, Schwartz, & Sechrest, 2000).

A Road Well Traveled but Rarely Mapped: Why Use Unobtrusive Methods?

Unobtrusive methods? The term, rarely encountered in methods texts, requires some clarification. While unobtrusive methods may be both qualitative and quantitative in orientation, they have been largely utilized in qualitative research. Unobtrusive methods draw on written records or what, following the postmodern turn (in which universal, normative, and ethical judgments have been subject to reevaluation and analysis), are referred to as *texts* (see Chaney, 1994). Unobtrusive methods were utilized to produce some of the earliest studies of prostitution, but these had usually been problem-solving exercises designed to produce generalized facts associated with prostitution that crossed geographic and temporal frameworks (see Henriques, 1962). I chose to examine a broad range of texts associated with prostitution, including published materials such as books, government records, journals, newspapers, photographs, sketches, newspaper illustrations, and magazines. Accessing such data did not involve direct intervention into lived environments.

The founding parents of the discipline of sociology, such as Karl Marx, Émile Durkheim, and Max Weber, spent almost all their time engaged with texts, largely conducting historical research. While the methodology of these scholars has been much written about and regularly subjected to criticism, it had not been taught. At an undergraduate level, I had regularly encountered unobtrusive methods such as participant observation or archival research, but I had not been trained in how to interrogate and use them. While all methods texts have some reference to common obtrusive methods such as interviewing, emphasis on how archival and historical research is to be conceptualized, let alone conducted, is scarce. As an undergraduate, I enrolled in qualitative methods courses but was not introduced to unobtrusive methods. It is as though unobtrusive methods should be known to the researcher in an intuitive or instinctual sort of way, a suggestion that would, under any other circumstances, run counter to the nurturing discourses championed by social scientists. This is surprising considering that most sociological studies contain a historical section, even if it is rendered as merely a brief, potted fragment of a much larger narrative.

Editors' Comment

Capturing Additional Voices

People often think that qualitative research only involves collecting data based on the here-and-now—interviewing or observing people—but John's study highlights how important insights can also be generated by studying the past through diaries, historical documents, and journalistic accounts. Within your own study, you can think creatively about alternative ways to access the phenomenon other than through direct conversation. In some studies, participants are asked to keep journals or provide diaries of their dreams, fantasies, thoughts, and feelings, all to enrich and expand the breadth and depth of data. The library, as well, is a repository for voices from the past that are screaming to be heard.

Do sociologists think about how they do unobtrusive research, such as historical records, before they conduct their research? It seemed to me that if they do, they do not think about it often. Take, for example, historical research in the social sciences. Rarely is an account provided of how data have been collected or on what terms a narrative has been grounded and built (see Wright Mills, 1970). And how should the researcher account for time? Are dates or epochs important? What about people or ideas—are they important (see Carr, 1986)? Should historical narratives progress chronologically, be presented as a series of events, or be accounted for in terms of cycles? What narrative runs below the passing of time: progress and advancement or discontinuity and ruptures? How should a narrative be spatially organized: according to nation states, cultures, or some other unit of analysis? The problem of using a nation state as a surrogate for culture is that cultures rarely have fixed boundaries. Where does one culture end and another begin? Is it justified to have a Western cultural bias? These issues confronted me as I began my doctoral program. An important issue in unobtrusive research is ensuring the topic is not so broad as to lose its focus.

Despite their relative neglect in the curriculum, unobtrusive methods have been particularly useful in research concerned with social change, politics, and stratification. These issues concerned me. They have also been successfully applied in areas associated with gender, sexuality, and crime and deviance—which are also areas with which my thesis was concerned. In recent times, unobtrusive methods had been used as a means to empower historically marginalized populations who are pathologized within scientific texts. Of great importance in my decision to adopt unobtrusive methods was that much of the existing research had concentrated on disadvantaged groups, especially street prostitutes. I did not see it as necessary to disrupt or intervene in the lives of people when the information I required already existed. What was important to me was not who these people were or what they did, but rather how they have been represented. Researchers had too hurriedly intervened in the lives of sex workers without adequately considering core research questions or how their research was framed conceptually.

Equipping the Journey

I adopted what is referred to as a genealogical method of historical research (Dean, 1994), which fitted well with my objective to examine the construction of social reality of prostitution. The method is highly contextual and provides what seems to be an appropriate compromise on issues of structure and agency, which are important to the historical researcher and archivist. I explored a contingent view of causality, which gave weight to a range of causal factors relating to economic, political, and sociostructural issues. Many historical studies in the social sciences and humanities have attempted to identify universal processes or relationships operating across all human societies or in a particular epoch. My research concentrated more on the limits of knowledge in a particular period and shifts in knowledge. I applied a historiographic approach, which writes a history of histories or, in my case, histories of the texts of prostitution. I wanted to understand the evidence and arguments used by writers when examining prostitution. The historical focus was especially important for opening up broader questions, and was a means to understand social and cultural processes over time. How does major social change occur? What fundamental features are common to most societies in a particular epoch? How do contemporary social arrangements appear in some periods and not others?

✻ ✻ ✻

I (Raymond) mentioned to John the importance of following the work of the French social philosopher and historian Michel Foucault. Foucault's genealogical method works could counter essentialist and linear claims that, in this instance, prostitution is in some way eternally problematic, the product of some unwavering form of gender domination, or that it is in some way bound to denigrate and exploit human nature. Linear approaches, some of which seek to normalize particular deviant phenomena, ultimately work to obscure the practices contributing to their contemporary problematization (Sawicki, 1988; Thacker, 1997). While particular types of behavior resembling female or male prostitution may be disposed to some historical consistency, the meanings associated with such behaviors have been variable and fluid. The questions asked about such behaviors change, as does the importance they are prescribed in moral and philosophical debate.

✻ ✻ ✻

Part of the genealogical task is to deessentialize: that is, to reveal the social foundations of something that appears to have a timeless or natural quality and appearance. It is this quality that links genealogical studies with the interpretive traditions noted above (Rabinow & Dreyfus, 1982). This is not to anticipate a descent into cultural relativism, but rather to move away from the questions most commonly asked—in this instance, about prostitution. Such questions are likely to be, Who is the prostitute? What are the causes of prostitution, and how might prostitution be prevented? How might the social body be protected from the ravages of prostitution? What is prostitution? Genealogy, by contrast, allows for an examination of how the prostitute is made possible. How the prostitute is visualized, objectified, differentiated, and documented. Genealogy undermines the surface representation to explore significations, but genealogy does not end by describing the process of signification: it also traces its effects. A genealogical analysis of prostitution allows the following questions to be addressed: What do we understand by the terms *prostitute* and *prostitution* today? Why have prostitutes, male and female, been represented and characterized in the way that they have? How is it possible to speak about prostitutes and prostitution in the way that we do today? What cultural and historical practices have allowed for meanings about prostitution to be produced and reproduced, and on what basis have these representations of them been made meaningful?

Editors' Comment

Talk of the Discipline

You can't help but notice that John and his mentor, Raymond, are heavily invested in using the language of their preferred theories. They use terms like *essentializing, social structural, cultural relativism, signification*, and *contemporary problemization*. There is no doubt that there is a challenge in this kind of discourse for readers who are unfamiliar with the disciplinary language of any school. This is no different from overhearing two physicians, psychologists, or physicists having a professional conversation using their professional language. Any research study introduces conceptual and linguistic concepts that must be understood before you can appreciate the deeper meaning in the findings.

If history is a series of interpretations, then it is interpretation itself that comes to be the focus of the genealogist. Genealogy seeks to understand the multiple ways in which prostitution has been problematized by examining what is true about prostitution and why it is true. A genealogical analysis of prostitution would describe how certain questions and truths associated with prostitution have gained sociopolitical significance. A genealogy of prostitution would not be concerned with whether or not prostitutes are at risk of sexually transmissible diseases, but rather with how an association between prostitution, sex, and risk was historically materialized and rendered factual in discourse.

✻ ✻ ✻

Unobtrusive methods provided a way in which to explore what was common and what was unique in social systems. John was not merely interested in historical notions of prostitution, but rather in contemporary meanings and forms of regulation in both official and popular contexts. Two primary resources were contemporary media and political archives. There was also a practical advantage in adopting unobtrusive methods, in that this approach could be undertaken relatively quickly and with limited expense, two increasingly important considerations in the context of research. Advantages included archives being easily accessible, there being fewer ethical constraints, and data being easily collected so that analysis might be commenced early on in the dissertation cycle.

✻ ✻ ✻

Scratching Around the Gray Path: Managing the Research Process

I soon discovered that lack of training in such methods presented significant difficulties. Like most researchers, I began with a review of the relevant literature. A key difference between obtrusive and unobtrusive research is the significance given to reviewing the literature. For me, the existing scientific literature was not merely a source of facts to be described, but was also an archive to be analyzed and critiqued. A difficulty here was being consistent in my treatment of the literature. Could some literature be viewed as a source of facts and other literature be viewed as an archival source to be analyzed and described? Did I have to be methodologically consistent in terms of how the data were framed? Could a text be simultaneously a source of knowledge and criticism? I had to be reflexive in terms of how I sampled data. How would I locate resources and organize the data?

✻ ✻ ✻

As supervisor, I (Raymond) emphasized the importance of planning and structure in addressing these problems. Goal setting was particularly important. There was no compartmentalization of library research, fieldwork, and analysis. It was important that writing be begun almost immediately, that it be regularly undertaken, and that it involve a process of regular revisions (Chan & Donovan, 2007).

✻ ✻ ✻

What emerged from this process was a disciplined curiosity, which placed limits on that insatiable appetite for everything that can consume the unobtrusive researcher. I engaged in an orientation reading to familiarize myself with each period under question. I had to understand the overall arrangements of thought in the period that shaped experience and social reality: how so-called truth was created by understanding the culture that spawned multiple truths. I had to develop a feel for the epoch, which is best done by drawing on primary documents.

✳ ✳ ✳

I (Raymond) emphasized that it was also important to reread documents. Evidence was to be interpreted by immersion in a temporal and cultural context. I urged John to begin with a preliminary analysis to formulate low-level generalizations. It was important that he adopt an approach that examined the data without having a fixed hypotheses. Instead, I told him that concepts should be developed through a dialogue with the data and that they should be used, little by little, to organize the evidence.

The Student-Supervisor Relationship

As supervisor, I had a hands-off approach. I did not tell John how to carry out his research, but was mindful—and regularly reminded him—of the stages to which he should be alert. This left John with no option but to be self-motivated in the research process, which involved continually evaluating and questioning sources.

✳ ✳ ✳

Raymond refused to tell me how to conduct my research; using his well-honed interrogative techniques, he questioned why I had made particular decisions as to sources, was quietly persistent that I justify why I sourced these and not other resources that appeared equally useful, and questioned the resources' methodological and substantive implications for the thesis. Whenever I was confident in my ability to outline a particular theme and to present supporting evidence, that was just when he would refract the problematic through a different lens.

✳ ✳ ✳

I suggested that John think less about the evidence *(in the sense of momentarily suspending its significance), and that he focus more closely on the parameters of the problematic or theme. As a thought experiment, I asked him, "If the parameters were shifted ever so slightly would you be as confident with the textual materials you have chosen? If not, then what in the sense of abstraction had changed?" The substance of the issue had not changed, but new vantage points might be seen, initial questions could be reformulated, and new avenues explored. Sometimes both of us were surprised with what followed from these ruminations.*

✳ ✳ ✳

In managing these issues, it is worthwhile dwelling for a moment on the student-supervisor relationship. I had a professional relationship with my supervisor in the sense that we had limited social contact outside the context of our student-supervisor relationship. This allowed both of us to be honest and critical with each other regarding the content and direction of the research without secondary influences clouding or limiting our ability to discuss issues in a forthright manner. This was in contrast to other postgraduates I knew who had a more personalized relationship with their supervisors. Although I did not appreciate it at the time, I have since come to see the benefits of this professional relationship. I was certainly encouraged to be independent, and this is important in unobtrusive research that has less social interaction than other forms of research. Indeed, it is a type of research that, beyond the research project, is undertaken by individuals as opposed to obtrusive measures, which are more likely to be conducted by groups. My relationship with Raymond allowed me to develop self-confidence as a researcher.

✳ ✳ ✳

At some indefinable moment, John was no longer my student. He became, in effect, my apprentice colleague. As such, he was called upon to justify and trust his own research judgments, and to take responsibility of own his research.

Editors' Comment

Soliciting Input

Students frequently talk about their solitary research journey. They report feeling alone in unfamiliar terrain, trying to find their way through a confusing forest of multiple paths, some of which seem to lead to dead ends or even to go off cliffs. This feeling of being lost and alone can be considerably lessened by the quality of relationships you develop with mentors and peers. One of the most exciting and constructive stages of the research process is one in which you discuss your findings and challenges with qualified others who offer feedback, provide suggestions, and critique your thinking. It is even valuable to explain what you are doing with friends and family members who can offer their own input based on a more unfiltered perspective.

✳ ✳ ✳

Relating to Texts

Archival and historical research projects are often lonely experiences in which the researcher must develop confidence in his abilities. While there is no recipe with which to counter the isolation of the experience, it is important that there be a high level of engagement with a supervisor, with regular interactions. On another level, fellow students also provide an important avenue for the discussion of ideas and difficulties encountered during the research process. Opportunities should also be taken to present work as it develops, such as in the form of seminars or conference papers.

Unobtrusive methods are asocial forms of research in that they avoid direct encounters in the sense of personal engagements. Again, as Foucault (1992, p. 139) puts it, archival research "is gray, meticulous, and patiently documentary. It operates on a field of entangled and confused parchments, on documents that have been scratched over and recopied many times." Doing a research project originates with a more or less crude formulation of a problematic that is explored through to the refinement of the problematic (the hypothesis).

✶ ✶ ✶

I viewed our sessions as opportunities to draw out ideas, rather than to foist them on John. This was purposeful on my part, which I suspect he sometimes found frustrating. It was important that he begin the research with an open mind and that he assume nothing. To be sure, in the historical and social sciences this is rarely the case. Even so, I encouraged him to question what he saw in the texts, and to justify his interpretation of this or that event.

✶ ✶ ✶

I had to unpack my cultural baggage and rethink my assumptions. In order to do this I questioned everything and assumed nothing. I adopted something of an anthropological approach by which I looked afresh at core assumptions associated with the sex industry and questioned the meaning, relevance, and validity of such assumptions. It was important for me to be reflexive and interrogate and, eventually, to suspend or dispense with my own moral assumptions. I wanted to suspend the tendency to evaluate social phenomena in terms of "good" and "bad" qualities, instead merely describing processes. It is not easy to suspend judgments and was extremely difficult to do so consistently, without resorting to commonly encountered normative assumptions associated with such things as health or sexual behavior. Indeed, these most natural and scientifically scrutinized aspects of social life are often the most culturally loaded. My task was to adopt what might be considered a *relativistic* or *pluralistic* view of matters relating to sexuality or health, digging ever deeper to account for cultural location of core truths relating these areas.

✻ ✻ ✻

It is important to know how to ask questions in order to unravel patterns. It was in this manner that John discovered alternative ways to analyze and prioritize, and to adjudicate empirical evidence with deductive reasoning. Conducting the research project involved discovering how to approach and understand problems in a different way. It required John to shift his position beyond his established range of comfort, to suspend assumptions, and to ask of the archival and textual materials he was dealing with how, legitimately, they might be reconceptualized or repositioned. Occasionally, this resulted not in discord but in disquiet between us.

✻ ✻ ✻

I wanted to include a longish piece on the management of leprosy in the fourteenth century that I had written for an earlier research project. It was a historical narrative that focused on the leper as the morally and spiritually polluted iconic outsider. Raymond asked how this might contribute to a study of prostitution and public health in the nineteenth and twentieth centuries. It clearly fell outside the boundaries of the timeframe. I argued that the historical narrative presumed a continuity between leprosy and the issues of prostitution with which I was concerned. My point, to say the least, was dubious and tenuous.

✻ ✻ ✻

Yes, we soft-shoed around this for six to nine months until, eventually, we reached a compromise. John would scale back the rich historical detail about leprosy per se, and refashion the narrative to focus on the leprosarium as an institution of demarcation between the impure and the pure. I proposed it be included as an appendix to a chapter, or an excursus within a chapter. Ultimately, it appeared as an excursus within a chapter.

✻ ✻ ✻

This is an instance of how the most delicate of issues we had to deal with related to the use of source materials. It was a situation about knowing where to go to find things. Raymond encouraged me to use primary sources, as opposed to secondary sources, for the historical material. If I was inconsistent in my presentation of data, Raymond would question what I had done.

✻ ✻ ✻

A typical issue was taking a primary source, presuming it to be factual, and simultaneously relying on a secondary source to critically deconstruct the primary source through analysis. I insisted John show consistency in his use of data. What rendered a particular text as a source of knowledge and another a source of criticism? Unobtrusive research involves assessing the materials that are available and those that are utilized. This practice constitutes the critical aspect of the research process. Assessments of data were based on issues associated with the representativeness of the data or its uniqueness. Problem analysis is less concerned with issues related to the plausibility, trustworthiness, accuracy of sources, and the concern of empirical historians from von Ranke in the 1830s to Sir George Clark in the 1950s. Empirical histories of this genre assume continuity, the linear unfolding of events, the progression from one state of affairs to a more developed progress, the teleological movement toward a resolved denouncement. Empirical histories of this sort give priority to the civilization of Western humanity as lawlike and "pseudo-naturated" developments. In contrast, John was encouraged to develop an expository approach that explains and analyzes ideas and events within the accompanying frameworks of discursive and genealogical ideas about prostitution.

✷ ✷ ✷

Major Lesson Learned

There are no set recipes for carrying out unobtrusive research. There are no tricks of the trade or magic bullets. Each research topic project presents a unique set of problems that are best understood when contextualized. No two voices are the same. However, there are what might be referred to as languages of unobtrusive research, which can be heard and deciphered. These languages direct the energies of the researcher toward certain methodological problems and issues and, eventually, situate the research within a particular intellectual milieu. As noted, here, methods texts have habitually failed to identify or interpret these languages.

I recognize now that unobtrusive methods cannot be taught or learned in terms of instructions or the provision of rules. Perhaps this is why unobtrusive methods have not been taught readily or effectively. To teach such methods effectively requires dispensing with didactic approaches to learning, and adopting what is sometimes referred to as problem-based models of pedagogy. But that is another story. In terms of my own supervision of graduate students, I have adopted what might be considered a flexible or strategic approach that embraces the uncertainty of unobtrusive methods and the pluralism embedded in their practice.

Conclusion: Comforting Uncertainties

Why had I decided to quit my research project? When writing my first draft, I was not as comfortable with uncertainty as I am now. Now I relish the uncertainty that goes with starting a new project. I enjoy discovering data and being surprised by them. Back in the early stages of my project, though, things were not coming together as quickly as I had been accustomed to expect when using obtrusive methods. It became harder to plan each phase of the research. There were no clearly defined stages to guide me so far as the thesis was anticipated or expected to unfold. It was the second year into my research project and still I did not have the answers I needed. There is a sense of achievement when completing an interview, focus group, or any other form of obtrusive fieldwork, a sense of having accomplished something that is difficult, something that has utility, something that cannot be taken away. This sense cannot be easily found in an archive or a library. There is something less defined and less solid about this kind of enquiry. It is in this sense that ambiguity can engulf the researcher and lead her astray or plague her with doubt. I was both lost and demoralized.

It had dawned on me that my approach lacked consistency. I had not discovered a voice that would distinguish my work and allow me at once both to immerse myself within and to stand above the field I sought to analyze. My supervisor understood this. He suggested that I was too intent telling other people's stories, trying to use their language, and becoming confused in the process. It was as though I was trying to speak for them but struggling to find the words. I had repeatedly attempted to analyze the data I had collected, with mixed results. I was frustrated because so many of my peers seemed to be well advanced in their research. They were doing fieldwork, but I was still reading. They had a sense, and so did I, that I had become bogged down in neverending cycles of literature reviews. My supervisor identified my problem: I had not sufficiently considered method. My approach lacked consistency. I had vacillated between problem solving and problem analysis. Methodologically, it was as though I was trying to write another person's story in two languages, jumping between them in a haphazard fashion. The solution was to go back and write about method. What was my method? This was not easy to formulate.

Too often unobtrusive methods have been neglected in qualitative research. Moreover, this impasse was by no means quickly fixed. Six drafts and six months later a small part of my confidence had been restored. Six years after that, I published my thesis as a book (Scott, 2005). The practice of qualitative methods is grounded in uncertainty. There are no simple or universal recipes, nor are there easy answers to complex ethical or practical dilemmas faced by the researcher. This is as much the case with unobtrusive methods as with any other methods. The critical relationship to be considered with postgraduate research involving unobtrusive methods is often the supervisor-researcher relationship, as opposed to the subject-researcher relationship. Questions relating to how data are sampled and the need for methodological rigueur are important issues for consideration throughout the research process. My first step in addressing these issues was acknowledging that they exist.

References

Benjamin, H., & Masters, R. E. L. (1964). *Prostitution and morality: A definitive report on the prostitute in contemporary society and an analysis of the causes and effects of the suppression of prostitution.* New York: Julian Press.

Bullough, V. L. (1964). *The history of prostitution.* New York: University Books.

Carr, C. H. (1986). *What is history?* London: Penguin.

Chan, L. K., & Donovan, R. (2007). The "social" and "cultural" in graphic design: Case studies from design postgraduate research. *Proceedings of the design education Asia 07,* Hong Kong Polytechnic University. CD-ROM.

Chaney, D. (1994). *The cultural turn: Scene setting essays on contemporary cultural history.* London: Routledge.

Dean, M. (1994). *Critical and effective histories: Foucault's methods and historical sociology.* London: Routledge.

Foucault, M. (1992). Nietzsche, genealogy, history. In D. F. Bouchard (Ed.), *Language, counter-memory, practice: Selected essays and interviews by Michel Foucault* (pp. 139–164). New York: Cornell University Press.

Henriques, F. (1962). *Prostitution and society: Primitive, classical and oriental* (Vol. 1). New York: Grove.

Lee, R. (2000). *Unobtrusive methods in social research.* Milton-Keynes, UK: Open University Press.

Rabinow, P., & Dreyfus, H. (1982). *Michel Foucault: Beyond structuralism and hermeneutics.* Chicago: University of Chicago Press.

Sanger, W. (1939). *The history of prostitution: Its extent, causes and effects throughout the world.* New York: Eugenics Publishing.

Sawicki, J. (1988). Feminism and the power of Foucauldian discourse. In J. Arac (Ed.), *After Foucault: Humanistic knowledge, postmodern challenges* (pp. 161–178). New York: Rutgers University Press.

Schnieder, J. W. (1985). Social problems theory: The constructionist view. *Annual Review of Sociology, 11,* 209–229.

Scott, J. (2003). A prostitute's progress: Male prostitution in scientific discourse. *Social Semiotics, 13,* 179–201.

Scott, J. (2005). *How modern governments made prostitution a social problem: Creating a responsible prostitute population.* New York: Edwin Mellen Press.

Thacker, A. (1997). Foucault and the writing of history. In M. Lloyd & A. Thacker (Eds.), *The impact of Michel Foucault on the social sciences and humanities* (pp. 110–124). London: Macmillan.

Webb, E., Campbell, D. T., Schwartz, R. D., & Sechrest, L. (2000). *Unobtrusive measures* (Rev. ed.). Thousand Oaks, CA: Sage Publications.

Wright Mills, C. (1970). *The sociological imagination.* New York: Oxford University Press.

A Transgender's Qualitative Journey 12

Deconstructing Gender-Based Social Opprobrium

Stacee Reicherzer and Dana L. Comstock

Because I (Stacee) am transgendered, my research on transgender issues emerged from both personal and political agendas. My thesis became a rite of personal passage. In retrospect, what intrigues me most is how I experienced growth in my understanding of myself as a transwoman in the context of doing research about gender-based social opprobrium, while working under the direction of my feminist (and genetic female) mentor. This story is about our connection as women, albeit women with different experiences of womanhood, which grew into a complex relationship that served to support the inception and execution of this research. Along the way, we each experienced opportunities to enrich and expand our collective social justice agendas.

I remember the first time I met Dana on the day I began my master's degree in counseling. I recall her waiting for me at the secretary's desk in the entrance to the department. I had a sense of being really welcomed by her. I am never sure what it is, but I tend to trust an unspeakable clarity that I have at times with certain people. On these occasions, there is a bit of an, "ah yes, there you are!" familiarity that taps some deeper way of knowing.

* * *

I (Dana) was, in fact, anxious to meet Stacee that day and worked hard to present my best self. Stacee was a legend in our department before she even set foot on our campus, having achieved the highest test scores we had ever reviewed.

Before ever meeting her in person, I had begun to strategize ways to encourage her to move immediately into an educational track that would allow her to work toward her doctoral in counseling, rather than stopping with a master's degree. This was the first of many ideas I would pitch to Stacee, the latest of which was the chapter for this text. The theme of my pitching ideas to Stacee has become commonplace in our relationship and is one in which we have learned to negotiate with a great deal of mutual care and respect. This is because of the ongoing overt oppression, harassment, and microaggressions she experiences on a daily basis.

There is nothing understated about Stacee. At our first meeting, I was acutely aware of how striking she was both physically and energetically. Although her long blonde hair and dress were within conventional standards, she was clearly a transwoman. Although she didn't just walk up to me and introduce herself as such, I recall feeling a deep sense of responsibility to provide her with a safe academic environment that would protect her academic freedom and human dignity. In spite of the challenges I was aware of at our first meeting, I was excitedly prepared for us to move forward with our work and our relationship.

* * *

At the time, I had a lot of doubt about my abilities. Perhaps more specifically, I had a great deal of doubt about my worth as a person. Much of my own history of trauma was interwoven in the work I did in my graduate courses and my dissertation. Dana, along with other faculty members, respectfully guided the fallout. My relationship with Dana gave me more than sort of a hand-me-down mentor-student knowledge base. In a very real way, my relationship with Dana became an avenue through which I learned to express, name, and live by my own truth.

Reconstructing Identity Markers

I was born male, which really sucked because I never felt male in any way, especially not in the conventional sense of what it meant to "be a man" in the gender straitjacketed culture of south Texas where I was raised. I experienced tremendous abuse and degradation, both physical and emotional, throughout my adolescence. I started taking hormones at nineteen, and had sexual reassignment surgery (SRS) at twenty-three. That was the best decision for me and really quite an appropriate action.

As challenging as this process was, I now know that I had it pretty easy. I was young, I could pass as a natal female (most of the time, anyway), and I had a career. The psychiatrists who evaluated my candidacy and readiness for SRS coached me on what I needed to believe and tell about myself: I was a woman, I had always been a woman, and because I was male attracted, I was also heterosexual. This is where it becomes interesting: clearly, most of this was completely fabricated. I had not been born female, I had been beaten for being a so-called sissy boy, and now I was supposed to omit this piece of my identity. My instructions were not unusual. In fact, this type of scripting was a common practice at the time for male-to-female transsexuals who sought sexual reassignment. Potential surgical candidates were to think of themselves as women, and had better be male-attracted so that they would be heterosexual after surgery. Those selected for SRS were strongly encouraged to invent stories about their lives growing up as girls and now women.

Given this strong indication of what it meant to have "good mental health" as an emergent heterosexual female, I found myself cut off from the gay and transreference group that had been such an integral part of my identity. My reality became a story of narrow identity markers that included being white, female, and straight. These reference points existed as a complete dichotomy to my lived memories of spit in my face, the word *Fag* written on my high school locker, and the assaults on my body and my spirit that I survived. Yet, because validation as a woman was such an important part of substantiating that I was fit to exist in a culture that had despised me as an effeminate male, and that had no room for a gender experience that existed in some purple space between pink and blue, I accepted my new identity markers with gratitude.

Editors' Comment

Preliminary Concept Development

There is a debate among qualitative researchers that the only valid and genuine conclusions that can emerge are those grounded in the data. Stacee developed quite significant preliminary findings based on our own transgender experiences. Her concepts about *identity markers*, *good mental health*, and *cultural and gender scripts* arose initially from what she had lived.

While such contributions to a study can be valuable and insightful, this preliminary personal reflection can also be obstructive if it limits the researcher's openness to the participant data. For instance, if Stacee assumed that her experiences were necessarily going to mirror those of everyone else, other emerging concepts would remain hidden. It is an interesting finding about human behavior that often the differences within particular groups are greater than those between groups. In other words, transgendered individuals are no more homogeneous in their characteristics and experiences than are Catholics, Latinos, or heterosexual, married men, as examples.

So, here I was, e ight years later, beginning my journey to become a counselor. I was pretty determined by this point that I wanted to work with gay, lesbian, bisexual, and transgender (GLBT) issues because of my awareness of how deep the wounding was for me and for others with similar experiences. Although I was still very invested in my heterosexual female identity, I secretly recognized that my own history held knowledge that was needed for the counseling profession. I was simply uncertain at the time what role any of that would play in my education or career. So, with part altruism and part missionary entitlement to change the world according to my own ideals, I began my doctoral program.

About the time I arrived at the university, Dana had contracted to create a textbook about lifespan development from a Relational-Cultural Theory (RCT) perspective. RCT's (Miller & Stiver, 1997) developmental basis posits that growth-fostering relationships are central human necessities, and that disconnections, both relational and sociopolitical, are sources of psychological problems. Dana needed an author for a chapter she wished to include about GLBT lifespan development that would discuss the complexities and struggles of "coming out and living out across the lifespan" (a phrase that eventually became the title of the piece).

✳ ✳ ✳

I was always aware of, and intrigued by, Stacee's complexity in its many forms. My experience of her is that she was then and continues to be helplessly and thoughtfully authentic. Early in our relationship, I realized that I needed to be cautiously respectful of her, even in the face of the confidence she exuded. I have since come to learn that her overt expressions of stoic self-confidence serve as a protective factor in the event she interacts with others who are uncertain of how to relate to her. This is a stressor I grew to understand, and is one in which she negotiates every day of her life.

At this point, she had not come out to me as a transfemale. Looking back, I was probably sensing some cautiousness in her, which I mirrored. In spite of my reservations, I liked her willingness and eagerness to write and followed her lead by inviting her to write the GLBT chapter for my book.

✳ ✳ ✳

Diving In

As a new counseling student, I had no idea what GLBT issues would look like from the RCT perspective. I also knew very little about the research in these areas, and had no clinical experience. All I really had was my lived experience, and what I knew about the lives of others. While it did not seem like a lot to go on, I was yet to realize how informative my lived experience would be to my journey.

I enthusiastically delved into GLBT mental health texts, journal articles, personal biographies, and historical documents and archives. While this was a relatively small composite body of literature, it was nonetheless meaty and memorable. There was another body of scholarship, however, that would resonate with a deeper part of me. For the purpose of informing my work on the section of the chapter that dealt with the sociopolitical struggle with heterosexism, Dana introduced me to a few specific RCT working papers that brought GLBT issues into a new light.

It's hard to name what exactly happened after being exposed to this work. It was as if, throughout my life, I had been waiting to see or hear something like permission to be. Although I was dissatisfied by the individualistic and overly patriarchal garbage that we read in the classrooms, I wasn't necessarily looking for a theory that fit my ideas about counseling. I was really searching, without knowing it, for permission to bring myself into my work. In the RCT working papers I witnessed therapists and scholars naming their identities as women, mothers, lesbians, and people of color, all for the simple reason that doing so was critical in understanding the context of their work. This led me to a point of inquiry: How would my subjective experience fit into this work? In what significant way could I as a counselor contribute something of value to this profession?

I eventually began my clinical training at the Gay and Lesbian Community Center of San Antonio. This was an interesting time for me because I was encountering *transgender* in a completely different way. I was meeting people that were markedly different from me, people who possessed extraordinary ranges of identifiers and complex convergences of sexuality, gender, class, ethnicity, and physical and mental abilities.

I began to realize how my educational status, professional position, physical health, and the fact that I'd had SRS at a young age were privileges. Having SRS at a young age is a significant privilege marker among transgenders because of the high financial and emotional cost of going through an extensive mental health diagnostic period, medical evaluations, hormone therapies, and surgical procedures. Before I had the opportunity to begin this clinical work, I'd had very little knowledge of or sensitivity to diverse transgendered experiences. This new awareness served as the cornerstone of my initial inquiries regarding potential research questions.

My work with Dana on the chapter for her book interwove with the clinical work I was doing and brought me to some important points. There was a naming of my experience that needed to take place in the work. I wanted people to read the chapter and know that I wasn't just making stuff up. I wanted readers to empathize with me when I talked about hate crimes. Just as I had seen women express their subjectivity and voice in the wonderful stories of lesbian women as counselors, advocates, and theorists in the RCT working papers, I too wanted my subjectivity, my voice. In the spirit of the chapter, I wanted to out myself publicly in my first publication—but I wasn't sure I wanted to pay the price.

From Tears to Truth

I remember the day I went to talk to Dana about my dilemma. I was naming this experience of what I was giving up to out myself as a transwoman in the chapter: my privilege in relative anonymity. I was ambivalent because this meant letting go of a lot of the manufactured identity I was holding. The idea of naming my truth evoked memories of cold, dark hatred. I said to Dana, "I just don't know what I'll do if somebody calls me a 'fag' again." With that, I began to cry.

I was really overwhelmed by my trauma presenting itself in the forefront. I wanted to demonstrate an air of competence to Dana, whom I had come to admire. Not only that—I also liked her. I wasn't sure I was ready for this to be brought into our relationship, but there it was, between us, present in the room as a naked truth.

I looked at her as I was crying and saw that she was crying, too. "Well," she said slowly, "I've taken a lot of risks in my writing, but I have never had to deal with the fear of somebody calling me a 'fag.'" We just embraced. I remember needing to feel held in that space knowing she needed to hold me and be held, too. That moment was pivotal for me; I realized through our connection that I was a person, worthy of voice, worthy of protest, worthy of human dignity and respect. At that point I did the only thing I could do: I said, "Screw it!" and named myself as trans in my chapter.

✳ ✳ ✳

That was a tough moment. On one hand, I felt a degree of guilt for pitching the idea of the chapter that ultimately served as the impetus for her coming out in her work. On the other hand, though, I was really excited about the direction she had chosen to take her writing and career. I had worked with other students regarding their coming out in relation to their professional lives, but this was different. I didn't fully understand the risks for Stacee or even my own responsibility until I became aware of the trauma she'd endured while growing up after reading the first draft of her chapter.

What was haunting for me was during that pivotal conversation she shared through her tears: "I had just wanted to live a quiet life as a heterosexual woman in suburbia." Indeed, she would be giving up a lot, and much of what she was sacrificing were privileged aspects of my own life. It was in that moment that I knew that for our own relationship to continue to grow we'd have to acknowledge and work through our differences as women, rather than pretend they didn't exist.

✳ ✳ ✳

Our shared vulnerability really moved us into something. We seemed to inspire each other. We'd start going talking about our work and our lives. A real bond was being built. There was so much I was learning in our relationship and so much was occurring in that connection for me. I was growing as a professional, and really loving that I started to feel a sense of belonging, simply as I was.

Beginning the Dissertation Process

The emphasis of my SRS as a source of privilege was being brought home to me by the continued discussions I was hearing in the trans community, as well as what my clients directly said to me. There was a great deal of anger and mistrust of the mental health profession. The source of this anger related to the mental health profession's lack of effort to ensure awareness of trans issues among its professionals; the pathologizing language used in work with transgenders, from the Gender Identity Disorder diagnosis to the use of incorrect pronouns; and the expectation of professionals that transgenders should teach them about gender issues.

The granddaddy of all points of contention (patriarchal symbolism intended) was the power that mental health professionals held in determining readiness for hormone replacement therapy and candidacy for SRS. I found myself experiencing a lot of curiosity and confusion about this contention and wanted to know what was really going on for transgenders that made the issue of mental health such a source of controversy. My curiosity led me to begin a review of the literature. This review became one of the first steps of my dissertation process.

It was interesting that two distinct bodies of literature seemed to exist. There were the cold, hard, mental health studies that used medical terminology of "patients" with "disorders" and "disturbances." The pronouns were all wrong to me. I felt marginalized by the literature, which called male-to-female transsexuals "he." There was no respect or care about our gender experiences. Interestingly, I wasn't the first to identify the existing body of mental health literature as hurtful. This would become apparent when I read the second major body of transgender literature: the biographies of transgenders themselves.

Revealed by my research, in vivid and horrible accounts, was a collective story of historical social opprobrium and neglect by the mental health community: the study of so-called sissy boys (Green, 1987); the public humiliation of model and actress Carolyn Cossey (1992), who had appeared in the James Bond film *For Your Eyes Only* and was discovered to be transgender following the release of the movie, and who was abused in therapy; and the distortion that is often made in the field in which transgenders are often described as having a "disorder."

Moving Forward

As I delved deeper, I became agitated. I was angry, helpless, disgusted, and betrayed by the awful and destructive body of research that referred to transsexuals as "sick" research subjects. The full force of social justice came to my work. As I continued to construct my literature review, I unapologetically exposed the cruelty and ineptitude of the profession through the juxtaposition of the mental health profession's research with the lived statements that transgenders made of their experiences in subverting this.

In the method section of my dissertation, I discussed myself as a researcher much the way I did in the chapter I had written. I acknowledged that the research was, in part, a subjective reflection that served to give voice to extremely marginalized individuals. There was no way around it: I was living what I was reading. What they were calling a sickness and the biased studies they used to back up their nonsense was about *me*. They used their power and privilege as mental health professionals to pronounce what was "sick" and what was "well" about gender and then referred to the whole mess as "objective."

Frankly, I do not think I could have conducted such intensely evocative research without Dana. This is the point at which I know that many educators, living in some myth in which research is supposed to be strictly objective, would have protested, and forced me to write the document without naming the intensity of my emotional interaction with the literature. Instead, Dana joined me in my anger. We spent plenty of time in her office indulging in a collective rage in response to the silencing and invisibilizing that had occurred. At the same time, we were philosophical.

We had wonderful, even-tempered discussions about power in our culture, gender straitjacketing, and the arrogance and bias that was in the literature. We reflected on how this played out in each of our own lives as women, albeit women with different gender lenses. We were moved by each other's experiences and perspective, we connected, we felt a shared pain, and we healed. Most importantly for the work, we used our anger to take it in the direction that it needed to go.

Creating a Socially Just Research Methodology

Marginalized groups have valid reasons to be angry about maltreatment. In fact, this is an understatement. Dana and I both recognized that the mental health professional practices with transgenders emerged from and ultimately perpetuated a limited and constricted worldview of gender. This is what Foucault (1965, 1972) called an *episteme:* there are limits to knowledge and conceptualization in every sociohistorical period. Foucault posited that there is not only a limit to science, but also a limit to philosophy. There have been strict boundaries that can now be crossed.

Concept was also key. My review of the literature revealed there was clearly a need for a new conceptual understanding of transgenders. What was missing was a consideration of the complex experiences of transgenders that involved the confluence of identity markers experienced in a cultural context of individualism, gender binarism, and heterosexism. There was certainly no conceptualization of how white supremacy and misogyny further complicated things. Finally, the mental health profession's reinforcement of gender binarism through a narrow system of diagnosis was not being addressed.

* * *

It is important to emphasize that as Stacee and I came to an agreement about the need for something to be done regarding the maltreatment of transgenders we partnered, in a sense, in her literature review and spent many hours dialoging about her findings. The collaborative nature of qualitative research calls for the research advisor to invest time and interest in every phase of the student's research activity. This might also mean that there needs to be some shared interest in the topic if the research advisor is going to feel motivated and interested in meeting the student's individual needs and her respective relationship to her area of study.

* * *

Something was needed so that we could conceive of a completely new way of thinking about gender. We needed to push the boundaries of the current gender episteme. Better yet, we needed a radical reconceptualization of gender. We needed a new gender episteme that would be grounded in the stories of people who lived the experiences of gender diversity. We needed it to reconceptualize how transgenders experience mental health practices. We decided we would get this new gender episteme from interviewing transgenders about what they had experienced from the mental health profession, and, more importantly, how they would want the mental health profession to treat them.

Hearing and Holding the Voices of the Invisible

Having obtained approval by the institutional review board, I needed next to approach the participants. There is a distinct advantage to being a part of a community when trying to access participants for this type of study. There is, first, knowledge of where and how to find participants, which is challenging for all researchers working with diffuse, marginalized, and otherwise invisible populations.

There is also the issue of trust: I would be conducting the interviews, at least in part, as a representative of a profession that has functioned as the lapdog of an oppressive culture that holds the pathologization of trans-genders in place. I would be approaching a group of people who were painfully aware of the diagnosis as well as the standards of care (Meyer et al., 2001) for diagnosis and treatment that required a mental health evaluation. In the midst of this awareness, I contacted the coordinator of a local transgender support group.

One of the things I do when faced with stressful situations is to create a lot of anxiety in myself by preparing for worst-case scenarios. I was relieved that when I attended the group to invite members to participate in my dissertation research I was lovingly received. Some even volunteered to tell friends so that I would have a wide sample of birth-assigned males and birth-assigned females. The reception I received told me a lot about voice: People wanted to participate in an experience in which they would be heard. I also sensed a desire to support me, a sister, in the work I was doing for all of us.

As evocative as the literature review had been for me, my interviews were even more so. People told stories of exploitation—male-to-female participant: "They asked me if I ever masturbated as a male and enjoyed it, because if I had I did not qualify for surgery." They told of erasure—female-to-male participant: "In twelve years of therapy in which I said repeatedly that I had never felt like a woman, nobody, *nobody*, helped me identify that I was a transsexual." And they told of degradation—male-to-female participant: "The counselor I went to at the college said to me 'You want to be a woman? You would be a really ugly woman.'"

Editors' Comment

Studying Marginalized Groups

One strength of qualitative research is the way it can help scholars to access phenomena and human experiences that might otherwise be difficult to grasp. The focus of the investigation is on the perspective of the other, giving the person's experiences a voice that is often suppressed. It isn't surprising that a literature search of qualitative studies reveals a consistent theme of exploring subjects that are considered forbidden and unconventional, and that are often ignored. Going all the way back to the earliest roots of qualitative methodology found in symbolic interactionism, the subjects investigated considered underground life in the black ghetto, the subculture of marijuana use, police brutality, homelessness, prostitution, suicide, poverty, and immigrants. Stacee's own study perfectly matches her methodology because it also deals with a subject that has been rarely discussed in an open and authentic way.

Sometimes, I was unable to process or believe what I'd heard until after I'd play back the tapes while reading the transcriptions. I remember going into Dana's office with a lot of what I'll call *verbosity*: "You're not going to believe what the son-of-a-bitch told her!" and showing her these scathing transcripts. Although I'd been angry and helpless during the literature review, these feelings were honored in my relationship with Dana. Looking back, I now realize my participants and their stories were also being held.

The experience of analyzing the interviews served as a sort of corrective relational experience in which my sister- or brother-participant, my sister-mentor, and I were healing from some of the hurt we had all experienced in a culture that separates everyone into artificial, divisive, controlling, and fear-based gender categories. We had cocreated a space for healing.

My participants grew through the invitation to voice their grievances to me, a transgender sister and counselor. I grew through the awareness of myself as a person who held relationship between all of us; in this way, I was healed, expanded, strengthened, and actualized through the fluidity of these connections in my life.

The Challenges of Categorizing a Sea of Complexity

In organizing the hundreds of pages of transcribed data, the traditional grounded theory method involves a process of coding into progressively larger themes that link together. The concept of categorization, given all of the complex relationships that were involved here, did not seem to fit neatly together in the way that I'd imagined they should. Blocking our way were the culture of marginalization and the system of mental health diagnosis. In addition, Dana and I as counselors experienced relational healing alongside the participants. The study and experience in its entirety was about relationships and context. I needed to create a language that captured the complexities of the results, and to categorize it all into progressively larger groupings of narratives.

Again, I didn't do this alone. Dana and I would conceptualize ("they both seemed to have said something that feels like this"), and then I would relate it back to the participants' voices to check in around various themes. I don't think this process would have happened as effectively had we not had the kind of relationship and history that we shared. Ultimately, what emerged was a process of analysis and experience that is more complex than what is traditionally thought of as *triangulation* in qualitative research.

My fear along the way was always, always of doing something wrong. Part of representing anything that's a departure from a traditional academic model is the awareness of heightened scrutiny that occurs, particularly for a person from a marginalized group who was, in turn, representing that group. As passionate and committed as Dana and I were to it, I feared that it was going to be rejected by another committee member, or worse yet, by the graduate dean.

Was it truly a grounded theory? It seemed like it to me, but I continued to worry that somebody in a position of power, somewhere in the process, was going to reject it. What would that mean? A denial of our truth? A silencing of our voices? What form, I wondered, would heterosexism, gender-binarism, and the myth of objectivity take in silencing me now? Every trauma trigger I had ever had was being activated. My research, I realize now, was a source of worth, and a lot of my complex experiences of trauma and marginalization were tied in to this.

Dana and I dealt with my anxiety, and our relationship was, once again, a source of comfort and reassurance. We talked a lot about the fears I had, and my need for reassurance about the legitimacy of my research. I needed it to matter and be of some worth to academia and to the profession.

✻ ✻ ✻

My relationship with Stacee was unique in that I had high expectations of a student who had proven, in my opinion, her capabilities before she'd even arrived on campus. But I did understand her lack of self-esteem because of the trauma she had endured, much of which I learned about during our time together. On a serendipitous note, my work with Stacee came at a time when I had become increasingly involved with the Human Dignity and Humiliation Studies Organization, a global network of scholars and researchers whose collective goal is to eradicate forms of humiliation around the globe (www.humiliationstudies.org).

In my work with this group, I had become increasingly aware of the global impact of humiliation and how it is used to incite fear, to silence, to control, and to wreak violence on interpersonal and international levels. I had become particularly aware of the role of humiliation in educational settings, including higher education. My interactions with Stacee were structured, and continue to be structured, in such a manner that I literally step out and into her world with her. That sometimes means I endure the occasional threatening stares of curious onlookers by virtue of affiliation. But most importantly, my encouragement of her and her work was always done with a sincere belief in the importance of promoting human dignity. This sometimes meant I challenged oppressive practices inherent in the so-called rite of passage of the dissertation process.

When, indeed, she vetoed requests by others to try to make the research sound more objective, when she stymied requests to rework a concept at which I had legitimately arrived, when she ultimately held the final piece together and said, "Don't change a damned thing," she was doing so in love and out of respect for the work that served as a demonstration of our connection and our mutual commitment to the promotion and preservation of human dignity for all people.

As I was walking down the hall and into the room where she waited to begin to defend her dissertation, I was stopped by another committee member who animatedly suggested she didn't have enough participants for her dissertation research to be grounded theory. I instructed this committee member to address the question to Stacee, and then stepped around this individual to make my way into the defense. After Stacee completed her defense, the issue was never brought up again. I later heard this faculty member had boasted to a research class that, "My role in our department is to keep the faculty 'honest.'"

I learned many things from this experience. One lesson is that the notion of triangulation *doesn't quite capture the full relational context or relational direction from which qualitative research data emerge. I believe that if researchers adhere to the idea of the results only being circular in nature, then there is the paradoxical potential to restrict the protocol for the collection and analysis of data.*

I also learned that categorizing data could perpetuate, in a very subtle way, our culture's need for separateness and individualism. If researchers aren't careful, there is the potential to illegitimize a broad range of equally important findings that can come to light from this methodology, many of which are the impetus for social change and human rights advocacy. For example, Stacee's research did not simply uncover the maltreatment of transgenders by the mental health community, but she also (a) composed a comprehensive history of transgenders that did not previously exist, (b) created a new gender episteme that indeed deconstructs the power and pathos of mental health diagnostics for transgenders, and (c) illuminated a system of gender binarism that has implications for human development and humankind.

By only appreciating that the researcher has "answered their research question(s)," other equally important aspects of the research can potentially be devalued much in the same way hierarchies are constructed and maintained in the larger culture. With all the important findings that emerged from Stacee's research, it makes sense she would experience her work as subversive and vulnerable to being dismissed. I have learned that the very potential for this to happen speaks to the need for researchers to join together, not only to pool their expertise, but also to find creativity and courage in connection.

✳ ✳ ✳

Conclusion

Reflecting on this experience now, a year and a half later, I am very much aware of how the relationship supported me in this process. While I realize in rereading this that it sounds and feels like a love story, in a sense it is. I don't mean that, though, in an inappropriate way. My point is that my mentor and I both recognize that I am a part of a maligned and misunderstood culture—and that I have never not been part of that culture. In approaching graduate school, I really did not believe in my legitimate right to earn a doctorate, let alone a career in academia. Thus, speaking extensively about my relationship with Dana is essential to understanding what made this possible. To say she empowered me would be cliché. In truth, she joined me as a sister in struggle who held the same level of passion for my research that I did.

References

Cossey, C. (1992). *My story.* Winchester, MA: Faber & Faber.

Foucault, M. (1965). *Madness and civilization: A history of insanity in the Age of Reason.* New York: Random House.

Foucault, M. (1972). *The archaeology of knowledge.* New York: Random House.

Green, R. (1987). *The "sissy boy syndrome" and the development of homosexuality.* New Haven, CT: Yale University Press.

Meyer, W., Cohen-Kettenis, P., Coleman, E., Diceglie, D., Devor, H., Gooren, L., et al. (2001, January–March). Harry Benjamin International Gender Dysphoria Association's: The standards of care for gender-identity disorders (6th version). *International Journal of Transgenderism, 5.* Retrieved June 5, 2005, from http://www.symposion.com/ijt/soc_2001/index.htm.

Miller, J., & Stiver, I. (1997). *The healing connection: How women form relationships in therapy and in life.* Boston: Beacon Press.

Lessons From My First Focus Group Project

13

Suzanne Lunn and Larry Smith

"It really doesn't matter how well you are capable of doing a job if you can't convince the employer to hire you in the first place." These words were spoken by my (Sue's) 18-year-old niece, Rosie. Along with three of her friends, we were chatting over lunch at a local McDonald's about the difficulties and frustration facing school graduates who simply want to get a job rather than go on to further study at a university or technical college.

I work as a policy officer for the nongovernment school sector in Queensland, Australia, and the discussion I was having with my niece and her friends was one I had heard many times in recent months. The high school curriculum in Australia now provides significant job-specific preparation for students who do not wish, for whatever reason, to go on to further study. The curriculum, for example, allows students in their final two years of schooling to gain foundation certificates from local technical colleges in a range of trade areas such as hospitality, tourism, hairdressing, and office administration. Nevertheless, statistics reveal that more than two-thirds of young Australians seeking to enter the workforce straight from school still do not have permanent employment six months later, irrespective of how well they did at school or what job-specific knowledge and skills they possess.

"Someone should do something about it," Rosie mumbled through a mouthful of Big Mac. "Exactly," I thought, "and that someone should be me."

Defining a Project

Well, now I was committed—absolutely determined in fact—to do something that would help young school graduates have a better chance of gaining sustainable employment. The problem was, however, that my knowledge about the issue was superficial, and I had absolutely no idea what it was that I might actually do to improve the situation for the graduates. "One step at a time," I said to myself. "First, find out what you can about the area."

Over the next six months, I read everything I could about job skills and youth employment. I spent weeks trawling the Internet, particularly Google Scholar, and hours and hours sifting through documents in university and public libraries. I read books, journal and newspaper articles, and government reports that had been written by academics, employers, union officials, employees, journalists, and politicians. I took copious notes, and at last I began to have a pretty good handle on the employment skills bucket. I knew the statistics, I knew the government policies, and I knew what the major issues were. What I found quite amazing, however, was that—except at a very superficial level—I had not unearthed research or opinion that provided any real direction about what could be done to address the problem that Rosie and her friends had so clearly articulated. It seemed that I was facing a brick wall. I needed a lot of help to move forward on my mission, but had little understanding of exactly what help it was I needed or where I could find it. Frustration was quickly leading to dejection, and I thought about letting the whole thing drop.

"You should enroll to do research at a university, and get yourself a supervisor who has a strong track record in this area. Let the supervisor mentor you through your project." My friend Robbie, always the pragmatic one, gave me the direction I needed. Until then, I hadn't thought about doing my research through a university—it was almost twenty years since I did my last study at postgraduate level. But Robbie's suggestion hit a chord. This would give me the strong mentorship I needed to pursue my goal, and completing a doctoral qualification along the way would not be without its advantages in terms of furthering my career.

✳ ✳ ✳

When Sue contacted me (Larry), she was bubbling over with enthusiasm and ideas for her research. She clearly had read widely around the topic of employability skills, and had a good understanding of the major issues and concepts. The problem, however, was that she was still at the wide end of the funnel: she was trying to include virtually everything she had read and thought about. Consequently, as a researcher with limited time and resources, she had little chance of addressing any one of the important employability issues at the depth needed to make a significant difference in the field. She needed priority and focus, as well as an acceptance that a lot of issues that she considered important might need to be put aside for later.

✻ ✻ ✻

Larry initially gave me just one task to do. I was to think about the situation a few years from then, after I had finished my project. I was to imagine someone asking, "What was your study about?" I was to frame my answer to that question in just one sentence, starting with the words: "This study is about. . . ." This seemingly simple task proved to be amazingly difficult. I tried a paragraph rather than a sentence, and got sent away to try again. I tried constructing the world's longest sentence: again, Larry sent me away. Then I tried using terms that were as broad and encompassing as possible, and recoiled to a verbal volley from Larry of, "focus, focus, focus." "What specifically did your study achieve?" Larry kept repeating. Eventually, my sentence read, "This study is about identifying the set of knowledge, skills, and attitudes required by school graduates if they are to maximize their access to and successful participation in the workforce."

Editors' Comment

Defining Moments

A defining moment in any project is when you settle on a working definition of the research topic. This is so critical because, initially, you are all over the place. Whatever enthusiasm drives the work is drowned in the apprehensions and anxiety about key questions: What can you possibly offer that is original? How can you possibly make up for your internal doubts and feelings that you don't know enough? What happens when your instructors find out your secret about how ignorant and unprepared you feel? These concerns are all part of the journey.

Whatever plan you think you have, whatever study you think you have conceived so well, you can be certain that things will change once you immerse yourself deeply into the work. This is the best and worst part of the experience. You have to learn to live with this complexity and ambiguity until things begin to come into clearer focus.

In hindsight, getting that single sentence sorted was one of the most important steps I took during my research. It made it very clear to me what I was trying to do, and in turn what questions I needed to answer in order to achieve the goal I had set myself. Just as importantly, it made it clear what I was not doing, so I was able to make the distinction between what was important and relevant, and what was important but not relevant to my current project.

Choosing the Method

"Choosing your research method," Larry told me, "is about identifying the most effective and efficient way of collecting the information that you need, in the forms that you need it, within the constraints of your own expertise and available resources." Once again, I started to doubt my capacity to complete the project. The reality was that I had little money, little time (I was working full time), and, in my view, little expertise as a researcher. Had I bitten off way more than realistically I could chew?

✳ ✳ ✳

It was at this stage that Sue articulated major doubts about her capacity to be a researcher. In particular, she was concerned that the research she had conducted up to that point lacked methodological rigor, that what research experience she had was almost exclusively qualitative, and that in the field she had really only used three research approaches: document analysis, survey, and face-to-face interviews. My advice to her was that before worrying about which research method was one in which she did or did not have expertise, she should address the question of which research method (or methods) was most appropriate for collecting the information she needed. It may be, I told her, that the most appropriate research method was one with which she already had experience or expertise, or one that could be learned quickly, given her existing research strengths.

✳ ✳ ✳

The information I needed was the knowledge, skills, and attitudes that school graduates would need to possess and demonstrate when they applied for a job or attended a job interview. It seemed obvious to me that the best source of that information, along with a review of the literature, would be the ideas, opinions, and perspectives of a selection of people who had relevant, direct, and recent experience around the issue. Suddenly, I started to be confident again about my study. I was well aware that written surveys and face-to-face interviews were the most widely used research methods for collecting people's opinions, perspectives, and ideas—and these were techniques I had often used in my work for the nongovernment schools.

The question I now faced was which was best: written surveys, face-to-face interviews, or a combination of the two. I quickly dismissed written surveys for two reasons derived from my previous experiences: First, return rates from survey questionnaires, particularly in the education sector where there is always someone wanting yet another questionnaire completed, tend to be very low. Furthermore, return rates from at least some stakeholder groups are sometimes zero. Second, surveys tend to collect broad-brush information, but don't assist deep exploration of many of the ideas and issues raised by respondents. Face-to-face interviews, in my experience, provide a way of overcoming both these problems: the researcher negotiates interviews to ensure all stakeholder groups are represented, and can probe the answers given by respondents at whatever depth necessary to ensure that the richest possible information is collected. Admittedly, one can sample many more people with a written questionnaire than by interviews, but the need in my project for rich information far outweighed any concerns about the number of respondents.

Then, in the middle of all this debating with myself about the most appropriate research method, I had a big win that largely overcame my other major concern—where to find sufficient money to support my research. The Queensland State Government announced funding for a research project to develop curriculum strategies and prepare students better for the workforce. I was the first to volunteer to undertake the research, and soon after was invited to be the senior research officer for the project. I quickly sought and was granted permission from the relevant authorities to use the project as the basis for my university study. This meant that not only was my study well resourced financially, but also that I could continue to use my supervisor to mentor me through all aspects of the journey in front of me. The government funding, however, was short term, and thus I was locked into a fairly tight timeline for collecting and analyzing the information for their purposes.

Editors' Comment

Trial and Error

This is another defining moment in Sue's journey, when she struggled to work out the fine details of her method. In your own study, you may have settled on a sampling procedure, recruitment technique, interview guide, and method of data analysis, but these are general decisions that must be further refined as you proceed. Suzanne is describing how she's working out the pragmatic realities in the execution of the plans. For example, she secured approval for her study by a government authority but then discovered she also needed the consent of individual participants who also had to be convinced that this study was worthwhile.

It is only through experimentation that you can find what appears to be the best combination of strategies specific to your desired goals. All methodologies are basic recipes that have to be improvised and improved with your preferred ingredients.

Now I had my funding and I had my research method—at least that is what I thought. I put together a list of the people I thought I needed to interview and why, and made another appointment to see Larry.

✳ ✳ ✳

It was an extremely enthusiastic Sue who arrived in my office. I had no major problems with her decision to use interviews as the basis for her research. She had thought the issue through, was comfortable that she had the expertise to use the method, and had considered the strengths and weaknesses of the alternatives. She did not seem to have considered, however, that interview methods are not just confined to one-on-one face-to-face encounters with a list of relevant stakeholders. With respect to her particular study, I considered there was at least one major concern about using a one-on-one approach to interviewing that she needed to think carefully about. "It is almost certain," I said, "that you are going to get significantly different perspectives from people around the same issues. How are you going to find a resolution to those differences? How are you going to decide whose views are the more or less appropriate and potentially productive? How are you going to use a plethora of diverse views to decide on your definitive set of knowledge, skills, and attitudes?"

Sue thought for some time, and proposed a number of solutions that she herself quickly discounted. Finally, she looked at me and said, "Instead of interviewing people separately, couldn't I bring them together into a single place at the same time so that each can express his views in front of the others, and in turn be challenged by the other participants about the strengths and weaknesses of what they have to say?"

"In your own way," I told her, "you have just defined what focus group methodology is all about. It is time for you to do some more reading."

✳ ✳ ✳

Selecting the Members of the Focus Group

Before addressing the issue of which individuals should be invited to be the members of the focus group, my first step was to identify the desirable set of knowledge and experience that the focus group, holistically, should possess. I set aside a white board and, over a period of a fortnight, wrote down every idea that came to me, no matter how seemingly trivial or irrelevant. Larry said this process is commonly called *brainstorming*. I then reviewed my list, identifying ideas as *critical, useful,* or *of little value.* I crossed off the ideas of *little value.* I then considered each of the *useful* ideas, making a hard decision about whether to keep or remove each of them. As a result of this process, I determined that members of the focus group should collectively demonstrate knowledge, skill, understanding, and experience with respect to

- contemporary and emerging workplace culture and operations,
- industrial relations,
- workplace health and safety,
- career planning
- personal development,
- interpersonal relations,
- systems thinking,
- critical thinking and foresight,
- student learning principles and processes,
- relevant legal and legislative issues, and
- current and emerging education and training systems and issues.

Sue now believed she was ready to contact a range of government and nongovernment agencies and organizations to ask for representative participants for her focus group. "Hold on," I told her, "there are a couple of very important things to think about before you start contacting people to be on your focus group. First, how many people do you want in your focus group? At what size will the group be too large to ensure robust discussion and debate? At what size will it be too small, such that there is insufficient diversity of opinion or individuals might feel they are being put too much in the spotlight? In particular, what will you do if the ideal size is smaller than the number of groups you want to be represented? Second, are you happy to have anyone from those groups on your focus group? Is representativeness the only key criterion for membership, or do you also want people who are prepared to engage in debate, who think creatively, and who can provide innovative ideas and perspectives? If so, how are you going to attract such people to your group?"

Larry challenged me to determine the optimal size for the focus group. This was a question I could not answer, because I had no previous experience with group interviews, so I turned to the literature. Highly experienced focus group practitioners such as Fern (2001), Kamberelis and Dimitriadis (2005), and Stewart, Shamdasani, and Rook (2007) gave a consistent message: focus groups ideally should consist of six to twelve members in order to ensure maximum interaction and input among all members of the group. The dilemma, of course, was how to identify six to twelve creative individuals with appropriate expertise from across the wide range of stakeholder groups that I believed should be represented. My process for identifying the group was to seek recommendations for focus group membership from key contacts I had in the school sector, employer associations, industrial unions, and relevant professional associations. When seeking these recommendations, I stressed that I was not only seeking individuals with high-level expertise, but also—in line with Larry's second consideration—seeking individuals who had a demonstrated reputation as innovative or lateral thinkers.

This process identified eleven potential focus group members. I then contacted each potential group member by telephone, and invited each to become a member of the focus group. I was delighted that ten of the eleven people accepted my invitation, and that when I crosschecked the demonstrated knowledge, skill, and experience of these people, they collectively covered my previously identified set of desirable attributes for the focus group.

The telephone calls were then followed by a letter detailing the processes to be followed before, during, and after the focus group session, and what would be expected of each person throughout that time. Accompanying the letter was a set of relevant reading materials summarizing the key findings from current research studies in the area of the transition from school to work.

Preparing the Venue

✳ ✳ ✳

It has been my consistent personal experience of group work, strongly supported by the literature, that the physical environment has a significant influence on the extent to which individuals will be free and open in discussion, as well as on the nature and productiveness of the interactions that will occur among the group. "Think very carefully about the venue you choose for the focus group," I told Sue, "and about how you set up that venue. Think about things such as the amount of light, outside noise levels, room temperature and ventilation, room size, the distance between seats, and the size, shape, and arrangement of tables."

✳ ✳ ✳

For the focus group session, I hired a small conference room in a hotel, thus minimizing the distractions for participants of their regular workplaces. The room was large enough to ensure participants would not feel that their personal space was being crowded, but small enough that they would not be intimidated by the amount of open space around them. It was bright and airy, carpeted, away from most vehicle and pedestrian traffic, and was equipped with an electronic whiteboard and photocopying facilities. I arranged the tables into a circular configuration so that all members of the focus group would have the capacity for continuous eye contact. Seating was arranged with a distance of approximately four feet between participants to ensure that personal space would not be invaded.

ROLE AS FOCUS GROUP LEADER

✳ ✳ ✳

"The basic purpose of the focus group leader," I told Sue, "is to provide the necessary level of direction and structure to ensure the desired outcome of the focus group session is met within the time available. This means maintaining a certain level of control over the nature and amount of discussion during the session. It is important to remember, however, that you must not allow yourself to become a participant in that discussion, except to stimulate further discussion or to probe ideas further. Above all, you must not assert your views or perspectives on the group."

✳ ✳ ✳

To begin the session, I provided a short overview of the purpose of the focus group, what we hoped to achieve by the end of the session, and the processes and procedures we would follow during the day. I then asked all the members in turn to provide their names, to talk briefly about themselves and their professional backgrounds, and to say what they believed their contributions would be to the session. My reason for this was to create a trusting and informal atmosphere for the session. I also sought and received permission to record the session so that I was not personally distracted by having to take notes when I should be actively listening and engaging participants.

Moving clockwise around the group, I asked each participant to identify just one skill, attitude, or component of knowledge that she believed school graduates should possess if they are to maximize their access to and successful participation in the workforce. I had one group member record each idea put forward on the electronic whiteboard. Group members could then seek clarification, indicate their support, or put forward arguments about why the idea should not be included. A group vote was then taken on whether to accept or reject the idea.

Once everyone had put forward one idea, the process was repeated in a round robin style until no further new items could be identified. By then, through a rigorous process of definition, clarification, and debate, I had accumulated a set of twenty-five skills, attitudes, and knowledge components that young people needed to access employment. I had achieved the outcome I had set myself for the project.

SOME IMPORTANT GROUP PROCESS ISSUES

✻ ✻ ✻

"There are four important process issues that will almost certainly arise during the focus group session," I told Sue, "and for which you should have prearranged strategies: ensuring that some participants do not dominate discussion, ensuring that even the quietest of participants actively engages in discussion, managing time of the discussions to ensure you cover all issues in the available time, and avoiding miscommunication of issues and ideas."

✻ ✻ ✻

I used, with overt success, three strategies developed from the literature for minimizing the extent to which the more confident and outgoing of participants dominated discussion. First, I ensured they were seated to my side rather than directly opposite me. This minimized the extent to which they could dominate my attention through eye contact. Second, I frequently interrupted what they were saying to redirect the issue to other members of the group for comment and confirmation. Third, I used the most dominant member of the group to record ideas on the whiteboard, thereby intermittently extracting that person from the discussion circle.

In order to encourage quieter individuals to contribute, I simply ensured that questions were frequently directed to them, such as, "What do you think about that, Mary?" "Could you explain that a little further?" "Could you give us an example of that?" "Why did you think that?" Initially, more reserved members of the group seemed a little intimidated by being challenged in this way, but the more that they found that their ideas were being highly valued, the more they warmed to this approach and the greater became the level and frequency of their involvement.

I found no magic strategies in the literature for determining when to cut off discussion around an issue, and did not come up with any significant ideas of my own either. Nevertheless, I did find that as more and more issues were discussed, my confidence grew in making a subjective judgment about when to cut off discussion. Perhaps the strategy for time management of a focus group simply is to accumulate as much experience as possible.

In a focus group, it is extremely important to be sure that the message that participants believe they are communicating to you is the same as the message that you believe that you are receiving. In order to avoid miscommunication, I used the four-part strategy described by Fern (2001): clarifying ("Could you please state that point in a different way?"), paraphrasing ("What I heard you say was . . ."), reflecting ("You appear to feel that . . ."), and summarizing ("Your major points appear to be . . ."). I found this technique extremely effective, as did the focus group members who praised the approach in their written evaluation of the session that they completed at the end of the day.

Editors' Comment

Authentic Disclosure

We admire Sue's honesty in talking about her feelings of inadequacy and self-doubt related to undertaking her research project. This is not only an expected and normal part of any journey into the unknown, but is also the reason why you would begin this process. You are supposed to be confused, overwhelmed, uncertain, and even anxious as you delve into areas for which you don't feel sufficiently prepared. One of the outcomes of completing a qualitative research study is that you will increase your tolerance for ambiguity and living with uncertainty.

Key Messages From the Research

I have spent a lot of time reflecting on my initial journey into the field of group interview research. My diary is full of all the different things that I believe I learned through the experience, but if asked to identify the five most important things I learned, they would be these:

1. Be passionate about your topic and what completing it will achieve. I would have thrown in the towel many times if I hadn't believed that what I was doing was so necessary and important.

2. Don't try to force a method to fit your topic. Choose the most appropriate method for the topic you are addressing and the information that you need to collect.

3. Choose your supervisor carefully, and then trust your supervisor to help you complete your journey, no matter how enormous the task in front of you may seem.

4. Value the strength of group processes, and the unique and important perspectives and insights that can be achieved through having appropriate people engage in focused group conversation.

5. Think before you act. Be sure of what it is you intend to do, and why you intend to do it, before you do it. Consider the strengths and weaknesses of alternatives, and plan strategies for addressing the various contingencies that might arise.

The best thing to come out of my first rigorous exposure to qualitative research, however, was the confidence I had about my own capacity to do research. When I look back, I really can't believe I went ahead with the study—I was so full of self-doubt when I took the plunge and committed myself to the research. The guidance and support of my supervisor certainly helped develop my self-belief, and got me through the troughs when doubt and despair seemed to engulf me, but above all it was the sense of achievement I got each time I successfully completed a phase of the study or found a solution to a methodological problem that most developed my confidence. I know I still have a long way to go to be a proficient researcher, but my experiences in that first project have given me the confidence to continue the journey.

✳ ✳ ✳

My major message to Sue was to approach each new research project as a major learning experience. "Realize that good researchers are experienced researchers," I told her, "and that you have only just set out on that experiential journey. Your confidence will grow as you confront more and more research issues, and find satisfactory solutions to them. Work with an appropriate mentor or critical friend whenever possible, and continuously reflect on what you have learned and what knowledge and skills you still need to acquire."

References

Fern, E. F. (2001). *Advanced focus group research.* Thousand Oaks, CA: Sage Publications.

Kamberelis, G., & Dimitriadis, G. (2005). Focus groups: Strategic articulations of pedagogy, politics and inquiry. In N. K. Denzin & Y. S. Lincoln (Eds.), *The Sage handbook of qualitative research* (3rd ed.). Thousand Oaks, CA: Sage Publications.

Stewart, D. W., Shamdasani, P. N., & Rook, D. W. (2007). *Focus groups: Theory and practice* (2nd ed.). Thousand Oaks, CA: Sage Publications.

Discourse Analysis 14

Effects on the Researcher

Pol Dominic McCann
and Victor Minichiello

Everyone hopes when commencing a research project that there will be no major disruptions. Most methodology texts focus on the practical aspects of conducting research, but gloss over how far from the original path the actual research can take you. While there are anecdotal stories from other higher-degree students about conflicts with supervisors, deaths in the family, and financial problems, there is little in the literature on doing research that prepares you for the possibility of a major disruption. However, as the research period can span a number of years, people's plans and career paths evolve. The main aspect of this chapter is to look at how one learns theory through doing research. I (Pol) also wanted to show how by developing a personal understanding of the theories I was reading I was able to piece together a cohesive picture from a mine of data I had collected. I struggled with how to comprehend discourse analysis as a technique and how to integrate its findings into the research from day one until late in the process: the change of supervision forced me to articulate what I understood discourse analysis to be and to come to terms with how to operationalize it. In effect, I learned the discourses of discourse analysis through articulating my understandings of the methodology to supervisors. In order to do this, I will first outline the research I conducted, and describe the supervisors who guided me through this process.

In 2003, I was awarded a scholarship to research the impact of homophobia on Western men. Because the scholarship had been funded through a research grant, which obviously required a full funding application to be submitted, the research methodology had been designed before I came onto the project. I saw the advertisement for the scholarship that described the project and applied for the job. The project described in the grant application provided me with a head start: I could concentrate on my literature review, in terms of both the masculinity and the homophobia, and engage in the literature on the methods chosen by the principal investigators. Had this not been the case, I would have had to scour methodology literature in order to find a means of investigating my topic, a process that would have taken up much time and required much thought in the early stages of a research project. Even with the advantage of having the methodology chosen, it still took months of reading to come to grips with the daunting literature on grounded theory and discourse analysis that had been chosen as the framework to guide this study.

✳ ✳ ✳

When David (the other mentor) and I (Victor) were assessing Pol's application for the scholarship, we were aware that his previous research background and experience were simultaneously positives and negatives. Positive because he was familiar with qualitative research, negative because his theoretical tradition was different from the approach we wanted to take for the project. We realized that Pol would need coaching about how to investigate the issues associated with homophobia and gender through the conceptual lens of theoretical traditions, with which he was not familiar. However, Pol was open to learning and expanding his knowledge of theories. Perhaps it was not as easy as he had envisioned because students often do not see the important connection between research questions and theory. Theory allows researchers to open up their minds and see things that they might not normally see. Learning how to use theory to read data was to become Pol's biggest challenge.

One more relevant point: Some students come to their doctoral work with their own topic—sometimes clearly articulated, sometimes not. Here the students often have the sense of ownership over the topic; supervisors assist in narrowing the focus of the study or moving the original concept to a more refined product. In other cases, as in Pol's case, supervisors have designed a topic and been awarded a grant to research it. In such cases, students have the sense that the topic is owned by others, and a negotiation process often takes places where the student and supervisor work out some shared ownership. This can include adding new dimensions to the study. As Pol commenced collecting his data, he wanted to focus on the role of sports and jokes. These points were added as important questions to the study.

Editors' Comment

Discourse Analysis

You already understand there are different types of theoretical traditions used by qual-itative researchers. Discourse analysis is another approach that focuses on interpreting text in order to discover cultural and social meaning underlying the surface messages. Rather than talking to people about their experiences and examining individual per-spectives, this approach analyzes existing text (newspapers, memoirs, letters, journals, advertisements, minutes of meetings, proceedings of conferences, and so on) on a macro level looking at broader cultural themes. This makes more explicit the underly-ing power relationships that affect policy decisions and organizational structures. It also highlights winners and losers in particular forms of communication. This lends itself particularly well to exploring the nature of homophobia because it uncovers how majority views shape the way that homosexuality is viewed by the dominant culture. This method allowed Pol to analyze how sports talk or the use of jokes in conversation represents the ways that men internalize homophobic behavior.

✳ ✳ ✳

As has been mentioned in earlier chapters, grounded theory is a method that aims to find new theoretical perspectives within the data collected. In grounded theory, theory is literally grounded within participants' stories. Discourse analysis is a means of interrogating documents, conversation, media, and the physical environment as they relate to the social world. The researcher aims to find the common themes pertaining to the topic of investigation. In the case of this research, it meant looking for where the dominant themes about gender and sexuality are found for Western men. Discourses are the commonly held beliefs that underpin a topic, the authorized accounts about it. They contain indicators of power that shape how we interact with concepts such as gender and sexuality. Discourses can be linguistic, such as a series of statements that carry a meaning about an idea (Cheek, 2004), or nonlinguistic, such as material bodies on which the results of the discourses can be seen to be at work (Kendall & Wickham, 1999).

My background at this stage was a degree in sociology; sociology uses an interpretivist approach. Interpretivist research attempts to understand the complex world of lived experiences from the point of view of those who live it. The main concern here is to understand meaning and the par-ticipant's definition of their situation and experiences. This involves what is referred to in the qualitative literature as *verstehen*, or understanding of the social world. If the social world is mediated by our interactions, then we can read and decode these interactions to allow the understanding of the world. I used in-depth interviews to examine socialization processes that gay men go through once they come out. I posited that in the absence of identifiable gay role models in their childhood and youth, gay men had limited or no concept of how to structure a relationship with another man. My research looked at times when these men began to absorb ideas about the differing types of relationships that they were exposed to following self-acknowledgment of their sexuality. The doctoral research proposal was initially challenging from two angles: First, I had expected to continue my research on sexuality and on gay men's sexuality in particular. As I dialogued with my supervisors, I was being asked to shift focus from sexuality to gender, and from gay men to masculinity in general. This was a short-lived challenge because it became apparent that this broadening of focus not only allowed my gaze a much wider view, but also would provide a fascinating comparison with my earlier research. Now I could also examine how men are socialized in gender roles and the impacts of different sexualities in the creation of modern masculinities. The second challenge to deal with was learning both grounded theory and discourse analysis, and then marrying the two.

Gaining Ownership of the Project

Initially I had a strange sense that I was receiving a scholarship to conduct someone else's research. However, I was assured that I had the opportunity to adapt the proposal—pending ethics committee approval—to shape the research in ways that I saw evolving as the research continued. This approach sits well with tenets of grounded theory that state that research is organic, and that both theory and research methods should be allowed to develop in parallel as each informs the other (Glaser & Strauss, 1967).

It was not simply a matter of signing on to the project and following the dots. The ability to shape the research as it went along became paramount during the data collection as I began to project myself into the discourses of masculinity. As I began to understand how discourses shape gender, I made important discoveries as to why this was the right research for me to do at this stage of my life. In retrospect, it seems strange how unaware I was of the interplay between my own life and that of the research that I was contracted to undertake. My journey into research involved climbing inside the lives of a diverse group of sixty-four men, but also involved climbing into my own relationships with men of different masculinities in my own history. It was by becoming aware of the role and impact of discourse on ideas of gender and sexuality that I gained a personal understanding of many of the events that shaped my life. Without this personal development, I would have been unable to complete the analysis of the data and pull the argument together. This journey will be presented later in this chapter, because it formed an essential aspect to learning how to do discourse analysis.

✻ ✻ ✻

I was aware Pol had a personal connection with this research but left this dialogue to take place between Pol and David. David was an expert on homophobia and able to help Pol understand the academic issues associated with this topic, as well as to use Pol's personal experiences to make sense of the research question. Their discussion over many months focused on making sense of people's experiences with the consequences of homophobia. David helped Pol locate his experiences within this context. Over the years, I saw Pol both struggle with this research and come to terms with his own issues with homophobia. This healing process was facilitated when Pol was able to explain homophobia within a much larger socially constructed experience influenced by gender. This personal level of understanding ultimately allowed Pol to make a unique contribution to the field.

✻ ✻ ✻

Getting Into the Project—and Stalling

The literature on masculinities and homophobia was vast, so my main challenge was ascertaining who the key theorists were and delving into hundreds of books and journals. It was a rich and largely fascinating read, although I found some authors such as Butler (1993) and Sedgwick (1990) to be impenetrable, at least for a novice researcher. The literature on discourse and discourse analysis, including the writings of Foucault (1990) and others, was also challenging with respect to following the conceptual arguments. The basics of discourse analysis appear simple—look for symbolic indicators of power in a social environment that is mediated by the ways that language conveys and constrains knowledge. In the context of gender, discourses can be found in texts such as books, newspapers, movie and television dialogue, and advertisements, all of which are replete with indicators of so-called correct gender performance. But discourses also exist in the material world, such as in the architecture of buildings that influence how different populations are shaped. In writing about dormitories and barracks, Foucault (1990) observed how the physical layout of the rooms and beds shaped and constrained the behavior—including sexual behavior—of the boys and men who inhabited these spaces. Architecture and furniture form part of the discourse of gender in these environments. I found the techniques for this sort of analysis as a research method ill defined and obscure, however. I have always had this problem with poststructuralist writers: Like many students, I find their writing style verbose and inaccessible; those who claim to find beauty and poetry in the meter of such authors simply added to my sense of academic insecurity.

The prime example of overwriting I cite is from *Epistemology of the Closet* (Sedgwick, 1990, p. 74). In this tome, the author crams 155 words, 13 commas, and two dashes into one daunting sentence. I lost count of the number of times I have reread that sentence and yet I still cannot follow her argument. I wonder if anyone can follow a thread so obtusely fashioned. When I asked David about this style, he said that he too struggled with poststructuralists. Although their ideas were often elegant (i.e., Foucault: power is everywhere; Butler: gender is nothing but a performance), he thought the style of conveying the ideas to be exclusionary.

David was calm and reassuring in the face of my increasing panic. He continually reiterated that eventually the entire project would come together as a whole: Once I began to collect the data, the masculinities literature would become clearer. I would be able to see expressions of theory in a local context and could then ascertain how my research could fit into this patchwork of international knowledge. And importantly, he reassured me that an understanding of both grounded theory and discourse analysis would unfold through the data collection and analysis phases: the techniques would unfold as I began to utilize them. I was prepared to acknowledge his trust in me. I understood the basic concept of multiple discourses shaping the social environment (Cheek, 2004) and how hidden motivators could be uncovered below the surface-level meanings presented in texts (Howarth, 2000). For example, I clearly saw this point when I viewed a photograph reproduced in a newspaper above a story on a rugby club's decision to ban cheerleaders from games. Juxtaposed to the now-defunct cheerleaders was the picture of the rugby tackle—one man's buttocks exposed while in an almost-passionate embrace with an opposing player. The text below the photograph read, "See what happens when you ban cheerleaders? Blokes get weird." The discourses on offer here are that men should play contact sports—but that some forms of contact are dangerous to their masculine image. In the absence of women, such a clasp can have dangerous homoerotic implications. Sports are the allowable form of male bonding, and women are present only as sexualized objects. In this example, both the photograph described and the codes of Australian rugby convey important discourses of gender and sexuality to a largely male audience. Discourses of desired gender are paraded on the field across the world, and in various epochs. Men are expected to be team-bonded, impervious to pain, homosocial but never homosexual. Messner (1992) illustrates the links between sports and empire, where the military used the sports field as a proving ground for soldiers, a training ground for officers, and the means of distilling into its corps the ideals of masculine behavior of that period. Beyond the sports field, these discourses were exported to the empire. Had I seen this photograph early in the research, I may only have seen the humorous undercurrent, and missed the levels of social control exerted.

The project continued into its second year. Although I had read extensively on masculinities and homophobia, I was still failing to connect them to the concept of discourse—due to my failure to fully comprehend what discourses were, how to read them, and how to make them part of my project. What David reiterated, though, was that this was a symbiotic process, wherein learning the techniques that I was using would be part of the actual analysis. He began to push me to start data collection and I resisted, saying I needed to read more. He virtually pushed me out the door with a data recorder and the jointly developed interview schedule. I gathered my sample through a combination of convenience and theoretical sampling. I started with men referred to me by colleagues, men who my colleagues thought would have interesting stories: a builder whose best friend was gay, a conservative minister who had worked in an AIDS ward in the late 1980s, a soldier. I began to feel more at home with asking strangers to open up about their lives, and began to see the indicators or power that underpinned aspects of their lives. I was interviewed on the Australian Broadcasting Corporation's radio network, and this brought in a flood of calls—from men on farms, to men in conflict with their fathers or partners, to men incarcerated, and from a focus group of unemployed men trying to recover a sense of masculine identity without the crutch of paid work to reinforce them.

Sitting face to face with a man who told of trying to kill his best friend who had made a pass at him was a chilling moment. It seemed best not to allow myself to show any reaction. I heard a man say he would be shattered if his two-year-old son was gay—but this could not happen because he would teach him to play rugby and cricket, for surely these would teach him how to be the right kind of man. Sports in this man's mind were literal insurance against abhorrent sexuality. The social dynamic of homophobia and the discourses of masculinity showed themselves in a focus group: one loud, jovial, but boorish man made continual jokes through the group, at times at the expense of the men present. Homophobic humor was one of his stock-in-trade techniques of belittlement. It was fine for me to sit and listen objectively, but far more jarring to have one of the most interesting men approach me after the group, fighting back tears, and expressing his frustration at not being able to challenge the other man in the group. This man, smart but uneducated, had heard these comments as a child, and the restrictive power of those comments still made him bite his tongue and seethe in anger. However, these ideas were disparate at the time of the interviews. It was late in the analysis that I understood what I was listening to at this still-early stage of the research.

I transcribed the first six interviews. My misgivings about this plan disappeared by the time the third interview was transcribed. Seemingly random comments in different interviews began to emerge as related concepts that threw ideas about acceptable masculinity into relief. Once the interviews were transcribed, David and I did separate readings, high-lighting what appeared to be items of significance and comparing our impressions. The interview schedule was refined at this stage, and I began to see how the theories of masculinity were played out in the lives of real people. I was still sequestered in my understanding of homophobia apart from how it had impacted on my life, though, and was in a deep fog as to what discourses meant in all of this.

Editors' Comment

Transcribing Interviews

Data analysis begins once you start transcribing an interview. Although some researchers might hire someone else to do this work, that some call busy work, we believe that the long, often tedious task of listening to tapes over and over, writing each word, helps to further immerse you in the language and content of the material. Even when you aren't systematically analyzing the tapes, you are still taking in the content and making both unconscious and intuitive linkages that will be incredibly useful later. You will also hear and see issues and insights that went unrecognized during the conversation because you were so concerned with managing the time properly.

During this first stage of data analysis, you will also make notes about themes you recognize, issues you want to follow up, ideas for improving your next scheduled ses-sions, reminders to check the literature, and, most critically for this process, identified patterns that form the first level of coding. In other words, transcribing is what brings you in most intimate contact with your data. Even the pauses, silences, "uhs," and "ums" can become significant in ways that you may have missed earlier.

✾ ✾ ✾

I recall this debate well. I have a policy that students need to transcribe their own interviews so that they get close to the data. I learned this lesson from my own data collection experience. You do an interview. You then listen to it and find yourself saying, "I do not remember hearing that when I was interviewing." You transcribe the interview and find that there are all kinds of things that you failed to hear, interpret, or pick up. The transcribing process forces you to look at the data and is the begin-ning of data analysis, and not a chore. David and I agreed that despite the money available from our grant, Pol would transcribe his first set of interviews to learn the ropes of interviewing and qualitative data analy-sis. As the saying goes, you need to get your hands dirty to really know what it is all about.

✾ ✾ ✾

Seeing Beyond My Own View

I already understood the importance of bracketing—that is, stating the history that the researcher brings to the research and being aware of how that may influence interpretation of the data: failure to do so had been cited by a marker in my undergraduate thesis. At David's suggestion, I began keeping a journal and writing up field notes after each interview. David did not want me to bracket my own history out of the analysis, but rather to use it as a sensitizing concept with which I could see layers of power in the interviews based on how I had personally experienced homophobic bullying as an adolescent. The utility of these reflections came to the fore as the research developed but never more so than after a major turning point, which occurred after Interviews 15 and 16. I interviewed two men, coincidentally on consecutive days and both in rural towns, with remarkably similar stories. While the literature indicated that homophobia impacted on perceived failures in gender presentation rather than actual sexuality, it was not until these interviews that I saw how profoundly it affected heterosexual men. Both Shane and Theo had moved to a different culture at about age ten—Shane from Africa to Britain, Theo from Melanesia to Australia. Both had different accents from their peers' accents, were smaller than their peers, were excluded from peer culture, and became increasingly emotional as the ostracism, particularly homophobic labeling, intensified. Hearing stories from heterosexual men and seeing the long-term emotional damage that was wrought on these men provided my first *Aha!* moment when theory became apparent in real-life examples. The literature took on an exciting new relevance at this point.

This removed the first of the blinkers that had been constraining my analysis. So far, I was viewing homophobia from the perspective of a gay man who had received this sort of teasing through childhood. Although I had read of its impact on all men, I still failed to understand its impact on men in general. I had read extensively on the theories of homophobia, but it was not until hearing the stories of straight men who had experienced it and hearing the crippling impact it had on their lives that I saw beyond my worldview and that of the textbooks: now I heard first hand of the impact on masculinity. I began to comprehend why my supervisors had insisted I research *gender,* not *sexuality*. The subsequent data collection proceeded with a greater insight to the whole topic, and the later interviews displayed this. I finished the data collection and settled in to full-time analysis.

A New Mentor

Initially, David and I had far more face-to-face time than Victor and I had. As David was leaving to take a new appointment overseas midway in my thesis journey, and although we remained in close contact as I continued working, Victor and I were thrust into close contact for the latter part of the data analysis and the vital period of writing up the results. Not only did Victor need me to brief him fully on where I was, but also we needed to develop a relationship in order to negotiate the vital final write-up. At this stage, I felt distant from Victor. While both men have intellects that inspire and daunt me, David's playfulness is in contrast to Victor's workaholic drive. I sensed that I did not measure up to Victor's standards, and Victor sensed that he had been excluded from the supervision process because David and I had worked so closely together. This was a valid concern of his, but there was a reason for his exclusion: his role as dean of the faculty placed strenuous demands on his time. I had believed that working closer to David would lessen some of Victor's time demands. Once this situation had been clarified in an initially tense meeting, we set about figuring out how to finish the project.

Two weeks later in our supervision session, Victor asked me to outline in detail what the major findings of the data analysis indicated, in my opinion. I was able to verbalize clearly my findings in terms of what the data showed about the lives of the participants, but was unable to articulate how they fitted into the formation of and participation in the discourses of gender and sexuality. Victor made notes as I spoke and began drawing circles and arrows around words to form a mind map. He was grouping the loose themes that I was presenting into a time line of the lives of men; this ultimately formed the four results chapters of my thesis. Victor works visually, and I work verbally. He transcribed my discussion into images that allowed them to be reflected back to me in a new fashion. I verbalized my ideas and watched Victor turn them into a flowchart chronicling the development from boyhood to manhood and the influences and power dynamics on that journey. As he did so, I began to see how discourse shapes the social world. I would have eventually made this connection, but expressing the jumble of ideas in my mind and seeing them coalesce into Victor's schematic was a major step toward developing my own ideas.

✳ ✳ ✳

It was clear to me that Pol was drowning in his data. He had collected a remarkable set of data, including personal and often hidden stories. Pol was getting men to talk about issues that they kept very secret. He had been successful in getting access to this data. This in itself was a significant achievement. I think Pol was aware of the uniqueness of his data and perhaps this created pressure for him. He wanted to tell the story from all angles. The problem was that there were so many issues to discuss and he was writing a thesis with a finite number of words and pages. I recall that Pol was racing with his thoughts. My job here was to have him tell me two or three new discoveries that were prominent in the data. With no trouble, he was able to cite these. We wrote them down using key words and making linkages between his ideas. The trick of using diagrams is something that I have learned myself. It helps to clarify ideas that appear disjointed in your mind; somehow, once they are on paper and connected with others ideas are much clearer and make sense.

This discussion provided the context for the next year or so for Pol to clarify what he wanted to say in his thesis.

✵ ✵ ✵

Over the course of that supervision session, we discussed how boys shape their ideas of successful masculinity by projecting fears of lesser forms of masculinity onto acceptable targets. Boys of lesser masculine status attracted a homophobic gaze. This formed the first result chapter.

The second result chapter examined a specific social process through which this *othering* occurs: through the use of language—specifically humor—to mark out with homophobic pejoratives those who are different. The use of humor as a technique for delineating social power later became the second fulcrum on which my understanding of the deeper theoretical aspects of the thesis pivoted.

The third result chapter looked at the impact that sports have in delineating masculinity, and how this impact elevates a physically dominant, aggressive form of peer interaction that is simultaneously homosocial and homophobic, but with a strong homoerotic aesthetic. The photograph of cheerleaders and rugby players with exposed buttocks in the newspaper illustrates the interplay between sports and humor: discourses of a physically dominant, team-based series of masculine activities are held up as the apotheosis of masculinity in this culture, similar to many other Western countries. The playful comment that "blokes get weird" shows in a joking manner that men must not allow themselves to get too close to each other—especially when partial nudity is public—or else risk having their hard-fought masculine status ridiculed.

The fourth result chapter discussed how many of the participants unlearned previously held homophobic attitudes, and described the precursors nominated for this change in attitudes to unfold. In effect, we charted the chronology of how boys come to be homophobic as a functional tool in creating a sense of masculine self by reflecting socially held fears of the fragility of masculinity, through to their ability to shuck this off in early to mid adulthood as they develop their own masculine identity. The outline of the chapters fell into place quickly, although the details took months of writing. The conclusion chapter took more introspection to pull all the ideas together and express fully how discourses ran through and around all these themes.

Progress, Stalling Again, and New Developments

I liked the structure of the thesis, but was still having trouble integrating the idea of discourse into the chronology. Adding to the confusion was the fact that some aspects of the analysis were contradictory; it was in examining the conflicting accounts that I formed deeper insights. The boys who teased those boys who were perceived to be gay made continual reference to it all being "just a joke." This was just boys having fun, no harm was intended, they said. This was at odds with the recollections of the men who had been targeted with this abuse, who described it as orchestrated cruelty. This jostling for supremacy, through both verbal put-downs and physical performances, were interpreted very differently depending on the boys' perspectives—victim or perpetrator. I wondered if the bullies were emotionally rewriting the abuse they had been involved with to assuage the guilt that they may have come to feel for their past actions. I also wondered if the boys who were bullied were reading too much into childhood events. At this point I had to examine my own history to see who was telling the truth—or if both were, how two conflicting truths could coexist.

Bracketing: The Researcher Is in the Research

During the first eighteen months of this project, I had wondered about the role of the researcher in research, especially when there is a personal resonance, such as my own history of homophobic bullying. Most men are targeted with homophobic teasing at some stage in their lives; Plummer (2001) lists a set of predictors that are likely to instigate this in boy culture. They include being academically inclined, being overly emotional, being artistic, acting like a girl, appearing different, being smaller or slower to develop than peers, being inept at sports, and rejecting peer affiliation in preference for adult approval. The last three points are closely linked: they speak of the physically oriented, team-focused style of interaction that is held up as the nadir of masculinity in the West (Kimmel, 1990; Messner, 1992). This indicates why the sports chapter was vital in discussing how boys learn ideals of Western masculinity.

I discussed the idea of personal introspection by the researcher with a colleague who was at a similar stage in her doctorate, and she warned me off in a laconic Australian simplicity: "Don't get caught up in navel gazing, darl." Through separate discussions with David and Victor, however, I realized I had to bracket my experiences. At the same time, I did not want to play a victim card in the research. Failing to examine my own motivations and understandings would have been as much of a failure as a researcher as failing to see the impact of homophobia on my heterosexual participants. This is what David was referring to as "sensitizing concepts" that could help me to use my own experiences to gain greater insight into the impact of discourses on others.

I was aiming for some way of understanding of the disparity between the recollections of the bullies and the bullied, between those who saw harmless fun and those who were "crushed" by it, to cite Theo's description of the events. Analyzing my childhood experiences and thinking about the boys I went to school with became vital parts of this analysis—and vital parts of my ability to see how discourse underpins all of these themes. To complete this analysis, I made contact with several of the boys who I went to school with and asked them about their childhoods. I shall describe them briefly.

Lawrence was tall and willowy, and the most effeminate boy I had ever met. As a result, he was the most obvious victim of emasculating language. Boys generally used a feminine pronoun for him and called him a poofter (the Australasian pejorative for *gay*, which is equivalent to, and to some degree now superseded by, the word *fag*). Lawrence seemed just to roll with the punches, laughing along at his own humiliation as if it didn't bother him. This was the major difference between Lawrence and me: he laughed in the face of teasing and to an extent joined in, while I retreated to the safety of the library. Yet when I telephoned Lawrence about twenty-five years later, he told me the laughter had been a mask for intense pain. He now suffered from crippling social phobia, and worked as a nightshift cleaner to avoid having to deal with people: more than two or three people would put him in a state of panic. Despite also being the target for abuse, I too saw what was happening to Lawrence as just "a bit of fun" because it differed from the abuse I received, and Lawrence's attitude indicated that he was part of the joke. If, in the midst of also being teased, I had failed to see the damage inflicted on Lawrence, perhaps the other boys had also failed to see it. I knew too well not to let the bullies see me cry, because this would have exacerbated the intensity—but my stoicism allowed them to continue this behavior blithely ignorant of its impact.

I found a prime example of this sort of attitude in a focus group of young building industry apprentices. One of the young men described the sort of bullying that Shane, Theo, Lawrence, and I had experienced, including his description of hitting boys who he described as "the fags": "It was only a little slap behind the ear anyway," he said. I was amazed to hear and reread this comment—and not see a monstrous thug, but a jovial, carefree, and funny young man who saw baiting and low-level violence as an accepted, harmless part of male socialization. Just as I did not see how Lawrence was crumbling under the strain of abuse, neither did these apprentices. This exchange allowed me to see that some boys did see that it was just a joke, where they did not realize the magnitude of the pain they caused. Besides, they were simply reflecting the socially acceptable putting down of a minority. The bracketing of my experiences here was vital in allowing me to listen to the story without my own history putting up barriers. My own anger at how I had been treated in late childhood and early adolescence had so far prevented me from reading the discourses of male socialization.

There was a similar disjuncture in the ways men spoke of sports in their childhoods. For some it was a joyous means of engaging with their developing bodies and an opportunity to share intense emotional connections to peers. For others it was weekly humiliation from the most physically and socially powerful boys. I called two other boys who I went to school with, James and Carl, both of whom were stellar athletes. While they expressed similar fond memories of team sports, they also noticed the sidelining of the less hegemonic boys. Sports became the authorized enactment of bullying. I remembered an incident where James had confronted me on the sports field, deriding my lack of skill, yelling at me as he shoved me off the field. To James, this was a minor argument. To me, it was a moment of intense humiliation that encapsulated my failure to be one of the boys. The meaning of the situation depended on which side of the fence you were sitting on.

Carl expressed concern about the impact of physicality on the emotional states of boys. He recalled with unease the role the coach forced him to play in picking the boys for their teams, being made to whittle through the pool of classmates until the smallest or least-capable boys—generally Lawrence, another boy, and me who was about my height—were the last to be picked. Carl knew this was wrong, and yet was unable to challenge the role of the coach or the accepted means of sorting the men from the boys through ritual humiliation. I was beginning to understand that this was how men inhabited the discourses of masculinity: that is, in ways that were often uncomfortable and difficult to challenge.

It was interesting to watch Pol shape his ideas. In this last year of the study, I consistently asked him to send me drafts. Pol wanted to talk about his ideas and at times was resisting putting his ideas on paper. However, once he started writing there was no stopping him. My role here was to read his work and ask probing questions that forced him to question his data and to support his arguments. I always enjoyed reading his material because it was about so-called men's business; in a way, I was able to relate to some of the stories shared by his informants about topics such as schoolyard behavior, being aggressive in sports, and using jokes to make statements about sex and the role of men and women in society.

Just as David had pushed me to start data collection when I wanted to read "just one more book" again and again, Victor pushed me to start writing. When I said I was blocked, his insistence was gentle and tempered with a valuable comment: he asked me if I could tell the story of the research. Well, I couldn't stop talking about it! If I was asked at a party about what I was doing, I could encapsulate an overview of the research in five minutes. At a conference, I could easily present for thirty minutes. With anyone who expressed more than a passing interest, I could engage in conversation for the length of his attention span. Victor told me that if I could tell the story, I could write it, and when I was blocked, to discuss it with whoever would listen. With each retelling, the themes became clearer and the story fell more and more into place. This simple advice negated a great deal of stress during writer's block, as did David's continual reassurance that he believed I was capable of completing this project.

Incorporating a New Worldview Into the Analysis

Learning how discourses shape the social world was a vital aspect in how the results chapters came together. It was by listening to all of the interviews, finding the common threads in these men's lives, and comparing them to my own history that I was able to move beyond my blinkered, somewhat damaged worldview and see that it is not just the gay boys who get homophobic abuse but that all men are constrained by homophobia in varying ways; that some of those involved in teasing and bullying really did not seem to see how damaging it was; and that many straight men are far nicer than my cloistered gay ghetto lifestyle allowed me to perceive—a fact that David had warned of from the start but that again I had to experience for myself to comprehend.

I was able to write up the chapters on language and sports based on the personal developments that I was going through. Reflecting on the stories that I had been told and combining that reflection with introspection about my own history gave me new insights. Until this point, I was, as Victor noted, drowning in my data. I realized how blinded I had been to Lawrence's pain, due to my own experiences. It was seeing how schoolboys James and Carl had viewed the experience of our joint schooldays, and comparing this to the young homophobic apprentices who I now no longer saw as monstrous that gave me clarity. Once I made these connections, my writer's block began to lift.

Editors' Comment

Data Analysis

In data analysis, you are asking yourself, What the heck does all this mean? You have taken in all this information, read everything you could find on the subject, transcribed at least a few of your interviews, all these words, images, thoughts, feelings, descriptions flooding into your consciousness. How do you possibly make sense of all this?

The answer is through a systematic, reasonably structured approach that helps you review the data, identify recurrent themes of significance, and organize them according to some meaningful schema. The particular way in which you do this depends, in part, on which qualitative method you've chosen. In grounded theory, you conduct at least three different levels of coding from the general to the specific. In phenomenology, you identify essences of human experience, meaning the core descriptions. In narrative analysis, you look for plots and stories that have been most prominent.

Now I needed to pull all of this knowledge into the realm of discourses. A friend who had previously worked as legal advisor to a federal politician also suggested that I examine transcripts of senate reports that he had worked on such as the Inquiry into Anti-Genocide Bill and the Inquiry into Sexuality Discrimination (see Christian Democratic Party, 1999). The vitriol expressed in these committees shows the levels to which homophobia is entrenched in society, although it is frequently found in small, conservative groups with powerful voices that are sharply at odds with the liberal attitudes of so many participants.

At about this same time, I found some blogs in *The Sydney Morning Herald* (2006) online edition where sexuality was discussed, and again while the majority of bloggers were accepting of homosexuality, a small percentage were expressing disgust in aggressive terms. The policy of the *Herald* disallows any post "which racially or religiously vilifies, incites violence or hatred, or is likely to offend, insult or humiliate others based on race, religion, ethnicity, gender, age, sexual orientation or any physical or mental disability" (SMH, 2006). And yet in all of the searches I made, homophobic discourses were present and had been published. None of the blogs advocated outright violence, although Kimberley Porteous, who manages the blogs for SMH online, did tell me of the more extreme blogs that had not made it online. Notwithstanding this, there was an unpleasant undercurrent in these postings and, importantly, a sense of self-righteousness in proclaiming hatred. I could not imagine similar statements on the basis of race making it to the blogs. As an example, I compared statements, but exchanged homophobic terms in favor of racist ones, and the disparity became even more apparent. While a newspaper was prepared to publish "all you gay people make me sick! get some help! . . . I'm not homophobic, I'm not scared of gays . . . I hate them" (wateva, 2006), it is inconceivable that it would have printed "all you black people make me sick! get some help! . . . I'm not racist, I'm not scared of blacks. . . . I hate them." While the policy of the newspaper was equally clear in objecting to racism or homophobia, only the former was enforced. Homophobia is still an allowable form of discrimination.

Seeing the Power of Discourse Over Informants

What was becoming apparent now was the disproportionate impact of homophobic discourses. A vocal minority had an unchallenged voice, which I also saw in operation in interviews where some men expressed homophobic opinions. These opinions were also apparent in focus groups and illustrated the social dynamic of homophobia: challenging homophobic discourses risks attention being focused on yourself in a new version of Darley and Latane's (1968) bystander intervention effect. At this point, I began to realize how to pull the final chapter and in fact the entire thesis together. I could now see how discourses shaped the behavior and attitudes of a community even when the majority of the community, when asked individually, did not admit to subscribing to them.

Any country is a series of contradictions on topics in the realm of morality. While increasing numbers of jurisdictions now support gay marriage or secular recognition of relationships, there is still a strong political resistance, including legislation passed the week I completed this chapter that bans gay couples from adopting babies born overseas. Similar legislation about protecting the family by restricting marriage to heterosexual couples or sheltering children from "dangerous social engineering" inherent in same-sex parenting permeates the political discourses of many "modern" Western democracies, especially at election time.

This was, for me, the major finding of the thesis: how discourses are incredibly controlling, even when most people disagree with them. It was not until I was able to look beyond the stories in the interviews that I could see how they fit into and were restrained by the discourses.

I had learned the theory of discourse analysis by reading theorists. I began to learn how discourse impacts on people's lives by finding the common threads in the participants' narratives. The full realization came when I saw how discourses permeate the national psyche and shape and constrain how people are allowed to behave. The major revelations were seeing the impact of discourses at a national level, where a comparative minority of people hold homophobic views whose impact is disproportionately large. The dynamic quality of discourses (Foucault, 1990) predicts that they will change in the face of a developing social environment. The new discourse of masculinity that people discussed was a more open and accepting one that spoke of both tolerance and a more mature understanding of their own masculinity. The power of the homophobic discourse still blocks other voices to some extent, but there has clearly been a change in attitudes to sexualities and gender in the late twentieth century. The next stage in this development will be when the open-minded attitudes of participants effect a new national discourse.

It was through developing an understanding of how individual voices in the discourses can be both silenced and overwhelmed or become prominent beyond their representativeness that allowed me to bring the four results chapters together in the final conclusion chapter. While there were several moments of revelation during interviews and analysis, the understanding of the role of discourse was a gradually unfolding process where I was able to see the interview data in the context of my understanding of the broader, social power of discourses.

✳ ✳ ✳

Students often want everything to fall into place from the beginning. This seldom occurs in any research. Pol's journey is about a struggle with making sense of both his data and his own understanding of the topic. I want to make an important point here: No topic stands still in time. There is always a context of time and space. How another researcher researching this question ten years from now will see the experiences of masculinity will be very much shaped by the context of her society at a particular point in time and by her experiences. Imagine writing about this topic, let alone researching it, in 1807. Discourse analysis did not even exist then, so this theoretical framework to analyze the data was simply not available. An obvious point maybe, but my point to Pol during our supervision sessions and others is that forms of analysis evolve over time, are very much grounded to the times, and not easy to see. Ideas and connections emerge from a reflective process and dialogue with the data and other scholars—from supervisors, other peer students, presentations at conferences, reading, and rereading theory. The results of your final version of the thesis or research papers are only obvious after the fact, never before, and yet they are always bound to some extent to current thinking in society. Everything fell into place for Pol because this is the normal path of discovery and research.

✷ ✷ ✷

Lessons Learned

What did I learn? Love your research. Become deeply connected to a topic that will engage you for however many years you will carry it. Obsess about it. Look for examples of your topic in the social world, and in media. Look at how your topic impacts on you. Qualitative research is about investigating social relations so there should be some resonances in what you are researching and the world you inhabit. Make that world one of the lenses with which you examine your data. For me this was the key to reading more deeply into the wealth of information that sixty-four participants gave me—and the key to finding the important linkages. If required, put yourself into the research to connect with those linkages.

Talk to whoever will listen, from your grade school teacher to your parents to your kids. Anyone will have a perspective that may illuminate an aspect that you have not considered. Or at least the telling to people with a range of understandings of your topic will force you to express it simply at a high school reunion, or with academic incisiveness to your favorite undergraduate lecturer.

In his final comments, Victor noted that no research stands still. So don't stop. Even when the research is finished, it can go on. Writing journal articles after completion will give you new ideas about what was contained in the data. Keep interrogating your data to find new developments that springboard off the completed thesis. Writing this chapter made me aware of how much more I have learned since submitting the thesis nearly a year ago. You are in a fortunate position to have this time to concentrate on your own project for a period of years. Use that time, but also extend it to the full extent of your mine of information. Who knows when you will have such a luxury again?

Trust your supervisors. While they push and cajole, they have your best interests and your career at heart. Tell them what you find and what you cannot see. Let them be the mirror against which to see your ideas. Tell them when you are ready to throw in the towel, and they will hold the towel until your panic subsides.

When you are embarked on a project like this, people become excited on your behalf. It's amazing and wonderful how generous people are with time and encouragement. Relish that generosity of spirit, and start thinking.

References

Butler, J. (1993). *Bodies that matter: On the discursive limits of "sex."* New York: Routledge.

Cheek, J. (2004). At the margins? Discourse analysis and qualitative research. *Qualitative Health Research, 14*, 1140–1150.

Christian Democratic Party (CDP). (1999). Christian democratic party submission senate legal and constitutional references committee: Inquiry into anti-Genocide Bill 1999. Commonwealth of Australia, Canberra, *1.1*, 92–104.

Darley, J. M., & Latane, B. (1968). Bystander intervention in emergencies: Diffusion of responsibility. *Journal of Personality and Social Psychology, 8*, 377–383.

Foucault, M. (1990). *The history of sexuality volume 1: An introduction.* New York: Vintage Books.

Glaser, B. G., & Strauss, A. L. (1967). *The discovery of grounded theory: Strategies for qualitative research.* New York: Aldine de Gruyter.

Howarth, D. (2000). *Discourse.* Buckinghamshire, UK: Open University Press.

Kendall, G., & Wickham, G. (1999). *Using Foucault's methods.* London: Sage Publications.

Kimmel, M. S. (1990). Baseball and the reconstitution of American masculinity, 1880–1920. In M. A. Messner & D. Sabo (Eds.), *Sport, men and the gender order: Critical feminist perspectives.* Champaign, IL: Human Kinetics Books.

Messner, M. A. (1992). *Power at play: Sport and the problem of masculinity.* Boston: Beacon Press.

Plummer, D. C. (2001). The quest for modern manhood: Masculine stereotypes, peer culture and the social significance of homophobia. *Journal of Adolescence, 24*, 15–23.

Sedgwick, E. K. (1990). *The epistemology of the closet.* Berkeley: University of California Press.

Sydney Morning Herald (SMH). (2006). *Terms and conditions.* Accessed November 30 at http://www.smh.com.au/articles/2006/07/26/1153816236184.html? page=fullpage.

wateva. (2006). Gay schmay? Or keep your mouth shut? Club Metro. *Sydney Morning Herald* online edition. Accessed October 30, 2007, at http://blogs .smh.com.au/entertainment/archives/club_metro/005281.html.

Integrating Theory and Method to Promote Social Change

Young Women and Physical Activity

Heidi Gilchrist and Gerard Sullivan

15

In Conclusion . . .

My (Heidi's) research centered on young women's life experiences in relation to their involvement in physical activity. I wanted to understand the meaning that physical activity has for young women, and how it is shaped by social institutions and relations that govern their everyday lives. While there is currently an international focus on physical activity promotion, and young women have been targeted as a group "at risk" of being physically inactive, my research was in stark contrast to many other physical activity studies that have either ignored gender or simply acknowledged it as an unchanging variable that affects physical activity participation, with little consideration of why. I chose to take a feminist perspective for my research, meaning that I saw young women's physical activity participation as inextricably tied to gender. The goal of my research was to better explain how gender influences physical activity participation. To assist my investigation, I drew on feminist theories and the work of

Michel Foucault. Adopting these particular philosophical perspectives allowed me to understand gender as a fluid and relational concept, meaning that the effect of gender changes according to situations. This was a large shift from my original intention to quantitatively measure young women's physical activity and develop an intervention to improve it.

Through my conversations with young women, I found that everyday social relations, gendered discourses, and institutions all act as regulatory structures and relations with regard to young women's physical activity. These relations and institutions are negotiated differently depending on how young women perceive and experience their bodies. Some women consider their body to be a feminine object to be gazed upon (creating a negative relation to the self) and think of physical activity primarily as a tool for body modification. Some women experience their body as an active subject and engage in physical activity for physical and social pleasure. These young women tend to have a more positive relation to the self, often as a result of their less-gendered social and emotional relations. This attitude allows them to incorporate an active physicality into their leisure and gender identities.

It was my use of poststructuralist theories of power and embodiment that allowed me to think about young women and physical activity in this way. This interpretation has in turn led me to assess critically the promotion of physical activity as an unquestioningly desirable health practice when it may often be connected to a negative self-concept. As a result, I considered how a feminist ethic of self-care could be incorporated into the physical activity of young women in order to offer them a more diverse, enjoyable, and potentially transformative understanding of physical activity.

What I have presented in the above paragraphs is a summary of where my research ended. This paragraph does not indicate where my research began, though, or the difficulties I overcame in reaching my destination. I would have struggled to read and understand the above paragraphs at the commencement of my studies. I would therefore like to provide some autobiographical context in order to convey both my motivations for undertaking this research, and then to discuss some of the challenges I faced on the journey.

In the Beginning . . .

My adolescent experiences of physical activity were diverse and ranged from the embarrassment and avoidance of running races at school to the thrill and enjoyment of playing netball (similar to American basketball) with my friends. Overall, I was a relatively nonsporty adolescent, although an interest in health led me to study for a degree in physical therapy, which I did even though it was a course full of sporty types. My only forays into physical activity at this point were intermittent trips to the gym motivated by sporadic attempts to lose weight. When I was twenty-five, however, I took a hiking trip to South America. In order to prepare, I began doing circuit classes and jogging to get fit. It was only then that something I had so studiously avoided when I was younger actually became enjoyable. I took pleasure in setting goals for myself such as running to the next tree or timing myself and taking less time to run a lap of the park. I enjoyed the feeling that I could do something difficult that I never thought I could do. My hiking trip in South America added to my pleasure. We carried our packs over high passes and through snow, and I was amazed at my body's newfound abilities.

✳ ✳ ✳

When I (Gerard) first met Heidi more than fifteen years ago, I knew nothing of her interest or disinterest in sport. Heidi was a physical therapy student and I was a sociology instructor. We met because Heidi wanted to do an honors thesis that focused on the social aspects of health care. Even as an undergraduate, Heidi was interested in improving health outcomes for minority groups. At the time, I was doing some research on discrimination against people living with HIV/AIDS and we devised an honors project that examined physical therapy students' knowledge about HIV illness and their willingness to treat people living with HIV/AIDS.

Most physical therapy students are academically well prepared for university study, and as an honors student Heidi was toward the top of the class. However, the course was scientifically oriented and emphasized the biological aspects of health care, whereas most of the research methods Heidi had learned as an undergraduate were oriented toward experimental designs. At the time she was beginning her project, qualitative research was rare in physical therapy and not highly regarded, so we used survey research. Another issue was the development of a solid theoretical basis for the study. The physical therapy course had a crowded curriculum that allowed little (if any) time for the study of social theory, which was largely regarded as an alien form of knowledge, useless for health practitioners who were focused on learning skills to assist patients experiencing ill health.

Heidi was energetic, enthusiastic, systematic, and diligent in the way she approached the research. We were both pleased when she was awarded first class honors and a university medal for her thesis. After graduating, Heidi joined the public health system as a physical therapist but we kept in touch intermittently as we developed the thesis into a published article (Gilchrist, Sullivan, & Heard, 1997). Heidi married then traveled the world for a couple of years.

✳ ✳ ✳

After my trekking adventures ended, I continued jogging. A female friend who was an experienced runner took me under her wing and became my mentor. She helped me choose my first race—it was a ten-kilometer women-only run through London; I loved every minute of it. I also cheered her on as she ran the London Marathon, and hatched a plan of my own to finish one some day. When I moved back to Australia, friends were impressed by my newfound enthusiasm for running and I unwittingly became the mentor for several female friends who wanted to begin running but weren't sure how to go about it. (Men never asked for my help!) At that time, I was working in a private physical therapy practice and spent a large part of my day encouraging clients (men and women) who worked long hours and had stress-related injuries to become more physically active in their daily lives. My desire to implement physical activity interventions on a wider scale than I was currently doing in my practice as a physical therapist led me to undertake a master of public health program, and then embark on my doctoral research. It was my personal experiences as a girl and young woman, my unintentional role as both student of and mentor for other physically active women that led to my growing sense of feminist responsibility and my research focus on women and physical activity.

✳ ✳ ✳

Heidi and I did not meet again until after she returned to Sydney. At the time, I was looking for a research assistant to work on a project examining youth suicide. After several years in the profession, Heidi was an accomplished physical therapist, but with her success, I sensed, the challenge of the occupation had disappeared. Though somewhat uncomfortable with both the topic and qualitative methodology, Heidi agreed to join the project and almost reluctantly (though always diligently) gained experience in interviewing and qualitative data analysis. Although I was aware that Heidi was becoming an athlete, even participating in triathlons, I presumed her interest did not extend beyond physical activity as leisure—I was one of the men who did not ask!

Heidi spoke of undertaking further study and I tried to interest her in a research degree, but she decided to enroll in a master of public health course in which she learned about epidemiology and statistics, and about a range of public health issues. The course required a treatise; Heidi decided on a very quantitative content analysis of the media portrayal of suicide. It looked as if Heidi might be interested in conducting research, but it would be quantitative and not specifically related to suicide. Heidi began to apply for doctoral scholarships. As luck would have it, the most lucrative one she was awarded was associated with the department in which I worked. It looked as if Heidi was stuck with me! If that were so, she was certainly not going to be stuck with suicide, and she chose instead to pursue a project on young women and physical activity. Heidi supplemented her scholarship by continuing to work on the suicide project; at the same time, we began working on her thesis.

✳ ✳ ✳

The Initial Plan

In spite of my personal experiences of the social, gendered, and embodied nature of physical activity, my background is in physical therapy and public health, both fields that are dominated by quantitative research with a positivist approach to the discovery of knowledge, and where the goal of research is to create universal laws on human behavior (Wright, 1996). Though they regularly deal with human health, discussions of concepts such as *embodiment* are uncommon in these fields, which take a scientific epistemological approach to knowledge. I did not want to stray too far from my academic comfort zone, so my initial plan for this research project was to use a questionnaire to survey as many young women as possible. My plan was to determine correlates of physical activity for young women aged twenty to twenty-five, or perhaps even to run some large-scale physical activity intervention measuring the results, and ultimately writing up my success at increasing women's physical activity levels.

A Change of Plan

I began reviewing the physical activity literature to find all sorts of alarming statistics about young women's exercise behavior (for descriptive statistics see Australian Bureau of Statistics, 2006; and Booth, Okely, Denney-Wilson, Hardy, Yang, & Dobbins, 2006). I soon realized, as other qualitative researchers had realized previously (for example, see Hall, 1996; Parr, 1998), that there were few studies in the mainstream health promotion literature that went beyond the statistics to look at why things are the way they are.

Editors' Comment

Reflecting on the Literature

Heidi's change of plan occurred, in part, as a result of the literature review she conducted. This stage of a research project is often quite time consuming; it involves researchers familiarizing themselves with relevant studies that have been conducted before they embark on a new project. This is important in order to avoid duplicating any existing studies. While conducting a literature review, good researchers question their assumptions and identify gaps in knowledge about the topic being investigated. This process can change researchers' understanding of their subject and the way they conceptualize and conduct their research. They may also gain insights into their personal experiences.

The health promotion literature suggested to me that the absence of strong theoretical bases in much of the research into physical activity has resulted in difficulty in fully explaining the importance of physical activity to young women in their everyday lives. This is particularly the case when it comes to linking issues related to gender with physical activity. Furthermore, as a woman who had been inactive in adolescence and who developed a "serious leisure" identity in my late twenties (Stebbins, 1999), I suspected that there was more to patterns of physical activity than could be revealed by survey research.

Both my personal experiences and my review of the literature suggested that a questionnaire was probably not the most suitable way of researching my topic. I had some experience with qualitative research through my work as a research assistant on a youth suicide project and I knew that it was a useful way of exploring the deeper meanings behind people's behavior (beyond the simple numerical classification of survey research). By *deeper meanings* I mean recognizing that the changing social and cultural context of young women influences the choices they make in their everyday lives. Rather than assuming that both the research and the behavior are context free, qualitative research accepts and explores their value-laden nature.

As I read more widely in the field of leisure, sports, and gender studies, I found that there were indeed researchers who were concerned with the social constitution of gender and femininity and their relation to physical activity. Their methodology was nearly always qualitative; they adopted a far more philosophical approach to understanding physical activity than did the health promotion literature. After some reading, I decided to address the issues of gender and femininity, and to try and make them relevant to the field of health promotion, in spite of the huge shift in my knowledge base that this required.

Gradually it dawned on me that a consideration of the subjective nature of gender and femininity and its influence on physical activity for young women could make a valuable contribution to the field of health promotion. I decided to embark on a qualitative investigation into the meaning of physical activity in young women's everyday lives and to explore my research question with the use of feminist and gender theory.

✳ ✳ ✳

The other chief investigators on the suicide project had moved to other universities and countries, and my time was increasingly taken up with administrative work. Another research assistant resigned for family reasons, so Heidi inherited a lot of responsibility for the project, supervised by me when I was able. Like it or not, Heidi was having to become more deeply involved in the project and consequently began to learn more about qualitative research. I was delighted when she expressed an interest in using similar methods in her doctoral research. However, more challenges lay ahead. From the beginning,

I was concerned about Heidi's agenda to find a way to encourage young women to exercise more. Though not opposed to this as a goal of health promotion, I worried that it compromised a fundamental goal of qualitative research to understand life experience from the perspective of research participants. A second issue to resolve (which turned out to be related to the first) was the establishment of a firm theoretical basis for the thesis. I regularly bleated about this and together we tried our best to work on this aspect of the project.

✳ ✳ ✳

Once I had decided on a qualitative paradigm as a more suitable method of discovering the deeper meanings physical activity had for young women, I was keen to start interviewing. I thought the big decision had been made and it was simply a matter of going out and asking young women why they were or were not physically active. My supervisor, however, thought there was more work to be done before I collected data. While always supportive of my choices, he often made comments about my research plan being "a good start" and "heading in the right direction." He explained I needed to decide on a theoretical approach to my interviewing and subsequent interpretation of data. I really did not understand what he meant: I thought the point of qualitative research was to engage in theory generation rather than theory testing. If not, how was it then any different from testing a specific health promotion theory? While sympathetic to my dilemma, my supervisor gently pointed out I would be unlikely to be developing a totally new philosophical way of thinking. What I needed, he said, was a framework or way of thinking about young women's experiences based on my findings that would provide direction to my research, and upon which I could then expand (or which I could then reject).

Having attempted a few fairly directionless interviews as part of a course I was doing, I could appreciate the need for a stronger framework for my interviews. I still wasn't exactly sure how to find that framework, though. Part of the problem stemmed from the qualitative research I had read to this point. I had read journal articles, primarily. These articles, for the sake of brevity, tend to deemphasize the theoretical aspects of their research and focus on the findings. I contacted experts in the field whose articles I had read. Several were happy to talk with me and some forwarded me their own students' research. I found reading other student theses and dissertations invaluable because it gave me an idea of the different types of theories being used with regard to physical activity, and how those theories could be applied. At the same time, I found reading this research quite daunting: it was full of language I didn't understand and discussions of philosophers of whom I had never heard. I decided first to try and come to grips with the basics of feminist and gender theory. The only way I found to do this was to take a rather dogged and blinkered approach to my knowledge acquisition and plow through several introductory texts and readers without allowing myself to be distracted by how much I didn't know. I always reasoned with myself that I was an intelligent person and I would arrive at my goal eventually (it was just a matter of when!). I kept reminding myself how far I had come.

✳ ✳ ✳

Whenever I took a conversation on theory I could see a look of uncertainty on Heidi's face. I had sympathy for Heidi: in my experience, integrating a theoretical perspective is often the most difficult part of a project for many beginning researchers. It often requires perseverance to learn new concepts and the language used to discuss them. However, I believe that the ability to work with theory is the mark of a scholar, and provides depth to analysis, so I didn't give up easily.

I spoke of the role of theory in research and referred Heidi to an introductory article on the topic that I had written with colleagues (Andrews, Sullivan, & Minichiello, 2004). I spoke of various theories and their lineages, but did not want to be too prescriptive in suggesting a particular perspective, in part because I wanted Heidi to be literate in the foundational aspects of her research topic. I encouraged Heidi to read other research and to find reports that she admired. Thereafter, we could explore these authors' use of theory, build on it, and apply it to her project.

Encouragement was particularly important at this stage of the research. Heidi would read some research at the intersection of feminist theory and sport or leisure, then write about her understanding of what she read and how it might be applied to her research. We went through a progressive refinement as Heidi's ability to read and comprehend social science literature developed. At the same time, we worked on other sections of the project in order to break up work on this aspect, and to gain a feeling of forward momentum. Although Heidi was attracted to feminist theory, her reading was wide ranging and general, so development of this aspect of her research was slow. In part, this was because Heidi's education as an undergraduate was more practical and vocational than conceptual and theoretical. That may be appropriate for the training of health professionals, but it leaves gaps for students wishing to work in the social sciences.

✳ ✳ ✳

Getting Theoretical

I have always considered myself a feminist; feminist research to me simply implied research done by women, on women, for women. While this is certainly true, there is a great deal of diversity and controversy within feminist thought of which I had previously been unaware. My decision to use a feminist framework as the theoretical base for my thesis gave me a new sense of purpose. Soon I had a draft of what I considered to be a good first attempt at my theory chapter on my supervisor's desk. I waited anxiously to see what he thought. Always encouraging, his feedback was something along the lines of it was "an excellent learning exercise" and "a process I needed to go through." He also sent it to a colleague with a specific interest in feminist leisure research (who subsequently became my invaluable associate supervisor). Similarly, her feedback was along the lines of, "while it displayed that I had read widely and had a good grasp on the basics, it read a bit like a 'cook's tour' of feminism." Although slightly disheartening, I also understood exactly what they were saying and agreed with their points. I was indeed overwhelmed by the number of what seemed like equally valid perspectives on the issue of femininity and so had planned to use them all, although I was still unsure exactly how. What I really needed to do was commit to a particular way of making sense of young women's experiences and explore it more deeply, using my data to further develop it.

Editors' Comment

Choice of Theory

Selecting an operating theory is very complex because there are so many choices available. Heidi chose feminist theory to guide her research. She explains that there were personal as well as academic reasons for her decision. This study about the influence of gender relations on physical activity is well suited to a paradigm that helps explain how women are positioned in regard to participation in any cultural context. All the other researchers included in this book chose their theoretical perspective based on prior experience, literature they consulted, their interests and values, and advice from their instructors and mentors. Choice of a theoretical perspective is best made following extensive reading, conversation, and reflection.

As part of my overview of feminist and gender theory (previously known as my theory chapter), I considered the work of gender theorist Connell (1987, 2002), who had proposed four dimensions of gender relations, all acting simultaneously. I will not go into the details of her theory here, but suffice to say that Connell's theoretical interpretation of gender appealed to me largely because it touched on all the key elements I had written about in my "cook's tour"—power, emotion, symbolism, and production. Using these four dimensions of gender as a theoretical framework in my research allowed me to commit to one theory (Connell's) while continuing to "fence sit," to some extent.

A Question of Method

Armed with Connell's gender relations theory and my supervisor's blessing (I knew he still had some reservations about the general nature of my theoretical framework, but he was happy for me to discover its limitations in my own time), I set off to interview my chosen population—young women who had finished school but not yet borne children. I knew that I would need some sort of structure for these interviews; Connell advocated the use of a life history method of interviewing because it allows for the consideration of the changing social and cultural context of a person throughout her lifetime. Simply put, life history method involves a person looking back at her past and recalling the meanings and significance of various events as remembered.

I found this method of interviewing easy and enjoyable. I began by asking about the experiences in each participant's life surrounding physical activity. I used both life course stages (childhood, adolescence, and so on) marked by significant events (starting school, first sport played, and so on) and life course experiences (school, sports, family, friends, interests, and work) as prompts for the participants to talk about their physical activity experiences. I developed an interview guide to this effect, but did not adhere to it with any strictness. It provided an excellent way of starting the young women talking, all the time trying to allow them to explore their own ideas and thoughts without interrupting them. The guide also served as a prompt when a young woman found it difficult to find words to describe her experience and feelings.

A life history method of interviewing served me well for my research and allowed me to consider how meanings are constructed about embodied subjectivity in the context of social relations, institutional practices, and young women's relation to self. However, an ongoing topic of discussion with my supervisor regarded the desirability of ethnographic research. He suggested that it would be beneficial to socialize with some of the participants and their friends in "naturally occurring situations" (Russell, 1999), in order to learn about and understand these young women and their lives, from their perspective. Such an approach would have been more feasible had I looked at specific types or groups of women in the initial stages of the research, but I was interested in a wide range of participants and I could not see a way of carrying out this type of fieldwork. The only way of studying my participants ethnographically would have been to ask for an invitation to their social events, which I was not comfortable doing. While I appreciated that some ethnographic data would have enhanced my research, it was not until I began to analyze my data in detail that I fully appreciated the shortcomings of my methodology for my particular research questions.

> **Editors' Comment**
>
> **The Interview Guide**
>
> Although an interview guide may function as a questionnaire, more often in qualitative research it is used as an outline that includes issues and themes to explore, as well as the possible prompts and cues that might elicit this information. It is often a loosely structured list that constantly evolves in light of each research conversation. In some interviews, all the points on the guide plus more are covered. Other interviews head in unanticipated directions. This is why it is called a *guide*. It is intended to lead discussions, but not to control them.
>
> The interview guide may be constantly edited, revised, and modified as a research project evolves. During qualitative research interviews, it is important to be flexible and responsive to what is happening at any given moment. Some of the best interviews delve into unanticipated territory.

By interacting with young women only through interviews, I was always asking them to consider their bodies in a situation removed from any significant embodied activity. I postulated in my thesis that women view themselves as an object in certain contexts, although this may have been more apparent to me due to my method than if the women were engaging in activity while I observed or participated. It was therefore hard to capture in a research process that privileges language (talking) and the articulate subject those embodied meanings that escape language, such as how shame related to body size may have moved or affected them in different ways. I now acknowledge an awareness of the particular context of my research and how this may have influenced my insights into the young women's embodied experiences of physical activity. (In other words, my supervisor was right!)

Getting More Theoretical

After I had conducted, coded, analyzed, and written up several initial interviews I was beginning to realize that I was still missing something. I could see that both social relations and social institutions, as well as understandings of self, were significant to these young women, but my use of gender theory was insufficient to explain why. I sensed that there was something just outside my grasp. I never became disheartened, though, because I always had a sense that any second it was all going to fall into place. (Even though I am not sure it ever did completely, it allowed me to cope better.) My supervisor helpfully suggested I had reached a point where I needed to sit under a tree, have a drink, and think about it.

(He also told me that when a supervisor had given him similar advice many years ago he was mystified by her suggestion, but he now saw the wisdom in it.)

Once again, I went back to reading recent literature in fields similar to mine. I also began to read some of the texts on which Connell had based her dimensions of gender, particularly those that addressed the concepts of social institutions, social relations, and relations to self, which had begun to interest me. In much of the literature I was reading, Michel Foucault was referenced. Early in my studies, I had attempted to read one of Foucault's well-known works, but had understood little of it and been scared off. I decided to give Foucault another go and was surprised this time to find his work far more relevant and manageable (three years of study had not been wasted after all . . .). In addition, when I had first come across Foucault in the substantive research, it was his earlier works that were being used. On their own, Foucault's early works seemed limiting, with little potential for my own research. When I returned to the literature a year or two later, though, I discovered some researchers were beginning to apply Foucault's later work in the field of sports and leisure studies in ways that were far more relevant to the direction my research was beginning to take. I had not read his later work, but dove in and began reading.

Becoming More Critical

As with most developments in my research, development of my critical ability was as much a personal journey as a professional one. From the outset, I understood the need both to have an awareness of how my own position influenced my research and to reflect critically on my findings in light of current research and practice. Although I knew that this critical perspective would be crucial if I was to contribute to the field of physical activity, however, it was really only with time and reading that I was able to do more than simply recognize that need. To gain a critical perspective, I found that it was important to have read widely enough on a particular topic to have an opinion on it. I needed to appreciate the arguments both for and against a perspective, not just be well versed in my own argument. In addition, I needed to be confident in my own assertions. Spending time reading and assimilating a variety of viewpoints, then discussing propositions with others, especially with those who may not agree, were important ways for me to develop a critical perspective. Whereas developing a critical perspective comes from a gradual evolution of thoughts, however, it was also true that at some point I had to take a leap of faith and commit to an opinion. It is difficult to give step-by-step instructions on how to be critical, but some concrete examples from my research might help. The two most obvious examples of my increasing critical awareness relate to issues on which my supervisor had commented and that I had largely chosen to ignore until something clicked and I got it.

The first was the issue of barriers to physical activity. In the mainstream health promotion literature, there is much discussion on the barriers that prevent young women from being physically active. In spite of the more sociological approach I was encouraged to take, I initially adopted this concept and coded my first interviews according to discussion of various barriers (in spite of my supervisor's hints that it might not prove particularly useful). It wasn't long before I began to recognize the shortcomings of such a concept, although it took me almost until the end of my study to be able to fully understand and explain why the concept of "barriers" was not helpful for my understanding how women are barriers to themselves, other than in a blaming way.

It was clear from my data early on that a barrier meant different things to different people: to the elite athletes in my study, bad weather was not a barrier, but bad weather restricted other women in the study from being active. It also meant different things to the same person at different times. For example, one participant grew up in England, where the cooler climate never stopped her from participating in regular physical activity as a young person. As an adult living in Sydney, however, she often considered it too cold to be physically active outdoors. A barrier, then, is a socially constructed and dynamic concept rather than a fixed structure.

Gradually, as my theoretical position developed, I began to recognize the implication of barrier as a negative, something that limits, constrains, or prevents young women from being physically active. From a Foucauldian perspective, conceptualizing barriers as singularly repressive involves a limited notion of power relations. Foucault (1980) acknowledges that power is not inherently either good or bad; therefore, gendered power relations have the ability to both constrain and enable women to be active, depending on the context.

The concept of barriers also removes the element of choice from these women and denies them their subjectivity; many of these young women make active and informed choices about their physical activity participation. To label their choice a barrier (although not all barriers of course rely on choice) undermines their experiences and indeed their lives. My study also suggests that choice and hence women's subjectivity is complex, messy, and contextually shaped by particular relations. Choices are not simply made by a freely choosing voluntary or rational subject, nor are they purely determined by structures, but are made by negotiating demands and invitations to "perform" femininity (as described by Butler, 1993) in certain ways that are or are not actively embodied. The notion of barriers tended to reify social relations and institutions as things to be overcome by individual choice or that determine individual choice in an unproblematic way.

✳ ✳ ✳

When Heidi had developed a deeper theoretical basis for her analysis, the material drew her into consideration of power relations, which changed her relationship with research participants such that she now saw the participants as embodied subjects having agency within a social and cultural context. The change in Heidi's thinking and in the purpose and structure of the thesis was dramatic. What began as a study to identify and overcome barriers to young women's participation in sports and purposeful exercise became a study in which the complexity of identity and gender relations was explored in order to better understand young women's lives, particularly in relation to their ideas about their bodies. Crudely put, one could say that the exercise police perspective gave way to an empathic understanding of young women's experience and a very good doctoral thesis. I began to be excited by draft chapters Heidi was delivering to us. Judging by the speed with which she produced them, Heidi had also found her stride. Heidi's analysis moved beyond a somewhat superficial summary and description of her data to explanation. At this stage, I knew that Heidi had had an epiphany and that she would produce a thesis of which we would all be proud.

✳ ✳ ✳

My increasingly critical questioning of some of the normative concepts of health promotion literature allowed me to take a more relational approach in my research. I did this by examining the way power is embodied in particularly gendered ways to constrain and enable active engagement as young women negotiate the process of becoming autonomous adult women with new responsibilities, desires, and relationships with others and with themselves.

Another example my supervisor is fond of discussing in relation to my ongoing "critical growth" is what he referred to as my role as "the exercise police." I was well aware when undertaking this research that I needed to consider my background as a physical therapist, public health professional, and social athlete. I have spent a large part of my personal and professional life embracing the public health teachings that support lifelong physical activity participation due to the multiple physical and mental benefits it has for the participants, and encouraging people to be regularly physically active. However, the public health ethic of adopting a healthy lifestyle for the greater good of the nation does not sit comfortably with my (more recent) recognition that meaning and knowledge are created by individuals within the discursive resources of society. It was important for me to recognize the idea of physical activity as desirable and necessary as my own (as well as the dominant media message). My desire to "make" people more physically active was based on an understanding of power that reified notions of subjectivity as unitary, and resistance as opposition (Munro, 1998), rather than the Foucauldian understanding of power to which I aspired in my research.

Therefore, my perception of the health professional's role as an agent of change was severely challenged. I struggled in my research project to work toward social change "without violating the rights of others to construct their own knowledge" (Munro, 1998, p. 26). My own ethical awareness grew through this process, although this was certainly not the initial goal of this research. It took me a long time to recognize these competing ideologies and to acknowledge that I could not hope to "make" women more physically active. The recognition of my personal and societal biases allowed me to propose what I believe to be a more sophisticated way of understanding young women's participation in physical activity as related to their embodied experiences and regulated by gendered practices. It also permitted me to conclude my research by moving on from traditional prescriptive models of physical activity promotion, instead proposing promotion of a feminist ethic of self that does not rely simply on telling someone what to do.

✴ ✴ ✴

A gracious supervisor would allow the new graduate to have the final word, so I hope I will be forgiven for adding a postscript. I would like to comment on how Heidi has managed a balanced life throughout her research. As if completing a doctorate weren't enough, throughout the years of her graduate studies Heidi has had two babies, traveled, run marathons, renovated a house, managed a family, and worked part time. Wow!

✴ ✴ ✴

References

Andrews, I., Sullivan, G., & Minichiello, V. (2004). The philosophical and theoretical context of qualitative research. In V. Minichiello, G. Sullivan, K. Greenwood, & R. Axford (Eds.), *Handbook of research methods for nursing and health science* (2nd ed.). Sydney: Pearson/Prentice Hall.

Australian Bureau of Statistics (ABS). (2006). *4364.0 National health survey: Summary of results 2004–2005.* Canberra: Commonwealth of Australia.

Booth, M., Okely, A., Denney-Wilson, E., Hardy, L., Yang, B., & Dobbins, T. (2006). *NSW schools physical activity and nutrition survey (SPANS) 2004: Full report.* Sydney: NSW Department of Health.

Butler, J. (1993). *Bodies that matter: On the discursive limits of "sex."* New York: Routledge.

Connell, R. W. (1987). *Gender and power: Society, the person and sexual politics.* Cambridge, UK: Polity Press.

Connell, R. W. (2002). *Gender.* Cambridge, UK: Polity Press.

Foucault, M. (1980). *Power-knowledge: Selected interviews and other writings 1972–1977* (C. Gordon, L. Marshall, J. Mepham, & K. Soper, Trans.). London: Harvester Wheatsheaf.

Gilchrist, H., Sullivan, G., & Heard, R. (1997). Physiotherapy students' knowledge and attitudes toward the treatment of people living with HIV/AIDS. *Physiotherapy: Theory and Practice, 13,* 265–278.

Hall, M. A. (1996). *Feminism and sporting bodies: Essays on theory and practice.* Champaign, IL: Human Kinetics.

Munro, P. (1998). *Subject to fiction: Women teachers' life history narratives and the cultural politics of resistance.* Buckingham, UK/Philadelphia, PA: Open University Press.

Parr, J. (1998). Theoretical voices and women's own voices: The stories of mature women students. In J. Ribbens & R. Edwards (Eds.), *Feminist dilemmas in qualitative research: Public knowledge and private lives.* London: Sage Publications.

Russell, C. (1999). Participant observation. In V. Minichiello, G. Sullivan, K. Greenwood, & R. Axford (Eds.), *Handbook for research methods in the health sciences.* Sydney: Addison-Wesley.

Stebbins, R. A. (1999). Serious leisure. In T. L. Burton & E. L. Jackson (Eds.), *Leisure studies: Prospects for the twenty-first century* (pp. 69–80). State College, PA: Venture Publishing Co.

Wright, J. (1996). The construction of complementarity in physical education. *Gender and Education, 8,* 61–79.

Focus Group Methodology 16

*Being Guided on a Journey
From Novice to Expert*

Jane Phillips and Patricia Davidson

Introduction

Embarking on a research project is somewhat akin to venturing on a voyage into the unknown and being constantly exposed to new encounters and experiences, many of which are unexpected and some of which are not desirable. Often this research journey is like riding a roller coaster, where there are moments of exhilaration and immense satisfaction, closely followed by feelings of despair and frustration when events are not going as planned. What I (Jane) have come to realize, though, is that this is the real world of research, particularly when it is conducted outside the laboratory and in dynamic settings, such as in hospitals and schools. As a novice researcher, the only exposure I had to research was through textbooks and pristine research reports. So having a mentor who was able to support and navigate me through this journey helped make it a less confronting experience. This mentoring has been an integral aspect of my learning experience.

The research student–academic supervisor learning partnership has existed since the ancients. Socrates' role as a mentor and teacher to Plato is one of history's legends. Over the ages, this story has been retold to numerous generations. It reinforces the role of the mentor in enabling and guiding the student through the journey to acquire knowledge. The student in effective mentoring relationships is attentive and respectful, yet forges his own path. To date, little has been written about the learning relationship in contemporary research settings. Most of the literature presents research as a series of linear, streamlined processes that can be followed sequentially. However, what is missing from this discourse is the activity behind the scenes: the relationships forged and the experiences that shape the student's research learning experiences, particularly in complex and dynamic research environments.

Selecting a Supervisor—Partnering With a Student

Before telling you about our experiences with focus groups, we will share with you a little bit about developing our student-mentor relationship. My having made the decision to undertake research, my next challenge was to secure an academic supervisor. As a mature aged student, I was aware that I wanted to work with an accomplished researcher in my area of clinical interest, palliative care. More importantly, though, I wanted to partner with someone with whom I could work collaboratively and who I could trust implicitly. As I mentally drafted these essential criteria and mapping out my next steps, a serendipitous encounter led me to meet my future supervisor. During this initial meeting, I was struck by Patricia's extraordinary skills and passion for improving end-of-life care for people with chronic heart failure. At the end of the meeting, we exchanged contact details and continued to converse over the next couple of months. During this period, I became aware of our similar worldviews with compatible values and beliefs. Her advice to me was that choosing the right supervisor was possibly more important than choosing the school or institution. Patricia encouraged me to seek a supervisor who would enable me to develop in my own way. She suggested that asking other students about their experiences was a good place to start identifying some potential supervisors.

✳ ✳ ✳

During my (Patricia's) first encounter with Jane, she expressed an interest in the applicability of palliative care for people with chronic heart failure. It also transpired that she was contemplating embarking on a doctoral program. During our conversations, it was apparent that Jane had a real commitment to improving the health and well-being of her local rural community. As an academic I was naturally interested in this conversation, but just as it is unlikely that I would sign up a new house mate without an interview and potentially some references, I did not want to accept a research student to work in my research program without the same background check. As callous as it may sound, a supervisor (mentor) needs to be convinced that the student (mentee) is someone who is worth the time and energy, particularly in academic settings where outputs are of critical importance. This for me means asking the tough questions: Will this student deliver? Can I trust this student to undertake a project associated with my name ethically and appropriately? And perhaps more importantly, Will I have fun and develop personally and professionally with this person? These are all questions I routinely consider when approached by potential research students.

When preparing students to embark upon a career as an independent researcher, it is important to prepare them as much as possible and to guide and enable, rather than control and contain. Many of the important strategies that promote a successful researcher are the things not readily gleaned from a textbook. It is sharing the art as well as the science of research that denotes the sharing and trust of the student-supervisor relationship. Effective communication and interpersonal relationships are critical in research, yet less commonly discussed. As you progress on your research journey, it is important that both the mentor and mentee respect each other's values and strengths. It is common for the student to become the expert, particularly at a doctoral level, and the supervisor can learn and develop accordingly if open to this exchange. It is important to recognize that the student's success is a true measure of your capacity as a supervisor and mentor. Unfortunately, from both the mentor's and mentee's perspective, success is not always the outcome. Sometimes, after considerable effort, students abandon their studies. Fortunately, this is the exception not the rule. As your career progresses, you mature in the mentor role and implement a range of strategies to maximize the potential for success and to mitigate failures. Therefore, choosing your supervisor and mentor is perhaps one of the most critical steps you can take in a research career. When choosing a supervisor, think about the skills this person has, not only as a researcher, but also interpersonally and professionally. If the mentor takes her role seriously, the mentorship is about developing you as an independent researcher, not building her own empire. I must admit, though, that basking in the reflected glory of your students is a wonderful emotion and a pleasurable sensation.

※　※　※

The R-PAC Project

To help contextualize our focus group experiences, I was drawing upon an earlier study, which forms the basis of my doctoral dissertation. This project was designed to address the palliative care needs of older people dying in *residential aged care*. *Residential aged care* is the term used to describe regulated accommodation available for older people who require ongoing assistance with activities of daily living and nursing care. This term is interchangeable with convalescent or nursing home, aged care facility, and long-term care facility. Sadly, for a range of reasons, many older people will spend their last days in residential aged care.

The R-PAC Project was designed to strengthen partnerships to improve the coordination and delivery of palliative care in local aged care facilities. A Critical Reference Group comprising key stakeholders provided direction in implementing the project plan. An action research framework was chosen to drive the project; this framework required energy and commitment on the part of both the student and the supervisor. From my perspective, utilizing action research required an acceptance that, unlike other forms of research, action research was unlikely to progress in a linear fashion and was more likely to follow a somewhat unpredictable research process that is not always continuous. It also required that I facilitate rather than direct the research process, which was something I was comfortable doing, having been previously involved in various community development initiatives. However, what was more challenging for me was tolerating considerable uncertainty and accepting that the action research journey and its final destination were somewhat unknown. The trade-off for this ambiguity was that an action research offered participants a potentially transforming experience.

✻ ✻ ✻

Adopting this type of approach requires appraising the skills and expertise within the student-supervisor research partnership. Effective communication is critical in ensuring that there is no role ambiguity or conflict in the research process, and that a trusting relationship is maintained between student and supervisor, researcher and participants. Considering these personal dynamics within the methodological and ethical parameters of the study was a critical step for Jane and me.

✻ ✻ ✻

During the extensive stakeholder consultation process of the R-PAC Project it was identified that that older people in local residential aged care facilities had unmet needs, particularly with respect to management of their pain, restlessness, and agitation. Having worked as a local palliative care clinical nurse consultant I was acutely aware of the limited opportunities that the specialist palliative care team had to provide expertise to improve the care of older people in residential aged care. This was of particular concern because older people in this care setting are more likely to have chronic debilitating conditions, such as dementia (60 percent), chronic pain (40 to 50 percent), and depression (40 percent) (Royal Australian College of General Practitioners, 2006).

As outsiders looking in, we saw many challenges in promoting a palliative approach in this environment. In the aged care settings, typically large numbers of unregulated and untrained workers provide personal care, which is particularly challenging when palliative care demands a skilled nursing response. There is also a high staff turnover in aged care, in some instances resulting in an increased use of agency staff and little continuity of care for residents, which can have adverse consequences. In spite of these challenges, it became readily apparent during the consultation process that all local aged care managers were enthusiastic about being involved as active partners in the R-PAC Project. The formation of this partnership offered us an opportunity to work collaboratively with these aged care providers to address their residents' unmet palliative care needs (Phillips, Davidson, Jackson, Kristjanson, Bennett, & Daly, 2006).

Selecting the Research Methodology and Identifying the Methods

When undertaking any research project there are a range of methodological perspectives that are accessible and appropriate. Choosing the most appropriate approach is largely dependent on the research questions and the study aims. I found that investing the time contemplating where I wanted the project to go and discussing this with my supervisor helped me select a suitable study method. I knew what I was interested in: improving the delivery of palliative care for older people. I believed that the research should focus on building the capacity of local aged care providers. It quickly became evident that what was required in the study setting was an approach that could act to empower the aged care workforce and help prime the environment for change. My supervisor had extensive experience in chronic disease management, health services research, and health-care reform, while I had considerable palliative care expertise and a background in health promotion. These two perspectives were melded to develop a study design overarched by an action research framework.

Editors' Comment

Implications of Research Paradigm

Action research is one particular paradigm for reframing and conducting research that is frequently used in designs in which the purpose of the study is not only to investigate a phenomenon, but also to influence a positive outcome for the unit studied. Jane

(Continued)

> (Continued)
>
> describes the rationale for using this approach that clearly demonstrates that her goal was to change organization policy and practices in order to improve the delivery of care. Once she made this decision regarding methodology, it shaped everything else she did subsequently, including the participants she recruited, the way she used focus groups, how she collected data, and, most critically, how she shared data with others in such a way that the data would be most useful to them. Had she used grounded theory, narrative analysis, phenomenology, or another methodology, she would have gone down a very different path. For instance, she might have used in-depth interviews instead of focus groups, taken a less participatory role in the sharing of information, and focused more on theory development (grounded theory), collecting individual stories (narrative analysis), or identifying core themes (phenomenology). Action research is concerned not only with studying issues, but also with impacting them.

The whole purpose of action research is simultaneously to gain an understanding of the social system in order to address the problems and to identify the best opportunity for change while generating new knowledge about the system. Collaborative action is a critical element of this process and helps to bring about change in a given situation. We developed a project in six phases involving continuous cycles of reflection, planning, acting, and evaluating (Street, 2004).

✲   ✲   ✲

Along the way, there was a juggling of pragmatic considerations and the methodological rigor recommended in textbooks. For example, Jane undertook an assessment of baseline knowledge. It was very tempting to include identifiers to facilitate the posttest process on an individual case basis. However, we did not want care assistants to think this was "testing" them. In these initial stages, I was keen to demonstrate to Jane how to effectively engage with aged care providers while generating baseline data from which to measure progress. Mapping this pathway required that Jane and I regularly teleconference to discuss these issues to weight the merit of these approaches. All of this is congruent with an action research approach. This enabled us to work in partnership with and for participants, rather than to undertake research on them. This involved listening carefully to their needs and involving them in decisionmaking. In spite of this, the project was still Jane's doctoral project; my role as her supervisor was to advocate for her needs and those of the study participants.

✲   ✲   ✲

Employing these collaborative processes also helped ensure that the research process and outcomes were more meaningful to participants and encouraged them to examine and reflect on their usual practice (Morrison &

Lilford, 2001). For example in the focus groups, participants were required to reflect on critical events, such as recent deaths of residents. This provided participants with an opportunity to consider whether the care provided was optimal or suboptimal, and to provide evidence to support their perceptions.

Equally important, our choice of action research as the process driving the R-PAC Project was also congruent with both of our personal commitment to principles of social justice and equity and striving for health-care reform. Having previously worked with marginalized community members, such as people living with HIV/AIDS and members of the indigenous communities, I was aware of how power, politics, gender, role, and status impact people's lives. Because women were one of the project's key stakeholder groups, having an understanding of feminist issues would inevitably be an integral element of the project. I was cognizant that my supervisor, an executive member of the International Council on Women's Health Issues, was committed to improving women's lives through participation, advocacy, empowerment, education, and research.

✳ ✳ ✳

I was all too aware of how these communities feel about (external), academics studying them. Often, what is a key driver to engage these communities is working on solutions with them, not just documenting barriers. I was mindful at the outset of the R-PAC Project of these issues, especially given that aged care nurses are often in a marginalized position within the health-care sector. I also was aware of the sensitivity of documenting potentially adverse factors in a highly politicized environment. It seemed that action research would allow Jane to adopt the role of facilitator and enabler and place her in the best position to provide aged care nurses and care assistants with a supportive and empowering environment in which they could collaboratively work to address their identified needs. I believed it was important that Jane debrief with me on critical incidents, and that Jane share her experiences of achieving change in the clinical setting. Together we would develop and negotiate a plan of action to address the issues emerging from the project.

✳ ✳ ✳

Focus Group Methodology

Action research is largely dependent on acquiring effective and appropriate data to empirically drive the project forward. Because action research is a conceptual framework as opposed to a specific method, I was able to use a range of methods; in particular, though, I chose focus group interviews as a method of both exploration and evaluation. The reasons for choosing this method were many, including the potential to access larger numbers of responders, to capture the collective and social characteristics of the setting, and, importantly, to capture the unique views and opinions of the study participants. Focus groups offered the potential of developing an understanding of aged care providers' perceptions and feelings about delivering a palliative approach to care within the individual facilities, while providing participants with an opportunity for reflective interaction in a safe environment with others who may have complementary or differing views about this issue. This method also placed me as the researcher in a less commanding and controlling role of information gathering, though I was actively engaging participants in a process that was focused on making a difference, appropriate for an action research project. Using this method also helped ensure that due attention was paid to the subjective meanings for participants. This level of involvement, along with having a voice and being heard, facilitated a sense of joint ownership of the R-PAC Project's process and outcomes.

The focus group methodology was applied extensively throughout the R-PAC Project because as a form of group interview it offered the potential to generate rich interactive data through the opinions expressed by aged care nurses, care assistants, and managers, individually and collectively. This was an action research project, so I anticipated the focus group data would guide the development of the intervention while ensuring that older people's needs were addressed. Exploring attitudes collectively rather than individually is a useful process, aiding in the examining of the social, organizational, and environmental contexts of nursing practice (Davidson, Paull, Cockburn, Davis, Rees, Gorman, et al., 2004). Given the complexity of the aged care setting, it was essential that I examine opinions, values, and beliefs in the context of the practice that is undertaken to help derive systematic clinical change (Roberts & Snowball, 1999).

For this reason, a strategic decision was made to ensure that all focus groups were conducted in an environment and at a time that best suited the participants. The advantage of using focus group methodology at the commencement of the project was that it placed me in the less commanding and controlling role of information gathering, while it actively engaged the participants in a process that was focused on making a difference. Focus groups provide an important opportunity for reflective interaction with others who may have complementary or differing views—in this case, views on palliative care delivery for older people in aged care.

Getting Started

As you can see from the information outlined above, our focus groups were nested within a range of other activities to engage the study setting. Undertaking any type of health service development involves anticipating people's reactions to change, from embracing to resisting. Anticipating these factors in the research setting is critical. It is also important to have a pragmatic attitude to research. Together, as partners, we were able to discuss these issues within our broader research team. Following an integrative literature review, we conducted a series of focus groups to investigate the collective perceptions and beliefs about palliative care in a purposive sample of nurses and care assistants working in residential aged care.

✳ ✳ ✳

As we began on this journey, a useful strategy I shared with Jane is the importance of scheduling adequate time to prepare for the focus group. It is common for the student to want to just start, but taking the time first to develop relationships within the study setting is critical. Environmental and technological considerations also need to be considered; researchers also need to prepare themselves emotionally and physically. As in most lessons in life, this comes from experience. I have noticed that when I do not do this preparation the project and participants are not well served in terms of data generation. Therefore, I spend a lot of time in preparation noting barriers and facilitators in the study setting. When I am conducting a focus group, I try to schedule my day so I am not rushed and tired. I want to be able to devote my full attention to facilitating and using all my senses to glean the perspectives of study participants. I encouraged Jane to read widely, and put her in touch with other research students who had utilized this method. We had numerous discussions about all of the necessary preparations required to conduct successful focus groups, such as purchasing a recording device, scheduling sessions, and working on strategies to engage participants. In addition, I alerted Jane to the need to be confident and prepared to manage interpersonal factors in the group setting, and to be prepared to monitor the flow of the conversation. Because we were dealing with a subject associated with sensitivities, Jane and I discussed how we needed to bear this in mind as well.

✳ ✳ ✳

The Critical Reference Group recommended that focus groups be conducted within local aged care facilities because this would enable those that were interested in this issue to participate more readily. Each residential aged care facility was provided with an opportunity to host a focus group. Invitations to participate and posters advertising the focus groups were distributed to all aged care managers, inviting aged care nurse and care assistants to participate. The focus group time was selected by management to fit in with the workload; the time coincided with an overlap of shifts to enable the maximum number of people to participate. The R-PAC Project team would provide refreshments.

Editors' Comment

Managing Focus Groups

Working within any group is far more complex and challenging than working with individuals. Group dynamics and process variables influence the ways that people share and interact with one another. Group settings for data collection can be particularly rich and stimulating, however. Participants build on one another's disclosures, reflect on what has been said, and come to consensus about shared experiences.

The structure and management of focus groups requires a specific set of skills to plan for optimal conditions of trust and safety, to operate efficiently, and to generate the most useful and varied data. Ideally, with approximately a dozen participants, you should consider how best to elicit interaction, record conversations, and manage the flow of discussion in such a way that everyone feels heard, understood, and respected.

The question route for these focus groups was designed to allow exploration and probing of key issues that had been defined from a literature review, needs assessment, and local key informant interviews. I hoped that the questions would invite exploration of different views, solutions, and suggestions and would help identify the strengths and resources that may be readily available in aged care to promote palliative care delivery.

A key strategy was to choose venues and timings to allow participants to feel free and open to exchange ideas and contribute to the discussion. However, I was aware that this consideration needed to be balanced with time, human, and financial resource considerations. We were concerned that some participants might be uncomfortable or anxious about outlining limitations of existing care models and challenging the status quo. For this reason, we interviewed managers and other nurses independently. The initial focus group consisted entirely of aged care managers. This not only provided information on organizational factors, but also was useful in consolidating support for the project and reassuring them about the project's aims. This group was followed by additional focus groups comprising nurses and care assistants. Participation in all focus groups was entirely voluntary and by self-selection. All of the aged care providers' voices were privileged and given an opportunity to be heard.

The Textbook Focus Group

My supervisor flew up from the city to the regional sites to spend several days mentoring and guiding me through this initial series of focus groups, which were scheduled to occur over a period of four days.

I consider that allocating a concentrated period of time is a critical investment in developing my students' research competencies. As part of this process, I intended to demonstrate how to undertake data collection and analysis concurrently as reflexive activities and then allow Jane to undertake this process independently. I reinforced with Jane the need to be unrushed and focused in these encounters to maximize our potential to engage with participants and glean useful information. This meant not scheduling activities on the day we were doing focus groups so that not only did we have sufficient energy to engage in meaningful discussion and listen intently, but also we had the time to reflect and process events and commence data analysis afterwards.

In the first focus group, my supervisor acted as the moderator and facilitated the discussion, while I took on the role of the assistant moderator. As an observer and scribe, I was afforded an opportunity to pay particular attention to the participant interactions, to listen, and to jot down notable quotes. I recorded all of these notations on a focus group template that enabled me to record the participants' names, roles, seating arrangements, direct quotes, time the session took place, and ideas in a systematic way. Collecting this information allowed for the issues of time and person to be included in the analysis. I noted that my supervisor took care not to ask leading questions or to make suggestions that could influence the participants' responses.

Editors' Comment

The Field Work Process

Field research is an ever-changing process that has a force and life of its own. You schedule focus groups and people don't show up. You design a consent form and people refuse to sign it because they don't like the way something is worded. You plan to use a tape recorder but the room you are using is acoustically dead. You want to focus on certain stakeholders but others insist on being a part of the group. You are listening to someone and she abruptly decides to terminate the conversation with no explanation and leave the group. You find yourself in the middle of a focus group when you realize that a certain participant is just playing games with you. You have an interview guide to cover various topics but the group has quite another agenda and tells you that they won't talk about issues that you've already identified are central to your investigation. In other words, you must not only anticipate, but also prepare for inevitable departures from your original plan. This is where the best learning about research can occur—through your mistakes and errors in judgment. That's what Jane means when she talks about the difference between what is in the standard textbook and what is in *your* textbook.

This initial focus group unfolded in textbook fashion: We had a good group size in a suitable meeting room. The room was in a safe environment within an aged care facility that was quiet and that had comfortable chairs and a low coffee table in the middle. A congenial lunch was followed by a lively, respectful discussion during the focus group with everyone contributing. Immediately following this focus group my supervisor (moderator) and I (assistant moderator) met to reflect on the group interactions, in particular on nonverbal clues endorsing values, opinions, and beliefs. I wrote down all of these thoughts and ideas.

✼ ✼ ✼

I encouraged Jane to start immediately to map out her thoughts and ideas from the focus groups onto separate PowerPoint slides on my laptop. A combination of the audiotapes and the field notes recorded on the focus group template allowed for data verification and validation, with direct quotes added to the slides. The use of PowerPoint in this way is merely a way of organizing information; other software applications can readily be used. I demonstrated how the findings from this initial group could be used to shape, inform, and drive the subsequent focus groups.

✼ ✼ ✼

THE CHALLENGES THEY DON'T TALK ABOUT IN THE TEXTS

However, as with all research methods, there are some limitations with undertaking this type of data collection. A focus group introduces many participants, which makes it an uncontrolled social situation where the researcher has limited control over the discussions, which have the potential to become tangential (St. John, 2004). There is also the potential for some participants to dominate the conversations while others may not contribute at all. Interactions also can be affected by personal characteristics and social factors such as class, gender, and race (St. John, 2004), which are important considerations given the composition of the aged care workforce. These were all issues that we encountered in the next focus group, held in a large privately owned aged care facility. To our surprise, thirty enthusiastic participants presented themselves at that focus group. It transpired that nurses and care assistants had come in from their annual leave and days off, and a few had risen early having worked the previous night to contribute to the discussion about the challenges associated with delivering palliative care to older people in aged care.

Given that the texts suggest that the ideal focus group numbers range from somewhere between six to twelve people, this turnout for a novice seemed like an unmitigated disaster. Suddenly the space we had been allocated in the residents' dining room seemed inappropriate and the treats purchased for afternoon tea insufficient to feed everyone. I was suddenly full of anxieties: Were there enough consent forms? Would the microphones be adequate to capture all of the conversations? Should the number of participants be limited? If I chose this latter option, I would need to turn some people away, which I didn't want to do. If I didn't, would everyone have an opportunity to contribute? Would we be able to adequately facilitate the discussion, especially given that the stimulation of interaction and discourse between participants and the researcher is critical to the focus group process? How could I create a safe environment for the free and open exchange of participants' opinions, which is an obligatory prerequisite for focus group research? How was I going to be able to listen to and follow all of the relevant threads? How were we going to manage to achieve our ideal with such a large group in such an open setting? Fortunately, my supervisor, an experienced focus group facilitator, was by my side and able to guide me through these challenges. On this occasion, my supervisor facilitated the focus group.

✷ ✷ ✷

As a supervisor, I did not see this as a potential unmitigated disaster. Instead, I was rather overwhelmed and overjoyed by the commitment and engagement of the participants in this study setting. This commitment and engagement of the participants invigorated me and I thought little of the textbook restrictions that concerned Jane. My level of experience in speaking to large groups was important in my confidence and I was grateful that I was there for Jane. To reiterate the points above, a level of pragmatism is necessary in research (Halcomb & Davidson, 2006). However, pragmatism does not mean sacrificing methodological rigor: it just means sometimes you have to go with the flow, especially because this is not the controlled environment of the basic science laboratory. I tried immediately to put the group at ease by acknowledging how delighted we were to have so many participants. I then outlined the process I would use to ensure that everyone had an opportunity to participate and contribute. Guided by the question route, I then endeavored to facilitate the conversations elucidating further detail from participants' important comments. I was mindful of paying particular attention to honoring and valuing the contribution made by all participants as a way of encouraging others to contribute.

✷ ✷ ✷

My supervisor's facilitation style ensured that, in no time, these nurses and care assistants were freely offering suggestions about how to address the challenges they encountered in delivering palliative care to older people in this setting. Watching this process unfold confirmed for me that participating in a focus group that is well facilitated and validating could be an empowering experience for the participants. There was a real sense that the participants felt that they were involved in a process that they believed could make a difference. Given that empowerment of aged care nurses and care assistants was one of the desired outcomes for the R-PAC Project, it seemed appropriate that focus groups had been utilized at the start of this action research process. I was convinced that by utilizing this method we had given a voice to this group.

At the conclusion of the focus group, my supervisor and I again met immediately to reflect on the interactions, group dynamics, and the beliefs and perceptions emerging from these conversations. I found this initial meeting quite tough because it required considerable discipline to concentrate further on the focus group conversations and interactions in order to distill the issues and themes that were emerging. The first step was to write down our immediate thoughts and ideas. On completion of that task, my supervisor and I brainstormed key points that we considered had emanated from the discussions. We sought validation of these ideas from the moderator's notes and replayed the relevant section of tape. Referring immediately to these references helped us to start to understand what we were discovering and to commence mapping out the themes. Our knowledge from the literature and preliminary investigations allowed us to filter this information. These thoughts and ideas, along with the notable quotes, were added to the PowerPoint slides. In no time, the data grew. This initial data generation was subsequently refined and validated from transcripts before we undertook member verification.

※ ※ ※

As we have discussed above, as well as feeling energetic and focused it is important to schedule time immediately following the focus group to allow reflection, clarification, and discussion. In my experience, this is the critical and important first level of analysis.

※ ※ ※

SEE ONE, DO ONE, TEACH ONE . . .

Competency based learning in medicine and nursing is often described as, "see one, do one, teach one." Having observed my supervisor conduct two focus groups in two distinct circumstances, it was now time for me to try my hand at facilitation. During the third and fourth focus groups, I took on the role of the moderator while my supervisor assumed the role of assistant moderator. I had had a valuable learning experiencing, having read the theory and then observed my supervisor over two days of focus groups. Given this close proximity in time, the techniques and approaches employed by my supervisor during the focus group were readily recalled. Having been supported to learn in this way I was comfortable taking on this new role.

Editors' Comment

The Learning Curve of Data Collection

As you would expect, the first experience you have conducting interviews, leading focus groups, or observing behavior in the field will be both awkward and inefficient. You will likely be nervous and frustrated that things are not going as smoothly as you had hoped. There will be dead silences that you don't know how to handle. You will try to overstructure, or worse, you will dominate the conversations. You will fire off way too many questions without providing participants the opportunity to respond fully. You will lose your ability to concentrate because you are so focused on what you're about to do next. When you review the transcripts, you will kick yourself over and over again with all the points made that you neglected to follow up. You will realize how many important themes and issues were missed that you now see so clearly. You will see how many times you interrupted the flow of the conversation or missed important signals or clues. This is all normal and expected for a beginner. The beauty of this process is that after reviewing your previous work, consulting with your mentors, and receiving feedback on your data collection skills you will improve significantly with every subsequent session. When later you review those first sessions, you will be amazed at the progress you've made.

Even though I was an experienced group facilitator, conducting a focus group seemed like a totally different experience, primarily because I wasn't sure entirely what would emerge from the conversation and I was mindful of not wanting to shape or influence the discussion. What took me most by surprise was how some of the information that participants shared really challenged several common misconceptions about aged care. These nurses and care assistants really wanted to provide the best quality care to these older people, who they viewed as being like family: "*We do care*" (Care assistant, Group 2), "*We only want the best for them*" (Enrolled nurse, Group 4), "*This is their home, this is where they should be cared for*" (Care assistant, Group 3). Above all, they wanted their residents to have a comfortable and dignified death within the aged care facility and not to die alone (Phillips, Davidson, Kristjanson, Jackson, & Daly, 2006).

While I was facilitating the focus groups, my main concern was to follow the lines of enquiry that emerged. At times, it seemed as though I might have "dropped a stitch." However, this probability was addressed by actively engaging my supervisor in the discussion toward the end of the focus group. This gesture provided my supervisor with an opportunity to explore the leads that she may have noted that I had missed. In addition, this brief diversion provided me with a moment to quickly reflect on whether there was something I had wanted to investigate with the group but had neglected to do before it ended. The inclusion of the assistant moderator is an important element of the focus group process. It is a demonstration of commitment that all parties have an opportunity to contribute fully to the conversation. The end of this process is often an ideal juncture to draw the focus group discussion to a close. Respecting and adhering to the agreed time frame is an important consideration for the moderator, especially when participants are giving so freely and generously with their time. Time in any health-care setting is a precious commodity.

Data Analysis

During my preparatory reading, I had wondered what "data saturation" looked and felt like and how long it generally took to achieve. As a novice researcher, I assumed that recognizing data saturation may present some challenges.

✻ ✻ ✻

I had suggested to Jane that in my experience it is useful to do one more focus group after you think data saturation has occurred. Our continual engagement with the study setting meant that if our assumption of saturation was challenged we could perform additional focus groups.

✻ ✻ ✻

Editors' Comment

Reaching Saturation

Everyone is mystified by what constitutes data saturation. How do you know when you've collected sufficient data such that you need to stop? This question is even more frustrating when you ask your mentors this question and they look at you with such confidence and say, "Don't worry. You'll know."

Jane provides several examples of the signs to look for. This includes when (1) your interviews seem so repetitive that you can anticipate what will be said next, and (2) your themes have already been identified and it appears as if you're getting more of the same. In other words, you have reached saturation when you aren't learning anything new.

There are also some practical norms that operate within each research context that provide parameters for what is usually considered acceptable to meet standards of rigor. For example, your mentor, instructor, or publication outlet may tell you directly that you must complete a minimum of interviews or sessions in order to meet their standards.

The danger of stopping data collection prematurely—before you have covered all the territory—is that you risk compromising the value of your study. So how do you know you know enough? Through trial and error—and supervision by someone who is more experienced.

As each subsequent focus group unfolded, it became clearer that the issues were consistent and congruent with our knowledge of published literature. We were impressed and humbled by the nurses' and care assistants' obvious caring attitude toward the residents. During the third focus group, no new issues emerged, so the fourth focus group was the final focus group. By this stage, the process of data analysis was well under way, so this final group was undertaken as an ongoing iterative process.

The field notes collected during the focus groups also helped to highlight significant themes and concepts. The use of transcripts allowed for all the data to be categorized before undergoing further revision, grouping, and reduction. Taking these steps meant that I was immediately immersed in the focus group data, which made it easier to tease out the themes and start to shape the data. This made the transition to writing up the data the next logical step in the process. Analyzing the data in a timely manner was a prerequisite of this action research study as the data was used to drive the next phase of the study. This timeliness meant that the final category coding of the broad analytic themes could be shared and confirmed with study participants. In accordance with the action research process, each phase of this study involved negotiating the outcomes with research participants to verify whether participants considered the interim and final research outcomes an accurate portrayal of their lived experience (Lincoln & Guba, 1985). All outcomes were then evaluated through data verification and member checking for their credibility, transferability, dependability, and conformability. Furthermore, throughout the project I was aware of the need for reflexivity and the use of a reflective journal assisted with this process.

✷ ✷ ✷

As a supervisor, I consider this a simple and logical framework for students to follow. As in most of these models, people do not always follow these initially in a linear fashion, but it provides a useful checkpoint to ensure that crucial steps are met. I was impressed with Jane's diligence with her journal. Her productivity is a measure of her organization and engagement.

✷ ✷ ✷

While analyzing the focus group data, I used the strategies of self-awareness and critical self-reflection to help minimize potential biases and predispositions that may have affected the research process and subsequent findings. Negative case sampling was another strategy that I employed to mitigate biases. This mitigation involved critically examining the data for cases that didn't confirm my expectations and for conflicts with tentative explanations about the findings. Sharing these ideas with my supervisor and the participants has been an important element of the data analysis process.

Using the Focus Group Data to Propel the Action Research Cycle

The initial focus group data informed the development and implementation of a multifaceted intervention. Focus group methodology was again selected for use at the midpoint of the R-PAC Project because we considered it a useful way of developing an understanding of participants' perceptions about intervention. Focus groups have previously been used to develop health service interventions and to inform evaluation strategies, so we anticipated that the data generated would assist in identifying action to be considered during the third phase of the R-PAC Project.

Another series of focus groups was undertaken with aged care nurses and care assistants. In addition, a series of focus groups was undertaken with general practitioners to explore their perceptions of a palliative approach for older people. Although the aims of the focus groups with both aged care personnel and general practitioners were to seek their views on implementing a palliative approach, these two tracks of exploration were reported separately. We did this because interviews with the aged care personnel had a greater focus on exploration of the process issues relating to the multifaceted intervention, while the focus groups with general practitioners discussed overarching issues in the delivery of a palliative approach. Furthermore, we decided to conduct these investigations concurrently yet separately to allow each of these key stakeholder groups to have a voice within her own professional context.

The same methodology that has been described earlier was employed. As time progressed, I became more confident and proficient in facilitation. Once again, all of the focus groups with aged care providers were conducted in local residential aged care facilities and audiotaped, to allow data verification and validation. Attending to the data immediately after each focus group meant that notable quotes were transcribed and that broad themes emerged. We perceived that the intervention had enabled aged care personnel to become more proficient and confident to deliver palliative care as part of routine care.

> On Tuesday, I had the chance to feel it all coming together . . . we were able to institute a program of care for the gentleman from the day he arrived. I have been in touch with the spiritual coordinator and I am about to get onto the palliative care girls [specialist palliative care nurses]. . . . So my [link nurse] education has given me the tools to institute a program of care for someone from the moment he walked through the door . . . whereas we would previously have waited and then looked at his pain, but that would have been about it. What has happened for us is that we are now onto [a palliative approach] straight away. This man has a terminal illness and what has happened [now] wouldn't have happened twelve months ago. (Link nurse, Group 3)

What I hadn't anticipated was the emotions that some of these comments evoked, especially the perception that the intervention had been empowering and increased nurses' confidence to deliver palliative care. Dealing with these feelings while facilitating the focus group required me to concentrate on the conversations instead of immediately processing the comments.

Undertaking any type of qualitative research can be an emotional and personal experience as you share and empathize with participants. These emotions can intensify as you try and solicit a range of views and opinions within a collective context, such as within a focus group. The group dynamic adds an additional complexity to the interview experience; it can be a challenge to integrate views and opinions, and to moderate conflicting perspectives in some instances, as well as to derive a consensus view where necessary. As researchers, both novice and expert, this form of interaction with participants enriched our understanding of the study setting. In the later stage of the project and immediately following one of the focus groups, we both attended a commemoration service that was a strategy implemented as part of this project. Both of us almost sobbed, we were so moved by the moment. We celebrated the achievements of participants and our own achievements.

An academic general practitioner moderated each general practitioner focus group, while the researcher acted as an assistant. We considered that having a general practitioner as a facilitator would create a synergy and empathy between participants and the researchers. These focus groups were much more challenging as the general practitioners, although enthusiastic to be involved, were difficult to schedule to participate. Engaging general practitioners in focus groups required considerable pragmatism, best exemplified by the first general practitioner focus group, which was held in a large medical center during lunchtime, in one of the general practitioners' rooms. Throughout this focus group there seemed to be a constant flow of medical center staff entering and leaving the room. They were busy tidying up from the morning session and preparing for the afternoon appointments with the examination couch sheets being changed, pillows fluffed up, bins emptied, and correspondences delivered. Throughout all of this activity, the focus group continued as the general practitioners actively contributed to the conversations, while signing forms and hurriedly eating their lunches. It was just another normal day in general practice except they had the opportunity to tell their story to people who were listening. In hindsight, I think that in-depth semistructured interviews with individual general practitioners, although more time consuming, would have been a more effective way of eliciting their perceptions. I suspect it would have been easier to schedule an appropriate time that fitted in better with their professional demands.

Lessons Learned

Within the context of this project, focus groups provided a unique insight into organizational and contextual factors of providing palliative care in residential aged care. This increase in knowledge of the practice setting was also reflected in my proficiency in facilitation, data analysis, and dissemination of study findings in the peer-reviewed literature. The critical lessons I learned from this process were the value of

- detailed planning and paying attention to issues of venue, timing, and participants in the focus groups;

- two consistent researchers to be involved in the entire focus group process;

- preparing and allowing space and time in which to immerse myself in conducting the focus groups and analyzing the data;

- pragmatism, which enabled me to successfully conduct focus groups in dynamic clinical settings while adhering to the theoretical and methodological considerations;

- preparation of systems that facilitated detailed field notes, noted seating arrangements, orders of speakers, and nonverbal cues, assigning a code to each participant and ensuring it is linked to all of their quotes;

- being prepared to be focused and disciplined and allowing time to meet immediately after the focus group to reflect on the discussions and recording thoughts and ideas in an electronic format, such as PowerPoint slides; and

- transcribing the data in a timely manner adding relevant quotes to the themes and subthemes in an electronic format and adding relevant details from the field notes to each theme.

Certainly one of the most gratifying rewards of research supervision is to watch your student develop and grow into an independent researcher. Watching Jane master the technique of focus groups was one of these experiences. Her expert clinical knowledge and issues of the local environment laid important foundations for generating information for guiding and informing the action research project that was the focus of her dissertation work. Common goals, mutual respect, and reciprocity within the research team, particularly between the student and supervisor, are important ingredients in the recipe for research success.

✳ ✳ ✳

Conclusions

We have outlined some of our experiences not just about conducting focus groups from a technical perspective but also about the key steps that are needed in the research setting. Taking the time to develop effective relationships that are internal and external to the research team is pivotal to conducting research. As in all relationships, adversity and success are managed more productively when there is respect, reciprocity, and mutual affection. Our partnership has been a success story; graduation is imminent, articles have been published, and, importantly, we have achieved our goal of improving outcomes for a vulnerable population. We wish you the very best in your research journey and hope we have assisted you in chartering the journey.

References

Davidson, P., Paull, G., Cockburn, J., Davis, J., Rees, D., Gorman, D., et al. (2004). Integrated, collaborative palliative care in heart failure: The St. George Heart Failure Service experience 1999–2002. *Journal of Cardiovascular Nursing, 19*, 68–75.

Halcomb, E. J., & Davidson, P. (2006). Is verbatim transcription of interview data always necessary? *Applied Nursing Research, 19*, 38–42.

Lincoln, Y. S., & Guba, E. (1985). *Naturalistic inquiry.* Newbury Park, CA: Sage Publications.

Morrison, B., & Lilford, R. J. (2001). How can action research apply to health services? *Qualitative Health Research, 11*, 436–449.

Phillips, J., Davidson, P., Kristjanson, L., Jackson, D., & Daly, J. (2006). Residential aged care: The last frontier for palliative care. *Journal of Advanced Nursing, 55*, 416–424.

Phillips, J. L., Davidson, P. M., Jackson, D., Kristjanson, L., Bennett, M. L., & Daly, J. (2006). Enhancing palliative care delivery in a regional community in Australia. *Australian Health Review, 30*, 370–379.

Roberts, D., & Snowball, J. (1999). Psychological care in oncology nursing: A study of social knowledge. *Journal of Clinical Nursing, 8*, 39–47.

Royal Australian College of General Practitioners. (2006). *Medical care of older persons in residential aged care facilities* (4th ed.). Melbourne, Australia: The Royal Australian College of General Practitioners.

St. John, W. (2004). Focus group interviews. In V. Minichiello, G. Sullivan, K. Greenwood, & R. Axford (Eds.), *Handbook of research methods for nursing and health science* (2nd ed., pp. 448–461). Sydney: Pearson Education Australia.

Street, A. (2004). Action research. In V. Minichiello, G. Sullivan, K. Greenwood, & R. Axford (Eds.), *Research methods for nursing and health science* (2nd ed., pp. 278–294). Sydney: Pearson Education Australia.

Prominent Themes and Lessons Learned 17

Jeffrey A. Kottler and Victor Minichiello

This book describes the qualitative journeys of more than a dozen neophyte researchers and their mentors. As such, the stories have embedded within them certain themes that can also be connected to reveal similar patterns. If you were going to analyze this data, ask yourself what stands out most to you across the narratives you've read. Just as the authors described the ways that they identified the most important plots (narrative analysis), codes (grounded theory), themes (phenomenology), and so forth, so too can we talk about what struck us as common threads that appear most significant.

One of the interesting (and perhaps disorienting) aspects of qualitative data analysis is that a variety of researchers may focus on different things within the material that they review. This can reflect their unique backgrounds, perceptions, biases, values, interests, and intellectual pursuits. In quantitative studies, such variations would be labeled a lack of reliability. In qualitative work, attempts can be made to address these issues through "auditing teams" in which different researchers identify themes independently of one another and then discuss their findings, eventually reaching consensus on common factors. If you remember that the qualitative research paradigm does not make claims about objectivity, but rather embraces subjectivity within certain academic standards, then you'll realize that any difference between what we focus on as themes and what you may notice is not a weakness but a strength. For example, as a sociologist, one of us (Victor) searched to understand the ways researchers used theories to frame their questions and shape their line of analysis; while Jeffrey, as a psychologist focused on how researchers' personal experiences influenced what they decided to research and their research journey. We are all unique individuals who see things differently and, as a result, put different emphasis on some aspect of what we see, hear, or read. This produces a triangulation of different kinds of interpretations about the same phenomena but seen from different lenses if we can use our camera metaphor again. All are valid observations and explanations. What can be constructively critiqued, like any research, is the quality of the methodology underpinning the studies.

Emerging Themes in the Narratives

What is the point of doing a research study if you already know what you're going to find? The beauty and excitement of qualitative research is that you take on a position of complete openness and flexibility, almost of naïvety, in which you want to be surprised by what you discover. This is quite unlike quantitative studies in which you must make predictions about what you think will happen (formulate and test hypotheses) and then measure the extent to which your forecasts were accurate.

As in most qualitative journeys, we started out with some preconceptions and expectations about what we thought we'd find and hear in the narratives. We have been doing this kind of work for long enough that we sometimes forget our admonishment about identifying, acknowledging, and "bracketing" our initial expectations. We thus thought we had a pretty good idea about what would be contained in the stories. We should have known better.

Our initial expectations took the form of imagining that we would receive chapters that were loaded with personal disclosure and revealing descriptions about the journeys the researchers followed. In fact, that may be *exactly* what you read in this book. Rest assured that many of these manuscripts did not look like this in their first drafts. We were surprised how difficult it was for some authors to talk about their internal processes and personal journeys; some preferred instead to focus on the pragmatics of completing their study, the intellectual challenges they faced, and especially talking about their results. This makes sense since the authors feel so passionately about their subjects and invested so much of themselves in the research effort. Yet we were surprised how reluctant some authors were to talk about the personal dimensions that led them to their research questions, much less explore the challenges, discomforts, and even crises they faced. A half a dozen chapters were abandoned altogether because the stated mission was beyond reach for the authors, or at least in such a public forum. We thought we had been so clear about what the unique purpose was of this project, that is, to discuss the process, *not* the content and results, but we hadn't realized how potentially threatening our task had been for some people.

On the other hand, we have been surprised by the courage and honesty of the authors who have been included in this book to talk about subjects that ordinarily remain quite private and unexpressed. We suppose that is why we undertook this project in the first place—to bring forth the most personal and exciting aspects of doing qualitative research.

Lessons Learned: A Thematic Analysis of the Research Journeys

Each of us reviewed the chapters independently, reading and rereading the stories several times over a period of several months. During this process of "indwelling" (as it is sometimes called) we immersed ourselves in the data, taking notes on material we considered significant, highlighting comments that seemed to capture essences (phenomenology), plotlines (narrative analysis), and codes (grounded theory). This led to the identification of initial themes—across chapters—that struck each of us as important.

Because we come from different disciplines (sociology and counseling), live in different countries (Australia and the United States), have different jobs (university administrator and professor/psychologist), hold different worldviews as a function of our sexual orientations, ethnicities, religious upbringing, ages, and other factors, it is not surprising that we focused on different dimensions of the stories. It should be mentioned that when we teach or supervise students together, we frequently find ourselves on opposite ends of an issue. We find this enriches our collaborations and believe it enhances our scholarly work.

Victor is a methodologist and so spent more effort devoted to identifying themes related to the studies. As a psychologist who was used to working with processes rather than content, Jeffrey seemed to gravitate more toward relational/process factors that emerged. Once we compared our findings and data analysis, negotiated and merged our observations, what resulted was a far more robust and comprehensive description. Yet we freely acknowledge that during your own data analysis—and whether you realize it or not, while you were reading you were also identifying your own themes—you may have noticed things that we missed.

Recognition of the Place of the Researcher in the Study

We arrive at a particular research question, not just because of professional interest, but often because of very personal motives. Often the things we choose to study are of great interest to us because of our own background and experiences. We began this book by locating ourselves as authors and editors of this volume, describing our motives and journeys that led us to undertake this project. You couldn't help but notice that we were hardly alone.

Theresa Smith-Ruig described how her vision impairment led her to function in a particular way while studying the experiences of business accountants. There were things within David Leary's life that were influencing the way he operated, as well as thirty years of background that impacted his choices and procedures. He initially felt sick at the prospect of investigating sex work and he didn't know why. Eventually, during the research process, many of his own unresolved issues (including an experience with a sex worker as a young man) emerged, forcing him to look at himself. A similar scenario unfolded for Stacee Reicherzer, especially since she intentionally chose the topic of gender identity that she lives every moment. Pol McCann, as well, felt he had to explore more deeply his role and place in the project since the things he was discovering about homophobia and bullying paralleled his own experiences growing up.

Given that the choice to investigate any research question can have—and usually has—a personal component to it, it is important that you become aware of these connections and perhaps even "own," explore, and write about this in your introduction or methodology sections. Heidi Gilchrist describes this challenge when she talked about how she had to increase her awareness of her own experiences with hiking and physical fitness in order to see how this influenced the ways she listened to the women she interviewed and examined the themes within the conversations.

Matching Methods

Not only can (and should) the subject reflect your particular interests and values, but also the choice of methodology. Heidi Gilchrist chose a feminist approach to investigate women's experiences with physical activity because it was well suited to her intention of exploring roles of gender and body image, but also because it fit her particular worldview. Jane Phillips selected social action research that allowed her to not only study a phenomenon, but also to initiate a program designed to make a difference, and as a nurse practitioner she was using this methodology in her work. Connie Malin used a "mixed method," combining questionnaires with in-depth interviews to find out about teachers' attitudes and perceptions. Certain students naturally gravitate toward methodologies that allow them to play to their strengths (collecting stories, studying documents or photographic images, immersing in cultures, advocating on behalf of the marginalized, using computer-assisted coding) or build their weaknesses (interviewing, leading focus groups, analyzing transcripts, deconstructing discourse, listening for deep meaning, identifying plots in stories).

Students and researchers often start out with one approach to their research, find that it is limiting or inadequate for their purposes, and then move on to something that is more appropriate or useful. You may start out with grounded theory and find it too confining or too focused on smaller pieces of the picture. Returning to the camera metaphor we introduced in Chapter 2, you may want to switch from a broad, wide angle view of the subject to one that is more focused—or feel handcuffed by the narrow focus you have taken in a case study or ethnography and prefer instead to expand your interest to broader landscapes.

You should fully expect that whatever you say you're going to do in the first draft of your methodology chapter will most likely not resemble what you actually have done by the time you have completed the study. Kiran Regmi thought she was going to talk to new mothers about their birth experiences and eventually ended up broadening her data collection to include conversations with other family members and health professionals, all intended to enrich the quality of her data. This is because your methodology will evolve as you carry out your study. You will need to rethink your assumptions, for example, about sampling, how to approach informants, what to include in your interview guide, what type of methodology is appropriate, and so on. For example, Myfanwy Maple originally had planned to use a grounded theory approach but as she began interviewing realized that a narrative approach would yield a richer data set and a more appropriate line of analysis that was related to parents plotting their experiences. Suzanne Lunn had to rethink her approach to recruiting informants for focus groups because the "best practice" textbook approaches she read about did not mirror the realities that she was facing when she tried to approach and recruit informants.

This leads us to make another observation. Often students selected methodological approaches because of their previous training or because it was the preferred approach of the supervisors. Interestingly, a number of the students changed their original approach because it did not fit with what their fieldwork experiences were telling them was appropriate. Slowly they realized the benefits of being open to alternative ways of approaching the data. There is a lesson here for both student and mentors; the important thing to remember here is to be fluid about what works because of what the "lived" research experience is telling you. This is what is meant by being "grounded" in the fieldwork process, rather than "blinded" by your current methodological preferences and practices.

Qualitative Research as Learning

One of the obvious themes emerging from all of the chapters in this book is that qualitative research as an inquiry process has been set up to be about learning. To inform the question asked in the study the researchers emerge themselves in collecting data, and through this intense data collection, they begin to see things differently. Frequently it challenges the assumptions they are making about people or about a particular situation. For example, rather than seeing older people as passive and in stereotyped terms, you begin to see them as real people, with needs like yourself. Terrence Hays realized that music could be studied as more than a therapeutic medical intervention in the lives of older people. He realized that older people use music to give them purpose, enjoyment, and identity, just as he does. These are challenges at a very personal level. Through his study he learned to better appreciate older persons as citizens with needs and contributions. He went on to organize a music festival for older persons that further validated the talents and contributions of older people. In other circumstances qualitative research allows us to see how we need to approach a topic differently from what is reported in the literature.

Qualitative researchers get their hands dirty, so to speak, by seeking answers to often loosely defined research questions via interactions with people in the real world. This sounds simple enough. But it is challenging to encourage people to talk openly and honestly about their innermost experiences. What should be obvious from the stories presented in this book is that it takes considerable time and effort to refine research questions, collect meaningful data, and locate an appropriate line of analysis. Researchers often get to this point by learning how to see, hear, and read the intentions and experiences of their participants and to interpret these as much as possible from the shoes of the participants. Trusting and honoring informants to guide them opens up the line of inquiry. For this reason, qualitative research is a personal experience that requires people to work with people and engaging them to tell their stories. As their studies progress over time, and grow from curiosity to understanding and knowledge sharing, researchers are transformed. For example, McCann discovered that homophobia is a learned behavior but it can be unlearned. Prior to his research, he was not aware that men who held strong homophobic attitudes can change over time. This realization allows him to revisit his own experiences as a gay man who was the object of homophobic behavior. It gave him hope that men can view gay people in more positive and respectful ways.

Negotiations With Mentors for Control of the Process

As you'd expect, there is a great variety of mentoring styles reported in the stories. Some teachers allow students to proceed in most any direction they'd like, as long as it has some academic legitimacy. Jane Phillips, for example, describes how she deliberately chose a mentor who would allow her to pursue her interest in using focus groups to explore health issues.

Yet mentors may feel very strongly about the ways to proceed, based on years of experience and expertise. Sometimes it is understood that if you are going to work with a particular faculty member, you will virtually be required to investigate a topic that is directly related to his or her lines of inquiry. There is a long-standing tradition in the sciences that whole teams of students work collaboratively to advance the research agenda of the mentor.

There often comes a time when students have to stand up for their own most cherished beliefs, supported by evidence and defensible rationales. Several of Victor's students—David Leary, Pol McCann, and Myfanwy Maple—struggled with the challenges of working with such a high-powered, renowned supervisor, who felt very strongly about what they should do and how they should do it. Pol mentioned that initially he felt like he was "doing someone else's research" rather than his own. There was a time when Myfanwy had to say, look, I need to follow my own path. Victor kept insisting that David stop doing interviews and collecting data and start writing but David felt a strong desire to keep exploring. Second, David never began a docturate with the intention or interest of studying sex work. He wanted to look at resilience among marginalized youth. It is a common scenario that mentors often suggest— or pressure—students to delve into areas that interest their mentors most, or further their own most cherished lines of inquiry. There is a long tradition for this within academia in which in some circles it is fully expected that you work in a particular area.

Of course it needs to be said that mentors also change through the rich experiences of being a supervisor. For example, Victor has learned to appreciate methodologies other than grounded theory and to expand his knowledge of qualitative research from the fieldwork experiences of his students. It is so easy to "profess" as a mentor and there is an expectation that you have all of the answers. What makes qualitative research so rewarding for supervisors is that there is always a different take on how people can be approached, and on how stories are given a different twist by others who are trying to make sense of these data. There is also learning from cosupervisors. For example, Victor had strict rules with respect to not including the personal journey of the researchers in the method chapter. But this changed once he saw the benefits of allowing people to be reflective in why they were pursuing certain lines of analysis. Jeffrey approaches *every* research project with the hope and expectation that he will be transformed by his interactions with the student and the research question.

Altered Professional Practice

Ideally, any study you complete would not only advance knowledge in your discipline but also influence your own professional practice. The most meaningful research journey is the one that provides you with new information to do your job—and live your life—more effectively. When Kiran began her study of maternal mortality, she had little idea that mothers-in-law were actually making the medical decisions in the family, and thereby often sabotaging opportunities to obtain needed health care. She made fundamental changes in obstetric practice within her hospital, and within her country, as a result of her findings. Dana Comstock was able to gather valuable data that helped her refine her clinical practice with clients. Connie Malin learned extremely valuable things about developmentally appropriate education that informed her work as a school administrator. Wendy Hu had to reexamine her own values, assumptions, and experiences as a doctor and this has had a profound impact on her practice and interaction with her patients and fellow practitioners.

Since you always have some degree of choice in what you study, and how you proceed (especially in qualitative journeys), it is important, even mandatory, that you find a subject that is driven by your passion. Suzanne Lunn, for instance, describes how she was "absolutely determined" to use her project as a way to help students find sustainable employment.

Finding Your Voice as a Writer

Fundamentally, completing a research project involves disseminating findings in the form of a manuscript, whether this is a thesis, dissertation, article, monograph, or book. It is an exercise in reflective thinking, for certain, but also in writing. Even though academic research has some rather strict requirements for the form, structure, style, and content of manuscripts, there is still plenty of room for a personalized narrative voice. For many students, producing a research manuscript is the first opportunity to write a book (loosely defined). In order to write fluently, you must be able to find your voice as a writer or the process will proceed as an exercise in futility and frustration. Prior to completing her dissertation, Kiran had thought of herself as a physician, an epidemiologist, a policy maker, but hardly a writer. Kiran's father is her country's national poet, but she had never before thought of herself as an author. That changed once she discovered that not only could she write from her heart, as well as her mind, but also that she enjoyed the process tremendously.

Relationships Between Students and Mentors

The relationships that develop between students and their mentors during the research process can often become quite intense, fraught with conflict, disagreements, and also intimacy. There are appropriate professional boundaries to establish in such relationships, yet it is not uncommon that friendships and professional alliances are formed after the research is over. You may coauthor publications with mentors and collaborate on future projects. Depending on the context and setting, you may also establish life-long connections that are both professionally and personally satisfying. David, Terrence, and Myfanwy continue to collaborate with both of us. Kiran and Jeffrey established a foundation together to provide scholarships for lower-caste girls. Stacee and Dana developed a friendship and professional affiliation that is mutually supportive and continues to this day. Danielle Couch described the mutual respect and reciprocal influence that took place with her mentor, providing her with the support, encouragement, and expertise she needed to pursue an exciting but unknown area (online dating) with qualitative methods that were unfamiliar to her. John Scott's journey was also guided by his mentor, but not directed by him; it was described as a "hands-off" approach. That can be a blessing at times, but also a burden if you are not receiving the input and structure you need. All of this must be negotiated so that all parties are in agreement and held accountable for their commitments.

Relationships are indeed the essence of what qualitative research is all about. During her ethnographic study in the medical profession, Wendy Hu talks about how important her mentors were during the journey, but also how critical her relationships were with those within the clinics in which she operated as a participant-observer.

STUDENTS CHANGE THEIR MENTORS

Change and influence in helping relationships are often both reciprocal and multidimensional. As much as students learn and grow as a result of their collaborations with mentors, so too do the teachers profit from these interactions. Both of us continue to supervise research students primarily because we so enjoy the intellectual stimulation, and personal growth and development that accompany being a guide during qualitative journeys. Every student brings a wealth of experience and knowledge, as well as curiosity, to the collaboration—sparking us to stretch in new ways.

Throughout the chapters, you couldn't help but notice parallel processes that occurred in which the mentors talked about all the ways that they were stretched, challenged, and transformed, as a result of being involved in the journeys. This is hardly surprising for guides in any exploratory enterprise. No matter how much of an expert a guide might be, no matter how experienced, no matter how many times she has been along a similar path, each and every trip is different in some ways—if eyes, ears, and heart are kept open along the path.

INTERACTIVE AND COLLABORATIVE DIALOGUE

Qualitative journeys, like much of research, involves constant dialogue, interaction with mentors and colleagues, and plenty of feedback, which must be somehow integrated and processed. Often the input is discrepant and contradictory. For instance, one of our current students (Alison Sheridan) was feeling a bit lost organizing her data now that she has reached saturation with her interviews. Alison asked Jeffrey about his thoughts regarding a particular series of books that she was recently introduced to: Did he think they'd be useful to consult since they introduce a new theoretical approach to the subject that might be relevant? Jeffrey's immediate response was that it would be best if she held off delving into more literature at this point, until such time that she had lived with her data longer and found her own themes. He believed there was a danger in consulting other sources at this critical juncture in the analysis when Alison was trying to grapple with her own thoughts and develop her own theories. He suggested that she hold off reading more theory until after she had finished her own thematic analysis or she might "pollute" her results with others' ideas instead of ideas grounded in her own data.

Alison thought this made sense to her, but then Victor chimed in with an *opposite* viewpoint—he could see some value to making ongoing connections to the literature since, after all, the qualitative analytic process is supposed to be recursive, circling back to the literature, the data, the analysis, and so on. He thought it might be useful for her to look at new developments and then dive back into her own material.

There are both functional and highly conflicted mentor teams. If big egos are feuding, if the committee members or supervisors are competitive, if the mentors "triangulate" the students in their own feuds, then someone like Alison could easily get caught in the middle and even experience collateral damage. Fortunately, we are used to taking different positions on issues, and doing so respectfully. We even see this as a way to enrich the experiences for our students and allowing them to become the ultimate arbitrators of the process and final decision makers. The key

point is that whatever you do in research—or in professional practice—
you'd better have a clear, defensible rationale that can be articulated and
supported with evidence. In this case, Alison was left to make her own
choice about how to proceed, negotiating a compromise that involved
holding off on reading additional literature until after she finished writing
more of her own reflections. Then she would swing back into new books
and articles before doing her final draft.

Struggle Is Part of the Process

Doing qualitative research is not just a sanitized intellectual activity—it
involves a degree of emotional investment and often corresponding arousal
that can be both joyful and excruciating. Stacee described the tearful experiences she had coming to terms with issues that came out in her interviews
that triggered other stuff in her life. She felt raw and vulnerable during the
data collection phase, an experience also described by David, Myfanwy, and
others. Pol described himself as "drowning in his data," feeling "stalled" and
absolutely overwhelmed with all the material he collected and stuck what
to do with it. Jane Phillips described the journey "like riding on a roller
coaster where there were moments of exhilaration and immense satisfaction, closely followed by feelings of despair and frustration when events are
not going as planned." Despair and frustration indeed. If you aren't
encountering such difficulties and challenges, you probably aren't going
very deeply in your investigation. When you read the journals and letters of
some of the world's greatest scientists, they are loaded with descriptions of
depression, despondency, frustration, anxiety, and doubts.

Because qualitative journeys tend to be organic and fluid processes rather
than rigidly structured procedures, beginning researchers are required to let
go of their need for certainty and clearly identified parameters. This was
especially challenging for Connie Malin, who took considerable time to trust
qualitative data gathering as a legitimate research tool. Danielle Couch
described how she was working in relatively unchartered territory (online
dating) using unfamiliar online interview methods to find out about people's
experiences. John Scott also described his struggles living with uncertainty
when using unobtrusive, qualitative methods that were unfamiliar to him.
Wendy Hu found herself continually pressed to argue the validity and use-
fulness of her ethnographic study to medical personnel who were suspicious
and skeptical. Many others found themselves ending up in a place that was
quite different from what they originally imagined; this was accompanied by
feelings of exhilaration but also a certain anxiety traveling into the unknown
with precious few guideposts along the way.

The Research Process Continues After It "Ends"

After the requirements for a course or graduation are completed, after the thesis or dissertation is done, all the data collected and analyzed, the process continues to unfold. The journey never really ends; a study lives within you for the rest of your life even after you move on to other projects. You continue to think about what you've done, what you neglected or ignored, what you could have done differently, and, most critically, what you learned that will help in your life and work.

Many of the students profiled in these chapters completed their very first comprehensive research study. This was only the beginning of their scholarly careers and the questions they initially explored may very well become the focus of a dozen or more subsequent studies. They may experiment with different ways of investigating the issues, learn new methodologies and data collection tools, and be part of the academic community as they grow into mentor roles.

As this project comes to a close for us, we've moved on to new studies of interest. Yet even after this book has gone to press we continue to reflect on the stories, to have conversations with colleagues, family, students, and friends about the things we have learned and the new insights they have generated. We've changed the ways that we teach research and mentor our students, focusing on many of the themes that are highlighted in this chapter.

By the time you are finished with your project you will have internalized many of the skills and concepts you learned. You have also become an expert in a particular area as a function of your study and investigations. Ideally, you will publish your findings, perhaps in collaboration with your mentor(s). This is the obligation and responsibility of a researcher to disseminate what you discovered so that others within your discipline can profit. It is also an activity that will take years to complete, given the additional challenges of writing and editing for successful publication.

How Doing Qualitative Research Changes You—as a Person and a Professional

In case you haven't noticed, qualitative research teaches you a method of making sense of the world, as well as your own experience. It provides a framework for examining *any* phenomenon more systematically and analytically, leading you to question that which you observe, sense, and hear, exploring at a deeper level.

Learning to do qualitative research changes the way you think and reason and solve problems. It teaches you to be more curious about things you don't understand and then provides a way that you can go about understanding them in a more meaningful way. When we introduced this book, we provided many such examples of this personally driven inquisitiveness in our own lives, how we felt motivated to pursue a particular line of research because of some issue in our own lives. If such human drives can lead to academic outcomes, so too can professional research change the way you operate in the world.

We highlight many of the ways that you can expect your training in qualitative research can change you, almost always for the better.

MAKES YOU MORE SKEPTICAL OF A SINGLE TRUTH

Most of us grow up being taught by our parents, teachers, and mentors that "truth" is something that exists in the world, and furthermore, that it is possible to discover it. Implicit in this lesson is that the truth we find is universal, the sort of thing that *everyone* would agree with. After all, if such truth varied from person to person, then how could it possibly be an absolute reality?

Somewhere along the line you had the bewildering revelation that your truth is not necessarily the same as anyone else's, or at least everyone else's. There are things that you consider most sacred that others hardly notice. The "facts" that you have come to hold as certain and unalterable might be considered mere opinions and theories by others who question your reasoning or conclusions. After all, there was a time in which it was believed that Zeus and Hera ruled the world, that outspoken women were witches to be burned at the stake, and that mental illness was caused by a spell cast upon someone (some of these beliefs still hold true in some parts of the world).

TEACHES YOU TO BE MORE FLEXIBLE IN THE WAYS YOU SOLVE PROBLEMS

Qualitative research relies on methods that are fluid, flexible, and adaptable. You are constantly changing what you do, and how you do it, in light of new data and experiences. You learn that what works in one situation, with one participant, won't work the same way again. You learn that problems are best solved by examining their context. You learn to appreciate and respect those who think differently than you do. And you learn to trust your own powers of intuition and critical thinking.

One of the most intriguing, and yet confusing, aspects of the qualitative research journey is the way that people make decisions about what they're going to research and how they're going to investigate those issues. There is rarely only one legitimate path to follow but rather a multitude of choices, depending on interests, goals, and responsiveness to the data. The method you choose, and the rationale for selecting participants, will tell you things that may be quite different from what you might have learned had you made different decisions. For example, in Kiran Regmi's study of childbirth experiences, she initially chose to interview new mothers about their experiences. When the data generated was only presenting one slice of the picture, she chose to expand the viewpoint to interview the women's mothers-in-law, then their husbands, and, finally, medical personnel. If a male gynecologist, or an American physician, had done this study, he or she may not have focused on gender/power relationships between women and the patriarchal system in place within Nepal and the health-care system.

YOU BECOME A BETTER LISTENER AND OBSERVER

Above all else, the quality of your data is based on how closely, carefully, and attentively you listen to what people have to say. You suspend your own beliefs. You monitor your biases and preconceptions and try to limit them. You use all your powers of concentration to really hear and see things that may have escaped notice previously. You respond with compassion and empathy to what you hear, communicating your intense interest. These skills will also transform all your other relationships, enhancing intimacy and improving the quality of communication.

These are just a few of the benefits that result from qualitative journeys. You may also:

- Become more sensitive to the inner, subjective world
- Learn how to deconstruct meaning in your own and others' behavior
- Search for deeper existential meaning
- Become more self-reflective
- Draw connections between disparate themes and experiences
- Become committed to helping the marginalized
- Learn how much fun research can be

Conclusions

All of the research students successfully completed their studies using a qualitative framework and all went on to have their results published in academic journals. This is testimony that qualitative research can not only be employed to gain significant knowledge, but also can be recognized as important contributions to various disciplines. However, as the stories reveal, this is achieved not without considerable struggles along the way. Doing qualitative research is indeed a journey, one with numerous unforeseen pitfalls, but also joyous surprises.

Because qualitative research follows a path that is considerably less defined than that of quantitative studies, it requires a different set of skills and qualities to flourish during the journey. These include tolerating ambiguity, living with uncertainty, being both personally and professionally reflective, and especially remaining flexible and responsive to both the informants and the data.

We chose to include research journeys that are diverse not only in the fields they represent, the topics selected, and the methodologies employed, but also in the kinds of challenges that were faced along the way. There are no templates in these stories that you can follow in your own research, but rather inspiration and encouragement to pursue this noble task with the same passion and excitement that you could not help but feel in reading the authors' voices. We wish you all the best during the research adventures that await you.

Index

  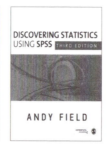  
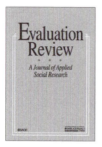